DISCOURSE MODALITY

Pragmatics & Beyond
New Series

24

Senko K. Maynard

Discourse Modality

DISCOURSE MODALITY
SUBJECTIVITY, EMOTION AND VOICE
IN THE JAPANESE LANGUAGE

SENKO K. MAYNARD
Rutgers University

JOHN BENJAMINS PUBLISHING COMPANY
AMSTERDAM/PHILADELPHIA

1993

Library of Congress Cataloging-in-Publication Data

Maynard, Senko K.
Discourse modality : subjectivity, emotion and voice in the Japanese language / Senko
K. Maynard.
   p.   cm. -- (Pragmatics & beyond, ISSN 0922-842X ; new ser. 24)
Includes bibliographical references and index.
1. Japanese language--Discourse analysis. 2. Japanese language--Modality. I. Title. II.
Series.
PL640.5.M39   1992   92-36878
ISBN 90 272 5036 7 (Eur.)/1-55619-292-4 (US) (alk. paper)   CIP

John Benjamins Publishing Co. · P.O. Box 75577 · 1070 AN Amsterdam · The Netherlands
John Benjamins North America · 821 Bethlehem Pike · Philadelphia, PA 19118 · USA

Contents

Part 2: Analysis of DM Indicators

Part 3: Reflections

Acknowledgments

The writing of this book was supported in part by a grant from the Joint Committee on Japanese Studies of the Social Science Research Council and the American Council of Learned Societies with funds provided by the National Endowment for the Humanities, the Ford Foundation and Japan-United States Friendship Commission. The conversational data analyzed in this work was collected in Tokyo in 1985 with funds made available by the Toyota Foundation. Rutgers University provided grant funds through the University's Research Council to assist in the production of the camera-ready manuscript. I take this opportunity to acknowledge their generous assistance.

Chisato Kitagawa read an earlier version of the manuscript and offered encouragement and critical commentary. Papers related to some of the chapters in this book were read by Sachiko Ide and Matsuo Soga who graciously shared their ideas with me. Paul Takahara read the manuscript and generously offered support and constructive commentary. He also encouraged my work by sharing his thoughts with me on similar research topics and by making available some of his works. I benefited from discussing with Takie Lebra and Jim Wertsch my initial thoughts, some of which were developed into ideas and are now a part of this work. Teun van Dijk offered a place to express my "voice" in his journal *TEXT* at the stage when my ideas on Discourse Modality were still being formed. I thank these colleagues of mine for their faith in me and their heartwarming friendship. I also would like to express my sincere gratitude to the series editors, especially Jef Verschueren, for their decision to include my work in the *Pragmatics and Beyond New Series*.

The summer of 1989 which I spent teaching at Harvard University holds special memory for me because of the good times I shared with the late Tazuko Monane. I thank her for her friendship and for discussing with me some of the earliest stages of ideas explored in this book.

In writing this book, many works in linguistics and related fields whose authors have long left this world have continued to inspire me. Although I have no way of conveying my gratitude, I would like to express my respect and admiration for their works reviewed in this book.

I wish to thank Rutgers University and Princeton University, two institutions I have been affiliated with during the time I developed the manuscript. Both have provided me an encouraging environment of scholarship in which I have been challenged to aspire to do my best.

Four papers that discuss issues contained in and related to the present study have been published. "Functions of the discourse marker *dakara* in Japanese conversation" (*TEXT: An Interdisciplinary Journal for the Study of Discourse*, 9, 389-414, 1989), "Pragmatics of Discourse Modality: A case of the Japanese emotional adverb *doose*" (*Pragmatics*, 1, 371-392, 1991), "Pragmatics of Discourse Modality: A case of *da* and *desu/masu* forms in Japanese" (*Journal of Pragmatics*, 15, 551-582, 1991), "Discourse and interactional functions of the Japanese modal adverb *yahari/yappari*" (*Language Sciences*, 13, 39-57, 1991). I thank the publishers and editors for their permission to use similar material in this book.

I wish to express my sincere gratitude to Ted Turner, the late Mary Turner, the late Almira Turner and the people of Corning, Iowa who gave me the first opportunity to come to the United States. My year as an American Field Service exchange student at Corning Community High School in the heartland of America continues to be the source of my inspiration and optimism. I thank my parents, Tsutomu and Harue Kumiya of Yamanashi, Japan, for their constant encouragement.

As always, my husband Michael has provided a warm and joyful environment where I can be true to myself and continue to pursue my academic interests. It is with my deepest sense of gratitude and respect that I acknowledge his continuous support and understanding.

SKM
July, 1992
Highland Park, NJ

Part 1

Analytical Framework

CHAPTER 1

Introduction

--Language, which is most easily misconceived to exist as an "objective" entity, must be understood to be the most "subjective" and the most "mental, psychological as well as emotional" existence.--Tokieda (1941:18, my translation)[1]

1. Introductory Remarks

Verbal expressions used in everyday interaction are known to simultaneously convey at least two integrated but distinguishable types of information. First, we describe the objects and events of the world in a propositional construction, and second, through the manner of presenting the proposition, we personalize the discourse as we express and reveal ourselves. These two types of information are often coded by linguistic signs, with some devices functioning primarily, but not necessarily exclusively, for an objective description of the world, and others functioning primarily for the language user's self-expression.

Some linguistic signs in modern Japanese fall into the latter category. Since these signs have no obvious referential functions--at least not in the Saussurean sense that the sound-image "tree" evokes the concept of a "tree," one may conclude, at first blush, that they are "meaningless." This conclusion, however, leads one to ask an intriguing question: How, then, do these "meaningless" signs "mean"? In order to answer this question, one needs to inquire into the relationship between the speaker's cognitive mode and these signs, the speaker's emotional involvement in these signs, the relationship between these signs and the world created by them, and the interpersonal as well as social motivations for using them. In short, in analyzing these signs we must rescue the concept of the speaking "subject" and consequently examine how one personalizes one's discourse. And ultimately we must integrate this aspect into the process of our theoretical inquiry. In real-life communication we rarely use linguistic signs merely to convey referential meaning; on the contrary we use language for communicating a wide range of non-referential meanings. This study focuses on these non-referential, i.e., emotionally expressive, personal and interpersonal, meanings of certain Japanese signs, with special attention given toward understanding their cognitive, psychological and social meanings.

Although every language is equipped with strategies to express personal attitude as reflected in the wide range of non-referential meanings, Japanese has a strong tendency to express this attitudinal stance, i.e., one's personal voice, by adding and/or avoiding a variety of linguistic devices. These devices include discourse connectives, modal adverbs, verb forms, interactional particles and so forth. In fact making a single utterance in Japanese requires the selection of a variety of linguistic devices which primarily express emotion and interpersonal feelings. Thus, when speaking Japanese, one simply cannot avoid expressing one's personal attitude toward the content of information and toward the addressee. Such personal voice echoes so prominently in Japanese communication that often in Japanese, rather than information-sharing, it is subtextual emotion-sharing that forms the heart of communication.

The primary question addressed in this study is this: How exactly is language designed to express one's emotion, to express one's voice? Conversely, why is an utterance designed in the way it is with devices that have little to do with propositional meanings? This study focuses on investigating how the Japanese language itself is elaborately built for expressing personal voice and emotive nuances. Consequently this study confronts the theoretical issues related to its analysis within the framework of humanistic linguistics.

Only recently have studies in expressions of emotion become the focus of modern Western linguists' attention. To view oneself as "rational autonomous self" represents a strong tradition in modern Western thought. Linguistics has not been an exception to this view as evidenced by the Chomskyan paradigm within which language is reduced to an abstract body of linguistic units bound by numerous rules. According to this view, language can be analyzed by appealing to the logician's formal semantics and it exists apart from the speaking subject and his or her partner, not to mention the emotional involvement of the speech participants. Indeed the distinction between the two opposing views toward language, that is, the "sentence" as a system on one hand, and "utterance" as a unit of interaction on the other, can be traced back to the inception of modern Western linguistics, to the Saussurean dichotomy of "langue" and "parole." Modern linguistics has been primarily concerned with "langue" and only marginally with "parole." As a result, until recently linguistics has focused almost exclusively on cognitive aspects of information processing while slighting the emotional aspects of language and communication.

The interest in "the emotional" has increased in the past two decades in various social sciences and humanities, including anthropology, sociology, psychology, and linguistics. As the voice of poststructuralist criticism has strengthened, some of the once unshakable confidence in purely formal linguistics has eroded. Within linguistics, branches such as text-linguistics, discourse analysis, conversation analysis, pragmatics and sociolinguistics offer some insight in exploring the functional and pragmatic meanings beyond formal semantics.

As much as the recent development in Western scholarship is significant in studying the emotionality of language, an important point concerning the scholarship in Japan must be raised. It is regrettable that the rich two-centuries-old *kokugogaku* 'traditional Japanese language studies' in Japan has been overlooked by the international community. The vast volume of scholarship, often referred to as the *shi/ji* dichotomy, is virtually unknown outside of Japan. Traditional as well as contemporary Japanese language studies have for a long time grappled with the distinction between these two types of linguistic signs-- often noted as "objective" and "subjective" expression. The distinction between *shi* (roughly translated as content words, and therefore more "objective") and *te-ni-o-ha* or *ji* (function words which express "subjective" voice and emotion), for example, originating in the works of the Edo period Japanese grammarians such as Fujitani (1960, originally 1778) and Suzuki (1979, originally 1824) and later reintroduced to the field of Japanese language study by Tokieda (1941, 1950) and others, is one such example. And it was Suzuki's (1979/1824) recognition of speaker's personal *kokoro no koe* 'voices from the heart' that has become a source of inspiration for many linguists to view language as more than a mere body of logically connected propositions which offer strictly referential meanings. According to this traditional view, in language lies the essential function of "expressiveness" which is the power of the speaking subject.

There has also been a tradition in Western linguistics, especially in Europe, that explores non-referential aspects of language such as modality and subjectivity. Works by Benveniste (1971), Lyons (1977, 1981, 1982) and Halliday (1970) exemplify this tradition. Linguistic analyses of German particles, for example have also inquired into modality (see Harden [1983] and Doherty [1987]). More recently Stubbs (1986) introduces "a modal grammar of English" and he analyzes English in light of modality which he considers a primary organizing principle in language. The development of pragmatics and discourse analysis in the past two decades has also contributed to the exploration of non-propositional meanings. Yet it is fair to say that analysis of language with modality and subjectivity as primary focus is yet to be fully explored and it is precisely this task that I hope to realize in the present study.

The goal of this study is threefold. First is to propose a new theoretical framework of Discourse Modality for analyzing the "expressiveness" of language in discourse and interaction. Discourse Modality conveys the subjective emotional, mental or psychological attitude of the speaker toward message content, to the speech act itself or toward his or her communication partner. I use the term "Discourse Modality" in a broad sense to characterize this expanse of meaning and I introduce four major aspects: (1) Information Qualification, (2) Speech Action Declaration and Qualification, (3) Participatory Control, and (4) Interactional Appeal.

Second, with the Discourse Modality framework I will concentrate on analysis of what I call D(iscourse) M(odality) indicators. DM indicators are in essence non-referential linguistic signs whose primary functions are to directly express emotion and personal voice. I have selected the following DM indicators of modern Japanese for analysis: (1) discourse connectives *dakara* 'so, therefore' and *datte* 'but, because,' (2) modal adverbs, *yahari/yappari* 'as expected, at any rate,' and *doose* 'anyway, after all,' (3) *da* and *desu/masu* verb forms, (4) interactional particles *yo* and *ne* and (5) *to yuu* in the clause-noun combination.

Third, in the process of my study I hope to introduce the traditional Japanese scholarship along with and in the context of Western scholarship. Due to the unavailability of translations of Japanese *kokugogaku* studies, Japanese scholarship has been ignored in the international community. The introduction of Japan's academic contribution, especially in the areas of humanities and social sciences, is overdue.

Another related goal is to search for social and cognitive sources for the view of language as conceived in this project. I will explore Japanese philosophical thinking as represented by Watsuji Tetsuroo, Mori Arimasa and Nishida Kitaroo.[2] These philosophers emphasize the social formation of non-autonomous Japanese self--the notion of "self" definable only in relation to its context, particularly "thou."

At this point a word of caution is necessary. Although my analysis is limited to the Japanese language, my intention is not to emphasize the commonly alleged "uniqueness" of Japanese. Rather, I explore the analysis of Japanese with a modality-centered view as opposed to the more frequently taken proposition-centered path with the intention of showing that the modality-centered approach can complement the proposition-centered analysis and has considerable merit as a way of more fully understanding language and communication in general.

2. Modal Characteristics of Language

The question--what is language--is a fundamental yet often ignored inquiry in linguistics. Linguists often assume that they know the answer to this seemingly simple question. However when we acknowledge that linguists have viewed language in a variety of ways--sometimes contradictory--often reflecting the then dominant philosophical and intellectual atmosphere, one doubts the validity of this assumption. Do we know the answer? Or, have we taken the question seriously?

In modern theoretical linguistics language has often been conceived as a system of propositions or logical relations. This view ignores or even denies the fact that language becomes psychologically, emotionally and socially meaningful only when one recognizes its speaking subject. Being socioculturally bound, acknowledging the speaking subject as a main source of language introduces into the study of language a whole range of humanistic factors that cannot be effectively explained if one analyzes the language only in formal theories. Introducing the speaking subject into linguistics forces us to answer the question--what is language--in a different way.

For one, we are forced to observe what actually occurs in real life when language becomes a part of human activity. Upon practical inspection, it becomes clear that language is created and consumed by the language producer as he or she addresses someone--regardless of whether or not that someone is actually present in real time and space. Even when one is engaged in monologic discourse, the language deployed is essentially dialogic in that one addresses oneself who is in part another self. This means that in order to communicate, one must organize information in such a way so that it becomes meaningful in its actual sociocultural and interactional discourse. For this reason language is equipped with devices and strategies that directly convey personal and interpersonal attitude and that are destined to express feelings of emotional involvement. These thoughts point to the view of language which necessitates a focus on the aspects of language beyond the system of propositions or logical relations.

Naturally I do not deny the importance of propositional formal analysis of language. It is true that one often constructs a proposition to convey propositional meaning which in itself expresses in some way one's personal point of view. Obviously even a choice of one lexical item over another and/or a choice of one syntactic structure over another certainly reflects the speaker's personal point of view. I believe that language can be meaningfully analyzed from a variety of perspectives including purely formal analysis. My point here is that for comprehending the essence of language, non-propositional aspects-- though often identified only as residuals--are also essential. For now, let me label these non-propositional aspects "modal" characteristics. Let us explore this view in more detail by focusing on the three modal characteristics of language, i.e., interactionality, subjectivity and textuality. The ensuing view of language, I hope, offers a partial answer to the question: What is language?

2.1. Language as Social Interaction--Interactionality

To say that an utterance is always made in social interaction is not particularly innovative. Sociolinguists in the past have drawn from the socio-interactional nature of language and have produced a considerable body of literature supporting this ideology. In this section I focus on limited aspects of the interactional nature of language, i.e., the social origin of thought as it is mediated by language. In this regard I briefly review two interpretations of this view--one from Russian psychology and the other from Japanese philosophy. I present these two views not simply because they have inspired me in many ways throughout the present study, but more importantly because they offer clues for understanding the inherent interactionality of language and its role in the socialization process of an individual. I hold the view that language provides an environment from which emerges an embryonic and consequently fully invested view of how one places oneself in society. For, ultimately language offers a mediatory device for an individual to identify himself or herself in the life-world,--the notion which serves as a basis for all other resultant psycho-social understandings.

The first is the view presented by a Russian psychologist and semiotician, L. S. Vygotsky (1896-1934). Vygotsky (1962) addresses the relationships between language, thought and society in the context of child development. According to Vygotsky, the cognitive development of a child is accomplished through a process of internalization of language--the result of which is "inner speech"--which is first used by the child for the purpose of socialization. Vygotsky emphasizes that the higher psychological processes as well as higher mental functions an individual attains directly reflect the social processes in which that individual participated at an earlier stage of his or her development--particularly through the dialogic use of language. In Vygotsky's words:

> We may even go further and say that all higher functions are not developed in biology and not in the history of pure phylogenesis. Rather, the very mechanism underlying higher mental functions is a copy from social interaction; all higher mental functions are internalized social relationships. These higher mental functions are the basis of the individual's social structure. Their composition, genetic structure, and means of action--in a word, their whole nature--is social. In their own private sphere, human beings retain the functions of social interaction. (Wertsch 1979:164)

According to Vygotsky, what mediates this process of social-to-private (which remains social) human ontogenesis are sociocultural means, most significant of which is the system of signs. The linguistic sign system possesses the transformatory power on two different planes, initially on the interpsychological plane and then, through mastery of internalization, on the intrapsychological plane. Language provides not only the source for actual socialization but also the source for inner and more private socialization. Clearly at the foundation of Vygotsky's psychological theory lies a strong view that interactionality is the essence of language.

The dialogic nature of language, however, does not end at the formation of, nor at a mere existence on a higher mental and psychological plane. Once inner speech is formed, it continues to interact with human consciousness and continues to regulate human cognitive activity. According to Vygotsky,

> The structure of speech does not simply mirror the structure of thought; that is why words cannot be put on by thought like a ready-made garment. Thought undergoes many changes as it turns into speech. It does not merely find expression in speech, it finds reality and form. (1962:126)

Thus we arrive at the understanding that language is interactional in two ways. First, language provides for socialization which becomes internalized to form our cognitive orientation. Second, language--in the form of inner speech--functions as a mediatory device between semiotic signs and thoughts both of which remain social, and as such, the process of semiotic mediation itself remains dialogic or interactional in nature. Vygotsky's view directs us to the conclusion that for language to be recognized and to function as such, it must be understood to possess its social and dialogic nature--that is to say, interactionality--as the most fundamental characteristic.

Culturally distant from Russia, Japan finds in Watsuji Tetsuroo (1889-1960) a contemporary who shares similar thoughts with Vygotsky. Watsuji's philosophical work is widely recognized in Japan and it offers some insight to our present concern. In his work Watsuji (1937) develops the concept that the social human relationship is that of *aidagara* 'betweenness.' The term *aida* 'betweenness' literally means a spacial distance that separates two items. The concept of space which makes the notion of betweenness operative was developed earlier in his work *Huudo* (1935). In *Huudo* Watsuji proposes that a person is realized as he or she closely interacts with *huudo* 'climate (and mores)' and this process of interaction and integration serves as the basis of human ontology. A person for Watsuji is also a betweenness in the social network found in social space, as reflected in the Japanese word for person, i.e., *ningen* (literally meaning *nin* 'person' and *gen* 'between'). Watsuji emphasizes that "self" cannot be defined without sufficiently considering the social relationship between the self and others, which in fact are definable only in their "betweenness."

In this regard, Watsuji defines the concept of *sonzai* 'existence' as the following:[3]

Son's fundamental meaning is a subjective self-preservation. The fundamental meaning of the word *zai* is the self's existence in some place. ... The place where the self exists is a social place such as lodging, home, village or the society. In other words, the place is (defined by) the human relationship recognized in groups such as family, village, town, and the entire world. Therefore, *zai* refers to nothing but an existence of self, dwelling in the (human and social) relationship as he or she circulates through human relationships...

and therefore,

Sonzai is the self's comprehension of self placed within human relationships. ... It is reasonable to say that *sonzai* is 'human relatedness realized by human action.' (1937:22-24, my translation)

Like Vygotsky, Watsuji finds the source of social relationship in the interactional nature of language. He comments that, in fact, as he writes his philosophical thesis, he is writing "for" or "to" someone. Even when one mutters a monologue, or one writes with no intention of having someone read it, this by itself does not mean that speech or writing exists without the listener or reader. In fact it is only by the existence of "reader," one is defined as the "writer." The relationship between writer and reader exists expressly as a relationship they themselves create; no "writer" or "reader" has existed before the establishment of this very relationship. Like Vygotsky, Watsuji maintains that one cannot realize linguistic activities without the other--pointing to the essentially interactional nature of language.

The interactional nature of the Japanese language is poignantly illustrated in a set of interactional particles. The particle *ne* is a case in point. While *ne* itself offers no propositionally characterizable meaning, it is nonetheless quite meaningful in conversation. *Ne* offers a mediatory device to connect the speaking subject with the other as it often solicits the other's confirmation and emotional support. It is only when we legitimatize the interactional meaning of language that the meaningfulness of *ne* can be fully appreciated.

2.2. Language as Subjective Expression--Subjectivity

The term "subjectivity" is semantically loaded with a variety of implications. I do not use the term "subjectivity" pejoratively as opposed to "objectivity"--as in "objective truth"--nor to refer to the metalinguistic use of subject in the sense of grammatical subject. Here I use "subjectivity" in a restricted way primarily as it relates to the language producer's subjectivity as reflected in the expression of his or her personal attitude and feelings.

As is widely known, formal theoretical linguistics has in general assumed a speaker who transcends the sociocultural and historical constraints that surround him or her. Under this assumption, the speaking subject is idealized, abstracted and consequently (and often conveniently) obscured. In fact the concept of the idealized speaker facilitates the theoretical position which views language as a formal abstract system waiting to be analyzed by appealing to strictly formal methods and models. I do not deny that language is referential and predicational (i.e., propositional) in part, and as such, abstraction and generalization are justifiable. Thus, for example, the formal analysis of propositional content in terms of the truth functional logic constitutes a primary research concern as advocated by many modern linguists. In fact, modern linguistics and philosophy of language have been dominated by the view that language is, essentially, if not solely, an instrument for the expression of propositional thought.

This view of language, however, is far from complete. Consider, for a moment, the category of modal adverbs. The Japanese adverb *yahari* or its nearly equivalent English adverbial phrases such as *anyway, after all, as expected* and so on do not "refer" to easily definable semantic content nor do they contribute to altering the propositional content per se. The speaker is motivated to use modal adverbs as a means for expressing his or her own attitude toward what is being said. Faced with linguistic signs such as this and many other so-called functional words and attitudinal phrases, we must somehow contend with how the language producer expresses his or her attitude through these signs, among other things, and confront the necessity to analyze them under some heading within linguistic theory. My position is that one can understand a language more comprehensively when one's theory of language becomes a thought-process that embraces the sense of the language producer's "subjectivity" as characterized in this work.

Particularly relevant to the "subjectivity" under discussion are the works of two linguists, one British and the other, Japanese, namely, Lyons and Tokieda. Drawing from the French-German linguistics tradition--especially Benveniste (1971)--Lyons' (1982:102) "subjectivity" refers to "the way in which natural languages, in their structure and their normal manner of operation, provide for the locutionary agent's expression of himself and of his own attitudes and beliefs." More specifically, Lyons (1982:105) proposes the notion of "locutionary subjectivism" which presupposes the following:

1. That the term "self-expression" is to be taken literally and cannot be reduced, theoretically, to the assertion of a set of proposition;
2. That there is a distinction to be drawn, in the structure and use of language, between a subjective component in which the speaker (or, more generally, the locutionary agent) expresses himself and an objective component comprising a set of communicable proposition.

By pointing out the difference between utterances (1) and (2), Lyons introduces the distinction between the "subjective experiencing self" and the "objective observing self."

(1)   I remember switching off the light.

(2)   I remember myself switching off the light.

While (1) indicates the subjective experiencing self, (2) may be interpreted as the speaker reporting the memory of something observed, i.e., objective observing self. As illustrated here the issue of speaker's subjectivity is far from simple. Nonetheless, it is undeniably clear that as long as a linguistic expression exists, we cannot ignore its creator whose subjectivity is somehow expressed in each and every linguistic expression.

Interestingly, a view similar to Lyons' "locutionary subjectivism" was presented earlier by Tokieda (1941). In presenting his theory of *gengo kateisetsu* 'theory of language as process,' Tokieda draws a triangular relationship for the three necessary elements which the existence of language is based upon. These are (1) *shutai* 'the speaking self,' (2) *bamen* 'place, situation inclusive of the addressee,' and (3) *sozai* 'material.' A word of caution here--in reference to traditional Japanese speaking subject, I prefer the term "speaking self" and I will continue to distinguish between Lyons' notion of speaker subjectivity and the Japanese concept of speaking self. The term "speaking self" here refers to the subjectivity expressed by the language producer regardless of whether the activity involved is "speaking" or "writing." Tokieda states (1941:40-431) that "language exists when someone (speaking self) tells someone (situation) about something (material)."

As for the "speaking self," Tokieda explicates his thoughts in the following manner. In a sentence such as *watashi wa yonda* 'I read,' one must recognize that this "I" is not the speaking self; rather, it is the objectified "I" which is part of the linguistic "material." In fact this "I" is, in terms of linguistic material, not different from the "cat" in a sentence "the cat ate a mouse." One may refer to this "I" as grammatical subject, but it is not the speaking self. The speaking self is never expressed in the same way as the linguistic "material" is expressed in language. The explanation given here is similar to the situation where the painter paints a self portrait. Obviously the self represented in the portrait is not the painter, but the objectified and "materialized" self. The subject is in fact the painter who paints. Likewise, the speaking self of the expression "I read" is not the "I." Rather, we must conclude that if one wants to know the subjective expression itself, one must consider the whole of the expression "I read" as *shutaiteki hyoogen* 'subjective expression,' created by the speaking self.

In developing the notion of the speaking self in his theory, Tokieda draws from the works of traditional Japanese grammarians who preserved consistently, sometimes vigorously, the concept of the speaking self. The clearest example of linguistic devices that directly express the speaking self's attitudes and emotions in Japanese, or what Lyons calls "subjective component" of the Japanese language is that of *te-ni-o-ha* particles or *ji*. Here we find a long philosophical tradition in Japanese language studies which takes the position that language is functional at least in two different aspects, one referential (or designative) and the other non-referential (or expressive).

Ultimately, linguistic expression is a power endowed solely to the speaking self. A linguistic expression does not simply "refer" to objects; it manifests thoughts. Therefore, an inquiry into linguistic expression essentially directs us to the speaking agent. In a sense no linguist would deny that natural languages have the property of speaker subjectivity. Few, if any, of the utterances we make on a daily basis are free from the property of the speaker's subjective voice. My point here is not simply to celebrate the obvious. Rather, along with Lyons and Tokieda, I emphasize the fact that some linguistic devices and manipulations primarily serve to express subjective voices and consequently speaker subjectivity must be incorporated in some way into the theory of meaning and into the theory of language in general.

Subjectivity of language has not been much discussed, at least in the terms in which Lyons and Tokieda have, in theoretical linguistics. This may be due, in part, to the fact that much attention has been paid to English which often expresses subjective voices extralinguistically, especially in phonological terms. I contend that some languages are more deeply imbued with subjectivity than others; and Japanese may be a primary candidate for a language that has many linguistic devices and strategies primarily committed to the expression of personal voice.

Admittedly, analyzing the subjectivity and the emotionality of language is controversial. One may question the validity of proposing an analytical framework by concentrating on the subjectivity and emotionality--notoriously elusive--of language. It is undeniable that certain proponents of objectivist theories of language believe that only an objective account of language is truly satisfactory. However, we must not limit ourselves by simply "objectifying" inherently subjective experience that is language for the mere convenience of academic accessibility. An inadequacy of truth-conditional semantics as a total theory of language derives from its restriction to propositional content and its inability to handle the phenomenon of the speaking self. For, ultimately an expression of personal voice cannot be reduced to the mere property of propositional knowledge and beliefs.

2.3. Between Interactionality and Subjectivity--Constructing the Non-autonomous Self

The two modal characteristics discussed in the preceding sections at first glance may appear contradictory. Interactionality emphasizes involvement of at least two individuals while subjectivity centers around a single individual. It is precisely these two notions, however, that play an important role in understanding some aspects of the nature of language.

It has often been said that the Japanese view of self differs from that of the Western tradition. Under the tradition of the Cartesian autonomous "ego," "ego" and the "other" constitute two polar extremes and this dichotomy is something that cannot be resolved unless one is willing to prioritize the existence of either "ego" or "other." In Japan, there is a tradition of defining self on the basis of the human relationship within the society of which the self is a part. This tradition emphasizes the social formation of non-autonomous Japanese self; the notion that self is definable only in relation to the other. Watsuji's work reviewed earlier is a case in point.

Mori (1979) takes a step further in characterizing the nature of Japanese ontology and develops the concept which he calls *nikoo kankei* 'binary combination' or 'binary rapport' (1979:66). According to Mori "binary combination" refers to the following; two persons construct an intimate relationship in the process of life experience, and that relationship itself serves as the ontological basis for each person. In Mori's words:[4]

> I mentioned earlier that among "Japanese," "experience" defines plural persons--more specifically two persons--or the relationship between them. What does this mean? This view of "defining two persons" leads us to conclude that it is impossible for us to analyze our experience to the extent that it defines an experience as an "individual" experience.

and,

> Essentially, among "Japanese" what opposes "thou" is not the "self," but rather, what opposes "thou" is also a "thou" from the point of view of your "thou." ... For example, if we consider a parent as "thou," it might seem obvious to consider the child "self." But this is far from the truth. The child is not the "self" which has its ontological root in its "self," but rather, the child experiences self as "thou" from the perspective of the parents, who in turn are "thou" from the child's point of view. (Mori 1979:63-64, my translation)

For Mori, what opposes "thou" in Japanese is not "self" but rather, a "thou" from the point of view of your "thou," thus defining Japanese self as *nanji no nanji* 'thy thou.'

Here I find a possible synthesis of the two concepts, interactionality and subjectivity. In fact subjectivity exists only when it is supported by interactionality. Thus the speaking self must be viewed as a metamorphic, fluid self which is defined partly in relation to the other.[5] Both the self and the other bring with them the complexity and the diversity of the life-world within which discourses come to life.

The reader at this point may question how this concept of "self" is relevant to the modal characteristics of language. Let me answer this question by making two related points. First, the modal characteristics of language encourage us to take modal meanings seriously. Since the modal meanings must always be traced back to the speaker attitude and ultimately to his or her personal views, how the speaker views and is viewed by the other and the society becomes critical. As discussed earlier, these personal and interpersonal views are reflected in the structure of language especially in its modality as well as in the way one uses the language. Therefore the concept of "self" and the language's modal characteristics are inherently intertwined.

Second, the linguist's view of self motivates, or sometimes forces, him or her into taking either the propositional or the modal aspect of language as a primary area of linguistic research. If one's definition of self is so interactionally ingrained, one cannot ignore the view of language as interacting between people, since language is the primary resource for human interaction. This leads to the view that language must be richly structured so as to accommodate the personal and interpersonal needs, which extend well beyond the propositional information exchange. Thus, extra-propositional aspects of language, i.e., its modal characteristics, become the main focus of one's research. Eventually, this task itself in turn becomes a device to manifest and to assert the researcher's view of self.

At this point I should warn readers that by the concept of Japanese non-autonomous self I do not mean that the Japanese self is weak/strong or inferior/superior when compared to the concept of "ego." Obviously all concepts of self and ego are in part based on a relationship with others. Thus the difference lies only in the degree to which and the manner in which each society endorses the autonomy of the self and ego rather more explicitly (through language, for example) or implicitly.

2.4. Language as Discourse--Textuality

The third modal characteristic of the Japanese language surrounds the issue of discourse and text. The term discourse or text has been used to refer to a body of linguistic signs, normally larger than the traditional unit of sentence, that constitutes a meaningful or cohesive whole. We often have an intuitive understanding of whether or not a group of signs is coherent. But to provide a theoretically based account for such judgment has proved to be persistently difficult. In this section I discuss two studies regarding the concepts essential in understanding discourse, i.e., cohesion, cohesiveness, and textuality.

Halliday and Hasan (1976) maintain that the primary determinant of whether a set of sentences or utterances do or do not create a text depends on "texture." According to Halliday and Hasan (1976:2), "a text has texture, and this is what distinguishes it from something that is not a text" and a text "derives this texture from the fact that it functions as unity with respect to its environment." For example, in a set of sentences given in (3),

(3) Wash and core six cooking apples.
     Put them into a fireproof dish.

the anaphoric function of *them* in the second sentence "gives cohesion to the two sentences, so that we interpret them as a whole; the two sentences together constitute a text." (1976:2)

Halliday and Hasan (1976) consider cohesion as a semantic relation, not any semantic relation but "one specific kind of meaning relation" (1976:11). For the creation of texture a semantic relation must exist in which "ONE ELEMENT IS INTERPRETED BY REFERENCE TO ANOTHER," (original emphasis) and "where the interpretation of any item in the discourse requires making reference to some other item in the discourse, there is cohesion" (1976:141). Although the interpretation is achieved on the semantic level, Halliday and Hasan seem to advocate that each case of cohesion, what they call a "tie," must be realized through a linguistic form. They appear to insist in the following passage that explicit linguistic realization of textual relations is required to achieve cohesion.

Thus the concept of cohesion accounts for the essential semantic relations whereby any passage of speech or writing is enabled to function as text. We can systematize this concept by classifying it into a small number of distinct categories... Each of these categories is represented in the text by particular features--repetitions, omission, occurrences of certain words and constructions--which have in common the property of signalling that the interpretation of the passage in question depends on something else. If that "something else" is verbally explicit, then there is cohesion. There are, of course, other types of semantic relation associated with a text which are not embodied in this concept; but the one that it does embody is in some ways the most important, since it is common to text of every kind and is, in fact, what makes a text a text. (1976:13)

This requirement of cohesive devices has been criticized by more than a few scholars. For example, Brown and Yule (1983:196) conclude that "'texture,' in the sense of explicit realisation of semantic relations, is not criterial to the identification and co-interpretation of texts." Obviously it is important to delineate the connections between items in a text from their explicit expressions within that text.

After a closer reading of Halliday and Hasan's work, however, we learn that they suggest a broader notion of cohesion beyond the textual level. They incorporate the Malinowskian concept of situation, i.e., the "context of situation," into the concept of "cohesion." The text is interpreted not only in the sense of semantic cohesion but within the context of "register," which describes the social, interpersonal and psychological nature of the context of situation. Halliday and Hasan write:

The concept of COHESION can therefore be usefully supplemented by that of REGISTER, since the two together effectively define a TEXT. A text is a passage of discourse which is coherent in these two regards; it is coherent with respect to the context of situation, and therefore consistent in register; and it is coherent with respect to itself, and therefore cohesive. (1976:23, original emphasis)

Although Halliday and Hasan intend to incorporate this broader concept of cohesion, the major part of their 1976 study focuses on the linguistic devices and strategies that signal textual ties and fails to develop this direction in detail.

The question remains: What concept of textuality is necessary for understanding language? How is such a concept of textuality related to the modal characteristics of language, which is our primary concern here? More recently Schiffrin (1987) proposes a broader concept of cohesion in discourse. Incorporating Gumperz' (1982, 1984) communicative view of coherence which includes all aspects of "contextualization cues," Schiffrin states:

Coherence, then, would depend on a speaker's successful integration of different verbal and nonverbal devices to situate a message in an interpretive frame, and a hearer's corresponding synthetic ability to respond to such cues as a totality in order to interpret that message. (1987:22)

Schiffrin then proposes "a model of coherence in talk," which is also called "a model of discourse" which includes (1) participant framework and (2) information status. Within the participant framework are three structures, ideational structure, action structure and exchange structure. For Schiffrin, then, cohesion encompasses aspects of communication ranging from the propositional content to the participants' turn-taking environment.

The concept of cohesion supplemented by register as suggested by Halliday and Hasan (1976) and Schiffrin's model of discourse cohesion are useful in identifying the modal characteristics of language. Cohesion--beyond the logical semantics of cohesiveness--falls under the concept of modality in language and it is in this sense that the meaning of textuality becomes important for understanding the modal nature of language.

The importance and the usefulness of the broader notion of cohesion becomes obvious when we begin to understand some of the Japanese connectives (or conjunctions). Although one may hasten to conclude that connectives in general signal logical connections such as cause-result or cause-consequence, this purely semantic characterization of connectives fails to capture some of their important functions. As will be discussed in detail in the course of this study, for example, the connective *dakara* in Japanese not only signals the existing cause-result relationship but also prefaces a discourse segment that offers supplementary explanation to the statement made in the prior text. This latter function can be identified only when the researcher incorporates the conversational exchange structure in mind. Thus the textuality realized here is not limited to semantics alone; rather, the textuality in pragmatic terms is also an essential part.

2.5. Modality-centered View of Language--Emotionality and Personal Voice

In sections 2.1 through 2.4, I have reviewed three modal characteristics of Japanese; interactionality, subjectivity and textuality. These characteristics illustrate my view toward language; language is interaction-based, subjectivity-conscious and textuality-bound. And above all, I hold the view that modal characteristics must be incorporated in the analysis of language. Thus, rather than a propositional and semantic approach, I take the modality-centered position and as the primary area of inquiry in this work explore an analysis of the modal aspects of language.

In essence the modal characteristics of language originate in the language's inherently social nature. One cannot escape the social nature of language even when engaged in a most private activity. A solitary thinker cannot separate himself or herself from the society of which he or she is a part. This is because it is through language, the most social of all resources of human life, that one learns to become an individual. Thus we can view language as a process which ultimately reveals the speaking self as a product of the society. Language in this sense is not unlike a narrative about the speaking self. In order to understand the personal message, one must discover, appreciate, and integrate non-propositional information which includes the expressions of subjectivity, emotion and voice of the speaking self. I go even so far as to state that the modal characteristics of language are primary and are more critical than propositional information to interpreting the message in Japanese communication.

3. Data

Faced with the decision as to what data should be analyzed, a linguist is confronted with the problem of circularity. Although the researcher has to know the theoretical framework before deciding on the type of data relevant to the research, it is also the case that the theory itself must be built upon the evidence gathered from the very analysis of the relevant data. As will be mentioned later in my discussion regarding the methodology for this study, data analysis and theory building feed on each other during the course of research.

For this study I made my initial decision on data selection--casual conversations--on the basis of the simple fact that the aspects of language I investigate are best expressed in spoken language. As the concept of Discourse Modality and the linguistic signs and strategies expressing it developed, and a broader data base was found to be necessary, I decided to add dialogues extracted from fiction. This made it possible to have access to a large number of tokens for analysis. Some linguistic expressions and strategies, for example, modal adverbs, appeared only a limited number of times in the smaller casual conversational data. The combination of actual casual conversations and author-created conversations in modern fiction offers a unique opportunity to contrast the results to observe whether or not data selection can significantly influence the overall interpretation of Discourse Modality.

Further, as my interest expanded to the sentence-final forms which had to include substantial written text as data source, I added literary essays. I believe that the broadened base of data sources as analyzed in this study brings insight to the understanding of how linguistic signs function across different types of genres and discourse. Specifically in this study I chose the following six types of data.

1. Videotaped casual conversation,
2. Dialogue portion of fiction,
3. Narrative portion of fiction,
4. Literary essays,
5. Created and sometimes manipulated data for discussion,
6. Miscellaneous sources.

The conversation data analyzed in this study was collected in Tokyo in May, 1985. All subjects were university students studying in Tokyo. Each conversation was performed by two speakers of similar age (between 19 and 23) and the same sex, totaling 20 pairs, involving 40 speakers. All conversations were video- and audio-recorded in a controlled situation with no outsider present, with minimal guidance given to the subjects. So as to minimize the degree of subjects' awareness of being filmed from being reflected in the data, with the assumption shared among conversation analysts in general (e.g., Duncan & Fiske 1977:37) that speakers grow accustomed to being recorded and that unnatural speech decreases with time, the initial 2-minute segments were categorically excluded from the data and the following 3-minute segments were selected as data relevant to this study.[6] Statistical information discussed in this work is based on a total of 60 minutes of conversation--3 minutes each taken from 20 conversations. It should be noted that data set (31) analyzed in chapter 3 is taken from the last ten-minute segment of the casual conversation when subjects were asked to discuss issues on which they disagreed.

The data taken from Japanese fiction consists of two types, (1) dialogue portions, and (2) narrated segments. All sources of fiction were selected from contemporary works of Japanese fiction--mostly from mystery novels, and some from short stories and a few from general interest novels. In all, 29 volumes of fiction representing 22 individual authors served as data source, totaling 7,638 pages altogether. (See data references for the list of sources). It should be noted that additionally, Ooe (1981) is included strictly for the purpose of contrast with its English translation and is not included in the statistical account of data.

I also chose 20 volumes of anthology of modern Japanese literary essays which I believe fairly represent the genre. The data sources for the segments of the essays analyzed in this work are given in data references. Additionally, some examples created by myself as well as some manipulated data examples are used to facilitate discussion. I should also mention that I discuss a few data samples from miscellaneous sources (utterances occurring in a television program, for example) where such samples are useful.

For the presentation of conversation data, the following guidelines are used.

1. Whenever there is a recognizable pause, the pause is marked by /.
2. The boundaries of the speaking turn are marked by square brackets.
3. Listener back channels are listed in parenthesis.
4. Identification of the subjects is in parenthesis classified by gender and pair number corresponding to the one identified in Maynard (1989).
5. Proper nouns appearing in conversational data are altered to protect privacy of the subjects.

The key transcription methods and conventions used for data presentation in this work are provided below.

1. Japanese transliteration is given in phonetic orthography referred to as the Hepburn style, except that *fu* is spelled *hu*, unless the use of *fu* is conventionalized. In presenting double consonants, before *cha, chi, cho* and *chu*, instead of adding an extra *c*, *t* is added, thus instead of *icci* 'agreement,' *itchi* is used. Syllabic *n* is written *n* unless it immediately precedes a vowel, in which case it is written *n'*. For long vowels, unless conventionalized otherwise, double consonants are used. Proper nouns appearing in this work also follow the transliteration method unless conventionalized otherwise.

2. When transcribing, not all morphemes are separated. Only those morphemes relatively important to the present study are separated with glosses given. When glossing, hyphens are used only when overt indication of the connection between grammatical and lexical elements is useful.
3. In data presentation the specific linguistic signs under discussion are underlined for convenience.
4. The identification number for authentic data is given in parenthesis; the identification number for fabricated and/or manipulated data appears in square brackets. The number for the data sample from other researchers' works quoted in this work is listed in parenthesis.
5. Square brackets are used to identify structural relations, for example, [X. *datte* Y] to show relevant segments [X] and [Y] discussed in the analysis of *datte*. Other uses of square brackets are explained in the main text whenever relevant.
6. The following abbreviations are used for the glossing of Japanese.

BE   the copula 'be'
COND   conditional marker
IO   indirect object
IP   interactional particle
LK   linker (linking nominals and nominal adjectives)
NEG   negative
NOM   nominalizer
O   direct object
PASS   passive
Q   question marker (assigned to final particle *ka* only)
QT   quotative marker
S   subject marker
T   theme marker

4. Organization of the Study

Following this chapter, in chapter 2 where I discuss Discourse Modality in detail, I propose that modality is best characterized as a mechanism to interactionally create a conceptual "scene." Included in chapter 2 are the introduction of the notion of D(iscourse) M(odality) indicators, descriptions of the aspects of

Discourse Modality along with the process of Modal Contextualization, followed
by a discussion on methodological issues. In chapter 3, discourse connective DM
indicators, i.e., *dakara* 'so, therefore' and *datte* 'but, because' are analyzed, while
chapter 4 explores two adverbial DM indicators, i.e., *yahari/yappari* 'as
expected, at any rate' and *doose* 'anyway, after all.' The two stylistic verb
endings *da* and *desu/masu* are analyzed from the perspective of Discourse
Modality in chapter 5. Chapter 6 focuses on interactional particles *yo* and *ne*.
Chapter 7 discusses the expression *to yuu* in the Japanese clause-noun
combination as it is used as a device marking Discourse Modality in subordinate
clauses. In chapter 8 I pose the larger question of how the theoretical
framework of Discourse Modality can be placed in its historical and social
perspectives, and I discuss some implications of this study to cross-cultural
communication.

CHAPTER 2

From Modality to Discourse Modality

1. Concept of Modality

Two distinctly different traditions in the study of modality are significant for our purposes. First is *kokugogaku* 'traditional Japanese language studies' in Japan which I review in section 1.1 and second, Western Linguistics reviewed in section 1.2. The reviews are limited since they cover only the aspects which are of immediate interest to the present study.

1.1. Modality--Japanese View

The general concept of modality has been in existence for quite some time in Japanese traditional scholarship. I find two haunting problems in explicating the concept of modality in this context. First, the concept itself is difficult to define in formal terms and therefore we must resort to a less vigorous, often metaphorical description. Second, many scholars have used the Japanese term *chinjutsu* 'modality' in a variety of ways, sometimes even in ways that seem almost contradictory to one another.[1] Terms such as *modusu* 'modus,' *muudo* 'mood' and *modariti* 'modality' have also been adopted by Japanese linguists and distinctions among these and *chinjutsu* 'modality' remain vague. Our first task in this section is to trace the history of the concept of *chinjutsu* by reviewing some of the earlier studies which touch upon the issues of modality in Japanese.

In tracing the sources of modality, I limit my discussion to the concept of *te-ni-ha* or *te-ni-o-ha* particles and the surrounding ideas. As for the rationale for this decision, let me point out that while many other aspects of traditional Japanese language studies are relevant to the concept of modality, it is the discovery of the *te-ni-o-ha* category that has inspired later studies. And it is the acknowledgment of the qualitative difference between *te-ni-o-ha* and other parts of speech that eventually leads to a prioritization of the concept of modality.

The first documented discovery of the category *te-ni-o-ha* is known to have appeared in *Teniha Daigaishoo* (ca. 1200) presumably (but being disputed by many) written by Fujiwara Teika. In this work the present day parts of speech--including the suffixes of verbals and adjectivals, particles, auxiliary verbs and conjunctions--are categorized as *te-ni-ha*. All other parts of speech, primarily nominals and the verbal and adjectival stems are known to belong to another category called *shi*.

The most important work related to modality and therefore more relevant to our discussion, however, is that of Fujitani Nariakira (1738-1779). The two major works of Fujitani include *Kazashishoo* (1938, originally 1767) and *Ayuishoo* (1960, originally 1778). Fujitani presents his view toward language in *oomune* the 'summation' section of *Ayuishoo*. First, Fujitani divides Japanese words into four basic categories, *na, kazashi, yosoi* and *ayui*, which he defines as the following:

1. *Na* 'nouns' identify objects;
2. *Kazashi* 'pronouns, adverbs, conjunctions, exclamations, affixes' assist other parts of speech;
3. *Yosoi* 'adjectives' describe objects;
4. *Ayui* 'auxiliary verbs, particles, suffixes' assist other parts of speech.

As is widely known, a literal translation of the last three terms reveals Fujitani's intention to associate his categorization with the linear order of Japanese expressions; *kazashi* means head decoration (appearing at the beginning), *yosoi* clothing (often the middle part of the sentence), and *ayui* the footwear appearing at the end of the sentence).

According to Nakada and Takeoka (1960:89), in *Koohon Ayuishoo* 'Ayui-shoo Manuscript' the terms used to define *kazashi* and *ayui* represent parts of speech that are particular to the speech situation; they are manipulated by the language producer in such a way as to represent one's personal voice. Therefore, if one is concerned with (literary) expressions and interpretation of literary works, as was Fujitani, the most important inquiry lies in understanding how an individual voice is represented in language. This voice is most prominently expressed by *kazashi* and *ayui* (and conjugation of *yosoi*), and Fujitani's most significant contribution lies in the study of these categories.

Ayuishoo is a collection of 164 particles, auxiliary verbs and suffixes which are hierarchically categorized into two large types being further divided into five intermediate and 50 smaller groups. Each item is semantically and functionally explained with frequent citation of poetry examples.[2] Beyond the fact that Fujitani's lifework is devoted to analyzing modality-expressing devices, perhaps most significant to our present concern, i.e., our search for the sources of modality, is his concept of *uchiai* 'echoing' introduced in *Ayuishoo*. *Uchiai* refers to the echo effect among different words within a sentence. When interpreting a poem, a mere understanding of each word is insufficient. One must grasp the larger framework within which one word echoes another, creating a resonance that reverberates throughout the poem. This echo effect is achieved as a result of two or more words functioning in combination.

Obviously the concept of *uchiai* is similar to *kakarimusubi* 'grammatical adverb-predicate correspondence' which was introduced earlier by Motoori Norinaga (1730-1801) in his *Te-ni-o-ha Himokagami* (1902, originally 1771). But *uchiai* is a larger notion covering a broader spectrum of phenomena than *kakarimusubi*. According to Fujitani,[3]

The master says: As I will explain in each chapter of this book, *uchiai* is regulated by a particular type of corresponding *ayui*. However, two additional types of *uchiai* exist that should be explained separately. First is the *nabikizume* and the second, *kakusu uchiai*. *Nabikizume* refers to the use of pre-nominal forms of adjectives and *ayui* which do not have corresponding particles or other corresponding *kazashi* and *ayui*. This happens when one admiringly exclaims with pre-nominal forms (rather than ending the sentence with usual verb endings). Such a case should be interpreted by adding phrases that express exclamation such as "how...," "what a..." and "I wish..." ... *Kakusu uchiai* occurs when one avoids using corresponding sentence-final particles. In this case the *uchiai* is suggested by the accompanying original poem or poetry citation, or by the *kakekotoba* (literary punning) phrase which hides the corresponding *ayui*. (Nakada and Takeoka 1960:97-98, my translation)

The essence of *uchiai* is an expression of personal feelings and emotion that cannot be fully explained by a mere compilation of word meanings. Here I find the early sense of *chinjutsu* realized by the sentence as a whole. Modality is not assigned to a particular linguistic item, but rather, it is the echoing effect of words (primarily *kazashi* and *ayui*) that can be understood only when one acknowledges an overall effect of modality that contextualizes the meanings of words.

Fujitani's work evidently influenced other scholars during the Edo period, most notably that of Suzuki Akira. In his *Gengyo Shishuron* (1979, originally 1824), Suzuki introduces four classifications of words; *tai-no-shi* 'nominals,' *keijoo-no-shi* 'adjectivals,' *sayoo-no-shi* 'verbals,' and *te-ni-o-ha* 'te-ni-o-ha particles.' Suzuki groups the first three into one large category, i.e., *shi* 'referential words,' and deems *te-ni-o-ha* to be an opposing category. Suzuki notes that the "refined" *te-ni-o-ha* system in Japanese is idiosyncratic to the language, and seems to, unfortunately, engage in celebrating the "uniqueness" of the Japanese language.

Suzuki delineates the contrasting characteristics between *shi* versus *te-ni-o-ha* as discussed below:

Sanshu-no-shi 'three types of referential words':
  1. They have referential function;
  2. These are referential words;
  3. They refer to objects and thus become referential words;
  4. They are like precious beads;
  5. They are like containers;
  6. They fail to operate (function) without *te-ni-o-ha*.

Te-ni-o-ha:
  1. They have no referential function;
  2. They represent voice;
  3. They are voices from the heart and are attached to *shi*;[4]
  4. They are like strings that connect precious beads;
  5. They are like hands that use or operate the containers;
  6. Without *shi*, they have nothing to be attached to.

Suzuki (1979:23-24/1824) summarizes that the voices of *te-ni-o-ha* distinguish and express states of one's heart, and the voices of nominals and other words distinguish between objects and describe these objects. Suzuki's *te-ni-o-ha* are linguistic devices that are non-referential and that describe personal attitude. Again, the concept of *te-ni-o-ha* is the key to understanding *chinjutsu* in Japanese. And the term "voices from the heart" warns us that language's purpose is not limited to a mere exchange of information. On the contrary, language is one of our most personal means for expressing our voice.

This very term "voices from the heart," however, turns out to be irksome to another major figure in Japanese language studies, Yamada Yoshio. Yamada (1908) is critical, if not seriously dissatisfied with Suzuki's work. Yamada comments as follows:[5]

> Since Suzuki distinguishes *te-ni-o-ha* from *shi* by metaphor alone, it is impossible to fully understand its essence. According to the metaphorical definition, it is defined as "voices from the heart attached to *shi*." What are voices from the heart? Are they sounds that express thoughts? If so, what words are voices from the heart? It is impossible for me to understand the description, "voices from the heart attached to *shi*." It could be that I am simply incapable of understanding a difficult concept, but I think it (Suzuki's concept of *te-ni-o-ha*) remains to be a mere riddle. (1908:24, my translation)

Contrary to this criticism, Tokieda (1941) reintroduces the concept of "voices from the heart" with enthusiasm in his own work. Tokieda writes in response to Yamada's criticism of Suzuki:[6]

> Referencing means conceptualized objectivization and "voices from the heart" means direct expression of concepts. ... I was astonished by the fact that Suzuki's thoughts are capable of providing answers to questions not answered in many linguistic theories available in the world today... Yamada's criticism of Suzuki ... is based on the structural view of language, and as long as one holds such a view, it is impossible to understand accurately the true meaning of Suzuki's concept. (1941:233, my translation)

Suzuki's work is indeed resurrected when Tokieda in 1941 introduces his theory of language, *gengo kateisetsu* 'theory of language as process.' Tokieda (1941, 1950) takes the view that language is the very process in which the speaking self expresses ideas by using linguistic sound. Instead of viewing language as a product (or an object) with its internal structure, Tokieda (1941:86) insists that language is *shinteki katei* 'psychological process.'

Based on this theory of language as process, Tokieda identifies two categories, i.e., *shi* and *ji*, and claims that all Japanese lexical items are grammatically categorized either as *shi* or *ji*. Tokieda (1950, 1954) defines *shi* as an expression which has gone through the objectifying process--representing an objective and conceptualized notion of referents, which includes grammatical categories of nouns, verbs, adjectives and adverbs. *Ji*, on the other hand, is an expression which has not gone through the objectifying process--representing the speaker's subjective perspective toward the referent and it includes conjunctions, exclamatory expressions, auxiliary verbs and particles.

Tokieda seems to associate *ji* most closely with the concept of *chinjutsu*. In his work (1941) Tokieda does not discuss *chinjutsu* directly; in fact although he uses the term, he offers no definition. From what I can comprehend of his writings, however, the power of *chinjutsu* is granted to auxiliary verbs (as well as zero auxiliary verbs, if not overtly expressed) and particles. Tokieda (1941:251-252) seems to equate the function of *ji* with *chinjutsu* as suggested in his statement that "the essence of *chinjutsu* is not an objectified element but the totally subjective judgment itself and therefore, *chinjutsu* clearly shares features common with *ji* (my translation)."[7]

Let us at this point examine some of the representative definitions of *chinjutsu*, the concept of modality in Japanese. Yamada (1922) views *chinjutsu* as the function of copula, logically connecting subject and complement (or object), which is perhaps best translated into English "predicate." According to Yamada,[8]

The most important characteristics of *yoogen* (corresponding to verbals and adjectivals) are that they express "*chinjutsu*." The power involved in *chinjutsu* is the function to unify human thought and to recognize differences and similarities between the primary and secondary concepts and to unite them. (1922:44-45, my translation)

In other words, for Yamada, *chinjutsu* and the subject-predicate unification are one and the same.

We have already noted that *chinjutsu* is understood differently by Tokieda. Recall that for Tokieda the subjective expression (often realized by *ji*) is the source of *chinjutsu*. Tokieda's ideas on *chinjutsu* are further elaborated by Watanabe (1971). For Watanabe, *chinjutsu* expresses the subjective speaker's view toward his *jojutsu* '(propositional) description,' and it is expressed by final and interjection particles. Here the term "modality" seems an appropriate English equivalent. Watanabe defines *jojutsu* and *chinjutsu* as *kotogara o egakiageru hanashite no itonami* 'speaker's act of describing facts and things,' and *sore o kikite meateni hyoogen-suru itonami* 'act of expressing that description toward the addressee,' respectively. Watanabe's *jojutsu* is further divided into *toojo* 'completing description' and *tenjo* 'conjunctive description.' In Watanabe's words:[9]

> *Chinjutsu* refers to a relational function that the speaking self finds existing between himself or herself and the description completed, description yet to be completed, as well as the relationship the speaker finds toward objects and the addressee. Internal meanings that realize the function of *chinjutsu* include speaker's judgment, questioning, exclamation, appeal and address (toward the addressee). (1971:106-107, my translation)

Haga (1954, 1982) further elaborates on Watanabe's *chinjutsu* by categorizing it into two types, i.e., *juttei* 'modality' and *dentatsu* 'communication.' For Haga *chinjutsu* is expressed by a variety of devices including auxiliary verbs, final and interjection particles, exclamatory phrases and intonation.

Notions of *chinjutsu* in common among Tokieda, Watanabe and Haga, are the following:

1. The speakerhood (the existence of the speaking agent), thus speaker subjectivity is emphasized;
2. Two qualitatively different types of linguistic elements exist in language, one of which is engaged in expressing *chinjutsu*;
3. The distinction between these two separate types of elements is used to explain the functions of sentence in communication.

Other works exploring the notion of *chinjutsu*, *modariti* and other related concepts include Hayashi (1983), Onoe (1973), Nakau (1979), Nitta (1989) and Masuoka (1991). While sometimes obscure and difficult to understand, it is clear that many scholars have attempted to systematize various aspects of *chinjutsu* 'modality' in Japanese. As will be made explicit in this chapter, although these studies offer insight and guidance into the study of modality I find the concepts developed in previous works lacking its scope and explicitness. Before discussing the necessity of introducing the concept of Discourse Modality, however, in the next section we turn to a brief review of literature on modality available in Western scholarship.

1.2. Modality--Western View

Within his functional framework, Halliday (1970) comments on modality in the grammar of English as follows. The expression *Smith died* expresses, beyond its content, "a role relationship between speaker and hearer." In making a statement, the speaker takes upon himself or herself a communication role, that of "declarer" and invites the partner to take the complementary role of hearer. Halliday (1970:325) states that the expression of these speech roles in a communication situation is "one instance of the wider function whereby the speaker enters into the communication process in its social and personal aspects"--that is, his interpersonal function. Modality derives from the interpersonal function and is frequently expressed by (1) the verbal (including modal auxiliaries)--e.g., *will* and *would*, and (2) lexical items (adverbs, adjectives and nouns)--e.g., *perhaps, possibly, possible* and *possibility.* These forms represent the speaker's assessment of the probability of what he or she is saying, or the extent to which he or she regards it as self-evident. These meanings are what Halliday understands by the term "modalities." In short, for Halliday modality is an assessment of probability.

Halliday is quick to add, however, that it is not in the specific words of English assessing the probability that we locate modality. In Halliday's words,

> There is thus no one single place in the clause where modality is located. It is a strand running prosodically through the clause; and this effect is further enhanced by the fact that in addition to the forms above it may be realized also by the intonation contour, or tone. (1970:331)

Grammatically Halliday sees modality as being outside the ideational meaning of the clause, and consequently outside the domain of tense. Halliday

(1970:336) adds that the modalities relate only to "speaker-now" and play a role primarily in the interpersonal function.

Lyons (1977:452) defines modality as "the speaker's opinion or attitude towards the proposition that the sentence expresses or the situation that the proposition describes." Lyons' view echoes that of Benveniste's (1971); Benveniste (1971:229) discusses the "indicator of subjectivity" being devices "suited to characterize the attitude of the speaker with respect to the statement he is making." Lyons (1977) divides modality into epistemic (necessity and possibility) and deontic (obligation and permission). Further, within epistemic modality, there are two types, objective epistemic and subjective epistemic. The objective epistemic modality refers to the logical conclusion of probability, while the subjective epistemic refers to the speaker's qualification of the I-say-so component of his utterance. Lyons (1977) explains that in subjective epistemic modality the speaker's subjective commitment to the truth or falsity of the proposition might be quite unrelated to his knowledge of the objective possibility or degree of probability--not unlike the gambler's subjective commitment to the probability of a particular number coming up in roulette.

Lyons' notion of modality, then, is closely linked to the concept of subjectivity. Lyons (1981:238) states that "subjective epistemic modality is nothing other than this: the locutionary agent's qualification of his epistemic commitment." According to Lyons (1981:237) this expression of the speaker's "own beliefs and attitudes, rather than reporting, as a neutral observer, the existence of this or that state of affairs," is "much more common than objective modality in most everyday uses of language." The close association between subjectivity and modality advocated by Lyons is an important ingredient in proposing my concept of Discourse Modality in this work.

While Halliday (1970) is mainly concerned with epistemic modality and Lyons (1977, 1981) mainly with subjective (epistemic) modality, Lakoff's (1972) work opens up a broader context for the concept of modality. For example, how does one account for the attitudinal differences observed in (1) (Lakoff's [31])?

(1.1) John says you must apologize.

(1.2) John says you have to apologize.

In (1.1), the speaker agrees with John that an apology is required, while in (1.2), he may be merely reporting John's demand, without agreeing. In (1.1) the speaker's participation in the obligation is one of sympathy. This feeling of sympathy cannot satisfactorily be explained without incorporating a broader notion of pragmatics. Even the then popular performative analysis seems to be unable to fully incorporate the speaker's attitude such as one of sympathy.

Additionally, modals are not the only grammatical category for expressing the speaker's participatory attitude. For example, examine (2) (Lakoff's [33]).

(2.1) It's raining.

(2.2) It's raining, isn't it?

Utterance (2.2) which contains no performative verbs or modal auxiliaries expresses the speaker's attitude similar to that expressed by a performative verb of a softened statement such as *I guess it's raining*. The concept of modality then is applicable to broad areas of grammar and its implication is not limited to the so-called epistemic or deontic modality.

More recently the concept of modality in pragmatics has been actively explored. Here I comment on two such works, Stubbs (1986) and Coates (1988). Stubbs' concept of modality is indeed broad as reflected in his words:

> ... whenever speakers (or writers) say anything, they encode their point of view towards it: whether they think it is a reasonable thing to say, or might be found to be obvious, questionable, tentative, provisional, controversial, contradictory, irrelevant, impolite, or whatever. The expression of such speaker's attitudes is pervasive in all uses of language. All sentences encode such a point of view, ... and the description of the markers of such points of view and their meanings should therefore be a central topic for linguistics. (1986:1)

Stubbs finds that the traditional performative analysis (which concentrates on performative verbs) can account for only one of the many ways of expressing explicitness or vagueness. He points out the necessity for developing a more general theory of "commitment" and "detachment." Utterances will fall somewhere within a continuum of commitment, whose extremities are complete commitment on one end and complete detachment on the other. Full commitment could be made by the categorical assertion that the proposition (P) is the case. Complete detachment from (P) involves some kind of quotation or mention--for example, an expression such as *for the sake of argument*. An utterance such as

(3) It could be that (P)

expresses only partial commitment.

By commitment Stubbs refers to a variety of speaker attitude including whether a proposition is presented as true, false, self-evident, a matter of objective fact or of personal opinion, shared knowledge, taken for granted or debatable, controversial, precise or vague, contradictory to what others have said and so on. The concept of commitment constitutes a part of what Stubbs calls "modal grammar of English," which contains topics such as (1) whether the propositions can be used or mentioned, and (2) the different sources to which the statements can be attributed. As for the grammatical categories that should be incorporated into the modal grammar of English, Stubbs lists simple versus -*ing* verbs, private verbs (e.g., *believe, think, imagine*, etc.), logical and pragmatic connectives, and sentence adverbs. Stubbs (1986:4) insists on the importance of developing a modal grammar of English since modality "can be seen as a central organizing principle in language." Still, Stubbs' suggestion is that discovering how utterances are qualified in modality and to what degree and in what manner they are qualified in different contexts calls for "a matter of prolonged fieldwork."

While Stubbs (1986), although insisting on the importance of the fieldwork, does not analyze data taken from natural language sources, Coates (1988) examines natural conversational data from the perspective of semantic-pragmatic modality. Coates (1988:9) includes hedges (as depicted in (4)--her [7]), for example, as a part of modality manipulation.

(4) Well isn't there a theory that that it, I mean I think it was
     your theory wasn't it that that it runs in families

Overall, Coates introduces the concept of modality which includes semantic-pragmatic aspects beyond those discussed by Stubbs. These include: (1) to mark speaker's shifting point of view, (2) to serve as a face-saving strategy, (3) to express negative politeness strategy and (4) to offer opinions without taking up a hard and fast position.

Through the observation of representative works on modality briefly reviewed above, one can conclude that the way, or at least one of the ways the study of modality is heading begs for an expansion of both the theoretical concept and of data in the area of pragmatics. Obviously any departure from modal logic as a primary source of analysis creates the possibility for opening up modality research and making it perhaps even chaotic. The neatness and comfortable order imposed by traditional analysis of modal logic is replaced by often muddled and sometimes confusing explanations. Here we must remind ourselves that one must not celebrate a neat and tidy analysis merely because of its neatness. For, when faced with the untidiness of real-life use of language, we are compelled to acknowledge the limitations of a cleanly definable modal logic. Resurrecting the speaking self and recognizing language as a self-expression negotiated in intricately complex multi-level actual human interaction leads us toward a pragmatics-oriented concept of modality.

2. Concept of Discourse Modality

2.1. Toward a Concept of Discourse Modality

The works reviewed in the preceding two sections simultaneously provide insight and reveal shortcomings. In this section I focus on two major shortcomings of previous studies thereby setting the stage for my proposal of Discourse Modality, the key concept and framework for this study.

First, most researchers build their framework for modal analysis on the basis of limited, often conveniently created data. While some research examines data taken from authentic sources, the types of data source are limited. More reliable analysis and its subsequent theoretical construction (and further data analysis based on said theory) are likely to be achieved by examining a broader data base. Once the researcher examines a broader data base, two important issues emerge which have not been handled satisfactorily in previous works. One is the issue of modality in social interaction which needs to be explored in more detail along the lines of Coates (1988). The study of modality in interaction can benefit from conversational analysis through the application of models such as turn-taking strategy, the exchange structure and conversational speech actions. The other is the issue of modality in its relation to the discourse structure, which has been given scant attention in previous studies. The modal meaning is bound not only by socio-interactional context but also by discourse structures--including cohesion, cohesiveness, discourse segmentation and discourse organizational principles. In order to fully understand the concept of modality, one must incorporate the concept of modality in discourse, i.e., Discourse Modality.

The second major shortcoming I alluded to earlier is that even when data analysis is presented, previous studies have tended to account for limited grammatical categories--modal auxiliary verbs and modal adverbs, for example-- without incorporating the results into a comprehensive view of language as a whole. The ad hoc results of an unorganized hodgepodge of research projects can be only marginally impactful. A framework enabling us to explain the modal nature of language across traditional grammatical territories must be found to present a systematic analysis of a variety of grammatical devices and strategies expressing modality. Analyses of signs expressing Discourse Modality, i.e., D(iscourse) M(odality) indicators, representing a variety of grammatical categories can be meaningfully interpreted when a theoretical framework such as Discourse Modality is put into place.[10]

In summary, although insightful many previous works on modality lack recognition of and attention to the broader data base, leaving us with no comprehensive framework with which to reckon with the critical interactional and discourse organizational aspects of modality. Previous works also fail to examine different modality devices in a systematic way within a single framework. As will be explained in what follows, my response to these remaining problems is to analyze Japanese language under a framework of Discourse Modality by using the concept of Modal Contextualization.

2.2. Defining Discourse Modality

I define Discourse Modality as follows:

> Discourse Modality refers to information that does not or only minimally conveys objective propositional message content. Discourse Modality conveys the speaker's subjective emotional, mental or psychological attitude toward the message content, the speech act itself or toward his or her interlocutor in discourse. Discourse Modality operates to define and to foreground certain ways of interpreting the propositional content in

discourse; it directly expresses the speaking self's personal voice on the basis of which the utterance is intended to be meaningfully interpreted.

In contrast to the concept of Discourse Modality are two terms, proposition and modality, which require some clarification. One can characterize the term "proposition" in various ways; here I borrow the definitions from Johnson (1987). When I use the term "proposition" or "propositional content" in contrast with modality and Discourse Modality, I mean the general sense of the term, i.e., a combination of what Johnson (1987:3) states--(1) something proposed, a statement, (2) a state of affairs in the world, usually one holding between an entity and its predicates (e.g., properties) or among a number of entities, (3) from model theory: (a) a function from possible worlds to truth values, (b) a function from possible situations to facts (where a "fact" is a property or relation paired with the entities that it holds of). I also find the following dictionary definition useful (Random House 1966:1153), i.e., "a statement in which something is affirmed or denied, so that it can therefore be significantly characterized as either true or false."

From this point on when I use the term "modality" in contrast with Discourse Modality, I refer to aspects of modality which are normally referred to as epistemic and deontic modality. I use the term modality in a way similar to Halliday (1970) and Lyons (1977) as reviewed earlier. The term "modality" in a narrow sense, then, refers to functional aspects mostly realized by English modal auxiliary verbs and modal manipulations such as declarative, interrogative, imperative, exclamatory and so on, which express speaker's opinions and attitudes. Modality operates primarily within a sentential boundary and has less impact on the discourse structure within which Discourse Modality primarily operates. Discourse Modality is a broader notion which includes not only the speaker's attitudes expressed by independent lexical items or combinations thereof but also those that can be understood only through discourse structures and in reference to other pragmatic means.

2.3. Discourse Modality as Scene

The best way of describing Discourse Modality and its relationship to the propositional content of the utterance is through circular imagery. I picture the propositional content as being situated within two concentric circles, one, the inner circle of modality and the other, an outer circle of Discourse Modality. Although this imagery identifies two distinct circles, modality and Discourse Modality, they are not mutually exclusive. The larger circle, Discourse Modality, completely encloses all modal features and provides the largest and most dominant circular territory. Thus, the relationship between propositional content and its surrounding territories is that the outmost layer of Discourse Modality provides the most dominant context and constraints for the semantic interpretation of the proposition.

When considering the structure of language, we are familiar with either the linear construction--for example, subject followed by verb followed by object--, or the hierarchical structure--for example, when subject and verb are placed under a higher node, sentence. However, in order to account for Discourse Modality these two images are less useful. For one, Discourse Modality affects the totality of the proposition in such a way that it constrains the overall semantic effect, including even the syntactically manipulated meanings. Second, Discourse Modality is often achieved not necessarily by an independent lexical item, but rather through a combination of lexical items, syntactic manipulations and all types of discourse strategies which involve the sentence as a whole, rather than the parts of a sentence. The traditional theoretical imagery, for example, the tree structure, which forces hierarchical relations directly linked to independent lexical items and concepts is therefore inadequate.

However, the primary reason I think circular imagery works most appropriately lies in the concept of "place," and the theoretical concept of "scene" derived from the notion of "place," both of which are critical to my view of language, and both of which require an image of space surrounding proposition in a circular fashion.

Let me now introduce the notion of scene as a part of the cognitive base for Discourse Modality and define it as follows:

Scene is an emotional and conceptual space established and activated by participants of communicative interaction within which states and events are identified, interpreted and described. To establish a scene, speaker's (or writer's) perspective must be recognized, and he or she must commit himself or herself to certain modes of expression. These include not only evaluation, assessment and personal opinions of the message conveyed, but also the speaking self's emotions, intentions, and feelings toward the content and toward the other, all of which provide a conceptual scene. Scene is a space in which speaker's (or writer's) subjectivity and the speaker-listener (or writer-reader) intersubjectivity meet. Semantically, scene contextualizes the meaning of and the interpretation of the propositional content, and therefore it is an integral part of language.

The process of scene-creation involves a personal commitment to the interaction. The process not only defines, introduces and describes the relevant phenomena with personal evaluation and assessment, it also adds emotional tone to the statement. This process of creating the scene is the very expression of the speaking self. Within this scene, and when this scene is moderately identified, a description of the event and state begins to emerge. This space itself is not predetermined to be either subjective or objective. As soon as a speaker makes a personal commitment and pursues his or her mode of description, i.e., a speaker chooses his or her Discourse Modality, and the moment he or she begins to form the scene, speaker subjectivity begins to take its shape. Within that emerging scene, description consisting of propositional statements are given direction. This description in turn substantiates and further defines the scene of which it is a part. This integrating process continues until subjective and objective perspectives fuse and characterize actualized utterances to whatever degree of speaker subjectivity is being expressed.

Another important aspect related to the creation and the subsequent establishment of scene is activating certain world knowledge and pulling it into the relevant "scene." When we construct a mental model for a piece of discourse, we use some of our pre-existing knowledge and experience to get a "picture" of the state of affairs described in the discourse. Obviously we do not activate all of our pre-existing knowledge simultaneously nor with the same intensity. At the same time one must compromise to obtain an appropriate balance between the knowledge being too detailed and too vague. The appropriate quality and quantity of information necessary for meaningful interaction must be incorporated into the "scene." The linguistic devices and strategies expressing Discourse Modality will serve as cues to activate just such knowledge.

While the image of "scene" developed above remains abstract, in more concrete terms one can link the concept of "scene" to the place of action one finds in a stage drama. Let me, for a moment, take advantage of this convenient theatrical metaphor and explain the characteristics of the conceptual scene as the following. First, a theatrical scene is always created with the intended audience in mind. So is the conceptual scene for language which cannot survive in a social vacuum, but which always expects a communication partner. The theatrical scene presents a spacial domain where an appropriate perspective is achieved by the differentiation between foregrounded elements and those that are backgrounded. The location of light and the degree of brightness, the color and the hue of the light and the props placed at various locations within the scene define the tone and the mood of the scene. Sound effects including music also add to the general atmosphere. In our conceptual "scene," Discourse Modality creates a certain tone or atmosphere for the interpretation of the propositional content. A particular theatrical scene is a part of a continuous flow of various places on the stage where dramatic personalities continue to interact. What happens in one scene is always interpreted relative to the whole. The same is true for the conceptual "scene" in which one must interpret its semantic significance in relation to neighboring scenes as well as the global scene of which it is a part. In appreciating a theatrical drama, one must interpret the meaning of what actually happens in the particular scene against the background provided by the very scene. This is also the case in the conceptual "scene" where one must interpret linguistically coded information in relation to the "scene" itself.

2.4. The Concept of Place in Linguistics and Philosophy

I have just introduced the concept of "scene" as a metaphorical device to characterize Discourse Modality. But obviously I am not the only one who uses this concept and concepts similar to it. In order to differentiate my concept of "scene" from the others, let us review a few of the similar ideas. I am aware that sociolinguists and ethnomethodologists, among others, have utilized and developed concepts similar to "place," "location" or "situation," including Malinowski's (1923) "context of situation" and Hymes' (1972) "components of communication." It is clearly the case that both sociolinguistically and cognitively some sort of common ground or common space must be acknowledged by communication participants for a meaningful interaction to take place. First, communication occurs in physical space. Second, this space is socially created and maintained. Third, beyond this sense of a sociolinguistic concept of "context of situation," there must also be a cognitive common space. This cognitively activated common space provides a background against which meaning is contrasted and interpreted. Therefore there is every reason to believe that the concept of "place" will continue to play an important role in theorizing on language and communication. However, it is the concept of "place" developed by Tokieda (1941) which comes closest to what I am alluding to here.

As mentioned earler, Tokieda (1941) claims that language requires three essential elements: the speaking self (*shutai*), place/situation inclusive of the listener (*bamen*) and the (semantic) material (*sozai*). In Tokieda's view *bamen* 'place' is not only the actual social situation for interaction but also as a rather comprehensive--almost psychological and emotional--"place" where linguistic interaction occurs. In Tokieda's words:[11]

> ...as opposed to the notion of *basho* 'location' referring only to physical and locative space, *bamen* 'place' includes the contents which occupy such 'place.' Thus, although *bamen* 'place' is similar to *basho* 'location' to the extent that objects and scenery are included, *bamen* 'place' includes far more than that. It includes the speaking self's attitudes (*taido*), feelings (*kibun*) and emotion (*kanjoo*) toward these objects and the scene. (1941:43, my translation)

For Tokieda the most important element of the "place" is the addressee. The addressee influences the speaker and "language is always expressed in harmony with that place." (1941:46) As important are the speaker's intentions, attitudes and emotions which identify the addressee and other objects existing in the scene.[12] Thus, according to Tokieda (1941:44) "the 'place' is not purely objective nor purely subjective; rather it is the world where subjectivity and objectivity fuse into one." While Tokieda emphasizes the importance of speaker subjectivity in establishing the linguistic place, the speaking self exists outside the place; it remains to be another necessary element required for language, i.e., *shutai* the 'speaking self.'

What exists in this "place," however, is not limited to the addressee only. According to Tokieda (1941:44-45) the "place" is filled with many other objects and environmental factors. Thus the same addressee will encourage different speech styles from the speaker depending on the context of the situation. The important point here is that all elements in the "place" must be recognized as such by the speaking self. Therefore, there is no concept of "place" unless we acknowledge the speaking self which defines it. At the same time, since the speaker is defined by the "place," primarily by the addressee, no linguistic action is possible without being situated in the "place." The place contextualizes linguistic expression, and in turn linguistic expressions characterize the "place." Tokieda concludes that it is because of this unbreakable chain between human action and "place" that the concept of "place" becomes indispensable to the study of language.

While Tokieda's concept of "place" remains directly linked to the situation of speech, my notion of "scene" is an abstract theoretical concept which is essential in interpreting the meaning. The conceptual "scene" which exists only in one's mind is ultimately owned by the speaking self. How the scene is identified depends entirely on each participant's way of understanding. In this sense a "scene" is a personalized "place" in the eye of the speaker. It is through defining this "scene" that the speaker personalizes the intended propositional interpretation. And it is in the process of building this "scene" that Discourse Modality most deeply engages itself. Exactly how we utilize this "scene" in the analysis of Discourse Modality will be addressed when we later discuss the process of Modal Contextualization.

At this point let us explore the philosophical background of the concept of "place" and "scene." Obviously one can recognize a philosophical source for the concept of "place" in Watsuji (1937) reviewed earlier. It seems natural to say that our self-existence is realized in some "place." As Watsuji (1937) suggests, the awareness of self is realized in relation to others which exists in a "place"-- both in a concrete and an abstract social sense. The notion of self, then, is not independent of the place in which it is recognized. Similarly, when language is used for communication, the propositional meaning can be appreciated only in its "place."

It is of interest to note that the two critical concepts under discussion here, i.e., the speaking self and the place, are interdependent and yet represent two opposing dialectical elements. As often proclaimed in Cartesian philosophy, it is the notion of the ultimate "ego" decontextualized and devoid of its existing place that has been glorified. As represented by the claim *"Cogito, ergo sum,"* in fact "ego's" independence from its environment--cut off from its intersubjectivity and its history--has welcomed the modern individual who satisfies himself or herself in the eagerly pursued prize of independence by reaching the state of an autonomous self.

In this context I would like to bring into our discussion a Japanese philosopher, Nishida Kitaroo (1870-1945) whose work addresses this very issue.

Nishida (1949, originally 1926) introduces *basho no ronri* 'theory of place/topos' which focuses on the place where the self is defined. Nishida pursues his theme, "the logic of the place of nothingness" in the following manner. First, Nishida maintains that logical inquiry should start not from the often assumed dichotomy between subjectivity and objectivity. Instead, it should start from self awareness which can be realized by "reflecting on oneself in oneself." For "self" to be conscious of something is to see oneself cast upon the screen of self's own field of consciousness. In terms of logic, this field of consciousness functions as a predicate. Given a logical calculus of "S is P," this means that S is defined by P which is the generally perceived characteristic of the object. That is, one interprets the proposition "S is P" by applying the general characteristic to the particular.

When one is conscious of oneself in the "place" within the field of consciousness, this place itself is not pre-determined, nor is it restricted or defined. It is a place of nothingness; a place of endless possibilities where nothing is predetermined. Nishida characterizes what occurs in this place as the following.

> That which is self-conscious must stand, self-consciously, in a dynamically expressive relation to an absolute other. This entails the biconditional structure of co-origination and co-reflection. Thus I repeat that I disagree altogether with the epistemological position that takes its point of departure from the logic of objects. I hold that thinking takes place within the structure of an interexpressive relation. Judgment itself occurs within the contradictory identity of subject and object. From A, A expresses B in itself, as something expressed by A. That is, taking B as grammatical subject, A predicates of B; alternatively, taking B as object, A predicates of B. But the converse is also true. It can equally be said that A is expressed in B, becomes a perspective of B's own expression. (Dilworth 1987:55)

For Nishida, the most important aspect of the self-identifying logic is not the a priori awareness of the subject of "*cogito*" but the self placed in the field of consciousness which is equipped with the power of predicating. Instead of building on the logic based on the concept of "subject" as the center of the universe, Nishida finds importance in "predicate" which identifies the "subject." Nishida continues:[13]

> Ordinarily one thinks of self as a subjective unification just as objects
> possessing various characteristics. However, self is not a subjective
> unification; rather it must be a predicative unification. It is not one dot, but
> rather, it must be a circle. It is not an object; rather, it must be a place.
> (1949:279, my translation)

The locative and the circular imagery I continue to use in describing my concept
of "scene" and Discourse Modality is influenced in part by this statement of
Nishida's.

How is Nishida's "logic of the place of nothingness" related to the concept
of Discourse Modality? I answer this question in three ways. First, Discourse
Modality is metaphorically identified as existing in a conceptual "scene." For
Nishida, the logical inquiry should exist in the "topos" within the field of
consciousness. Both Nishida's philosophy and my concept of Discourse Modality
share the importance of place/scene. Second, Nishida's claim that the predicate
defines the subject resembles my view that Discourse Modality defines the
proposition. Just as the predicate provides conditions which define the subject,
Discourse Modality provides the possible context which defines the meaning of
the proposition. In fact it is not difficult to provide linguistic evidence
supporting this position. In Japanese, grammatical subjects are easily deleted
while the predicates marked by DM indicators (or *ji* in a traditional grammatical
sense) are not. The speaking self always exists behind the predicate which
defines the subject, and not vice versa. Third, in both Nishida's and in my views
the importance of self--whether it is the thinking or the speaking self--is
emphasized. Just as one becomes aware of self by reflecting on oneself within
the consciousness of oneself, the proposition becomes meaningful by being
contextualized in the "scene" of Discourse Modality.

So far I have presented some philosophical background for the place-related
image of Discourse Modality without mentioning linguistic studies adopting
similar concepts. In fact the term "scene" has been used in linguistics and in
related fields. How then does my concept of "scene" introduced here differ from
those available in the field? In an attempt to answer this question I contrast my
concept of "scene" with representative notions of "scene" in Western linguistics.

Fillmore (1982) uses a term similar to "scene," i.e., "frame" as a part of
"frame semantics." According to Fillmore (1982:111), frame refers to "any
system of concepts related in such a way that to understand any one of them you
have to understand the whole structure in which it fits" and "when one of the

things in such a structure is introduced into a text, or into a conversation, all of the others are automatically made available." Fillmore uses the term "frame" as a general cover term for the set of concepts variously known as "schema," "script," "scenario," and so forth. Since frame semantics is introduced primarily as a descriptive framework for the analysis of word meanings and the combination thereof, it does not include the psychological and emotional aspects of communication. Similarly to the earlier concept of "scene," the concept of "frame" as it is fails to provide sufficient resources for our analysis.

Other related concepts include (1) "script" developed by Schank and Abelson (1977), (2) concept of "setting" appearing in the narrative schema introduced by Rumelhart (1975) and Thorndyke (1977), and (3) concept of "stage" developed by Longacre and Levinsohn (1978). Overall, although the term "scene" has been used in different ways in the recent history of linguistics and related fields, my concept of "scene" differs significantly from the others. As explained earlier, my concept of "scene" includes the broader modal aspects of communication. And what lies at the heart of the "scene" is the speaker's desire to create an environment where the speaker can successfully express his or her personal voice.

3. Discourse Modality Indicators

In this study I concentrate on analysis of what I call Discourse Modality indicators (DM indicators). First I define DM indicators in a way which allows me to identify tokens by a principled set of criteria. This makes it possible for me to address the issues of: (1) how to find the indicators and (2) how to group linguistic signs based on their similarity.

First I present the definition of DM indicator.

D(iscourse) M(odality) indicators are non-referential linguistic signs whose primary functions are to directly express personal attitude and feelings as characterized by the concept of Discourse Modality.

By "non-referential" I mean that DM indicators do not refer to or designate an object in the Saussurean sense. Although some DM indicators often possess referential meanings, referencing is not their primary function. Instead, non-referential uses are primary. DM indicators do not carry truth-functional value in their primary meanings. DM indicators, being expressions of the speaker's personal voice, normally occur in direct discourse and represent the speaker's subjectivity, emotion and voice. In this sense they "directly express" personal attitude and feelings as given in my definition.

I must confess, however, that specifying a precise range of DM indicators may be impossible both in principle and in practice. This is because given an appropriate context, some referential devices may operate non-referentially as DM indicators. Therefore, in some cases one must examine the context of a linguistic sign in order to identify a DM indicator as such. Some DM indicators, for example, interactional particles *yo* and *ne*, are genuine in that they possess no referential function. Others, for example, the discourse connective *dakara* is a functional DM indicator in that although it has no referential function by itself, it marks logical connections between propositions and is therefore referentially functional as well. As made evident by my definition, DM indicators do not belong to a single grammatical category; as long as a linguistic sign fits the description given above, we consider it to operate as a DM indicator. Here we should remind ourselves that DM indicators are not the only category of devices to control Discourse Modality. In fact the way a proposition is constructed or even the selection of one specific lexical item over another can influence the effect of Discourse Modality. Even so, it is possible to identify linguistic signs and strategies which function in significant ways to enhance the effect of Discourse Modality. Other discourse modality strategies include extralinguistic features as well as some syntactic strategies as listed below. This study analyzes only limited types of DM indicators, categories 3 and 5.

Types of DM Indicators

1. Paralinguistic DM indicators:
   This category includes paralinguistic features of verbal communication such as intonation, tonal effect, voice quality, speech rhythm and speed, as well as all nonverbal signs such as eye-gaze, head movements, and so on.
2. Syntactic DM indicators:
   Although Discourse Modality is expressed primarily through non-syntactic strategies, the choice of syntactic structure itself can influence the overall modal effect of the sentence. For example, whether an

utterance is expressed in an active or passive construction reflects the speaker's perspective toward the event. So does the word-order which reflects different information structure.

3. Independent DM indicators:
    This category includes all independent linguistic signs which express subjective and emotional aspects including:
    Exclamatory interjections--*maa* 'wow,' *saa* 'well,' etc.;
    Interactional particles--*ne, sa, yo, na, zo, ze*;
    Modal adverbs--*yahari/yappari* 'as expected, at any rate,' *doose* 'anyway, after all,' *sasuga* 'as might be expected,' etc.;
    Discourse connectives--*dakara* 'so, therefore,' *datte* 'but, because,' *demo* 'but, still,' etc.

4. Complex DM indicators:
    This category includes auxiliary linguistic signs which express subjective and emotional aspects of the related lexicon including:
    Auxiliary verbs and auxiliary adjectives which are combined with verbals when used--*rashii* 'it seems,' *daroo* 'perhaps it is,' *soona* 'it appears.'

5. Multi-phrase DM indicators:
    Included in this category are *da* and *desu/masu* alternation--DM manipulating device functioning in discourse organization and narrative manipulation, and *to yuu*--DM manipulating device functioning in clause-noun combination.

I should mention at this point a term similar to DM indicator, i.e., Schiffrin's (1987) "discourse marker." The concept of DM indicator refers to a larger body of devices that includes discourse markers. A DM indicator may have functions represented by discourse markers but it may also have broader functions spanning across many aspects of Discourse Modality--such as Perspective, Information Status, Personal Emotion and Sociolinguistic Style-- which will be introduced in the next section.

The rationale for paying special attention to DM indicators in this study has already been pointed out, i.e., to explore often neglected non-referential meanings of language. But another fundamental reason for analyzing DM indicators extends beyond the obvious. Consider that language offers multiple linguistic signs and strategies that can, in purely grammatical terms, occur in an identical context. The optional use of the *to yuu* phrase in the clause-noun combination in Japanese, for example, is a case in point. The speaker's motivation for either the use or non-use of *to yuu* cannot be explained in terms of formal analysis alone, since both are grammatically correct. To understand the nature of language and the way the language is used in communication, one must be able to discover the speaker's motivation for either choice. Since aspects of Discourse Modality offer a semantic, pragmatic and social basis on which such motivation is predicated, analyzing a linguistic sign as a DM indicator within the framework of Discourse Modality can bring into the open the speaking self's motivations for a specific linguistic choice. Whereas the issue of choice has often been neglected in the field of linguistics, this broadened framework can explain why one linguistic form or style is chosen over another.

4. Aspects of Discourse Modality

In this section I present four basic types of aspects of Discourse Modality whose functional domains differ qualitatively. As will be mentioned repeatedly, these domains are not necessarily meant to be mutually exclusive. In fact differentiations of categories themselves are fuzzy. An identical DM indicator often operates in multiple, if not all, functional domains. Obviously Discourse Modality permeates every aspect of language and communication, making it difficult to systematize each of its possible facets. It is useful, however, to separate aspects of Discourse Modality into four broad categories for the purpose of elucidating the qualitatively different kinds of domains that Discourse Modality governs. My purpose here is not to present a detailed taxonomy of all possible aspects of Discourse Modality. Rather, my concern here is to present an organized view of the aspects of Discourse Modality, each of which will be discussed in detail later whenever it becomes relevant in the analysis chapters. The aspects of Discourse Modality discussed in this work are limited to those relevant to the DM indicators analyzed in this study.

4.1. Information Qualification

This category functions to express the speaker's attitude toward the information itself. Let us assume, for convenience's sake, that (P) represents propositional information in an utterance. Then the information qualification of Discourse

Modality functions to qualify--semantically, pragmatically and functionally--the relevant information defined by (P) itself. In what follows I present four different ways information (P) may be qualified; (1) Perspective, (2) Information Status, (3) Epistemic Modality, and (4) Discourse Cohesion.

4.1.1. Perspective

It is often said that every art form expresses the creator's point of view, or what Uspensky (1973:2) refers to as the "viewing position." In producing a linguistic expression, one must take a certain viewing position or positions which determine what one sees and what one expresses. The particular viewing position one chooses is an important aspect of linguistic message, for it reveals the language producer's personal commitment to the actual mode of expression. I use the term "perspective" in the sense of Uspensky's viewing position, i.e., the position where one locates oneself in relation to the world expressed.

In actual linguistic expressions, perspective may be expressed through syntactic choice, including case assignment, active versus passive voice and so on.[14] It may also be expressed by assigning a morpheme to identify the theme or non-theme in the text that one is in the process of creating. The concept of "staging" (see Maynard 1980, 1987) introduced as a discourse function of the Japanese theme marker *wa* is one example of perspective. *Wa* assignment itself does not change the referential meaning, but it expresses the different perspective one takes toward the event described. Although I introduced the concept of "staging" on the basis of narrative data in Maynard (1980, 1987), the staging effect can be expanded to other genres beside the narrative. Distinction between the thematic and the non-thematic plays an important role in the qualification and organization of information in all types of discourse and therefore it is a vital part of Discourse Modality.

In narrative discourse--and I include casual narratives in conversation--a specific perspective is at play. Rather than identifying different viewing angles an observer may take toward the observed, the viewing position of the language producer may be found internal or external to the narrative scene. When taking a narrative internal position, one locates oneself internal to the scene as if witnessing the event right there and then. When taking a narrative external position, the language producer describes the event as an outside observer. This external/internal positioning of the narrator in relation to the events described constitutes narrative manipulation, the so-called narrative "point of view." We must be cautioned, however, that the concept of "point of view" is one of the

most troublesome terms in literary criticism and therefore it becomes necessary
here to use the term "point of view" in a rather limited as well as practical way.
Here I mean by "point of view," the language producer's viewpoint expressed
through and reflected in various positionings he or she takes toward the
narrative event. This sense of perspective is one aspect of Discourse Modality.
For example, the mixture of the DM indicators *da* and *desu/masu* verb endings,
among other things, operates for this purpose as will be discussed in chapter 5.

4.1.2. Information Status

By information status, I refer to the concept of given (shared, or old) versus new
information. The terms "given" and "new" have been used by scholars in
different ways as pointed out in Maynard (1980, 1981), and I should offer a brief
explanation regarding these concepts. Weil, as early as 1844, argued that in
order to carry out successful communication, it is necessary that speech
participants "lean on something present and known, in order to reach out to
something less present, nearer or unknown" (1887:29, originally 1844). More
recently the given/new distinction has been examined by linguists such as
Halliday (1967), Kuno (1972), Chafe (1976), Prince (1981), Yule (1981) and
Brown and Yule (1983). The notion of given/new that I adopt here is closest
to Chafe (1976:30). Chafe defines given (or old) information as "that knowledge
which the speaker assumes to be in the consciousness of the addressee at the
time of utterance."

The concept of given and new information and related qualification of
information status are useful in understanding the information status because its
distinction is often linguistically marked. For example, the DM indicator,
interactional particle *yo*, functions to request the addressee's attention to
information that is relatively less accessible and is therefore often new. Since
it is by the process of incorporating new information into the "old" or "already
activated" information that one accumulates knowledge and interprets the
meaning of the linguistic signs, identifying the information status which is an
aspect of Discourse Modality, becomes essential in communication.

4.1.3. Epistemic Modality

For the concepts of epistemic modality I adopt Lyons' (1977) views. According
to Lyons (1977:800), (subjective) epistemic modality can be accounted for "in
terms of the speaker's qualification of the I-say-so component of his utterance"
which expresses opinion rather than fact. This contrasts with deontic modality

which "is concerned with the necessity or possibility of acts performed by morally responsible agents" (1977:823). More concretely, in English, epistemic meaning is expressed by linguistic forms which indicate the level or the lack of speaker's confidence in the truth of the relevant proposition. For example, in an utterance *she may come*, the use of the word *may* indicates lack of confidence in the proposition "she comes." Lexical items such as *may, must, perhaps, probably, possible, I think, I suppose*, as well as certain prosodic and paralinguistic features are used to express epistemic modality.

DM indicators that qualify the propositional information by expressing degree of speaker confidence toward the proposition fall under the category of Epistemic Modality. Among the Japanese DM indicators analyzed in this study, modal adverbs *yahari/yappari* and *doose* contribute to this aspect.

4.1.4. Discourse Cohesion

By cohesion I refer to the concept of cohesion in the sense of Halliday and Hasan (1976). However, as mentioned earlier, I hold a broader view of cohesion than the one Halliday and Hasan (1976) have focused on, although they allude to a broader notion that is similar to my view of cohesion. For this reason I prefer the term "discourse cohesion,"--especially in the following sense. First, agreeing with Brown and Yule's (1983:196) point, I find that an explicit realization of cohesive relations by a linguistic device (which according to Halliday and Hasan create a "tie") is not a necessary condition for the existence of cohesiveness. Second, discourse cohesion includes not simply the cohesion realized by specific relations between two items within a text; it also implies that the text is coherent with respect to the general discourse structure. Thus the utterance is expected to be coherent intersententially as well as intratextually. The features characterizing this broad notion of discourse cohesion fall under Discourse Modality because they qualify the propositional content by signaling the inter-connection among multiple propositions as well as between these propositions and their statuses within the global discourse structure.

Segmenting discourse into meaningful units and organizing them hierarchically reflect an aspect of discourse cohesion. Foregrounding and backgrounding certain information within a text also contribute to discourse cohesion since these strategies distinguish between greater and lesser cognitively and interactionally focused information. As will be argued in the course of this study, among the DM indicators, *yahari* is an example which contributes to this aspect by signaling anaphoric relations. So do the verb-final forms *da* and *desu/masu* which may distinguish between main and subordinate information in a long speaker turn and in literary essays.

4.2. Speech Action Declaration and Qualification

By Speech Action Declaration and Qualification I refer to the notion that the language producer declares and qualifies the speech action itself implicitly or explicitly, marking the speech with linguistic devices. I adopt here the concept of speech actions or "verbal interactions" as proposed by Labov and Fanshel (1977:60). Labov and Fanshel (1977:61) introduce four groups of speech actions including "meta-linguistic," "representations," "requests," and "challenges." These actions differ from the traditional categories of Speech Acts associated with Austin (1962) and Searle (1969). They also differ from the kinds developed by Bach and Harnish (1979) which include Constatives, Directives, Commissives and Acknowledgments. These actions are the kind "which have to do with the status of the participants, their rights and obligations, and their changing relationships in terms of social organization" (Labov and Fanshel 1977:58-59). Additionally, I incorporate the categories of discourse arguments--some overlapping with Labov and Fanshel--introduced by Schiffrin (1987). Schiffrin (1987:18) discusses three parts of argument--"POSITION," "DISPUTE," and "SUPPORT."

In analyzing Discourse Modality, qualification of speech actions--or more accurately, assessing the intention for the speech action qualification--becomes essential. Only by identifying the speaker's intention for the speech action itself and by integrating that information into the comprehension of the propositional meaning, can one reach the utterance's true discourse and interactional meanings. In reality, speakers use every available strategy with the intention of convincing the partner to achieve the goals of interaction. For example, in order to "SUPPORT" one's or someone else's "POSITION," a language user may declare the speech action of "(self-)justification." Similarly, one may offer the speech action of "explanation" in order to support one's position. As I will argue in the course of this work, the former is achieved in part by the connective *datte* and the latter by the connective *dakara*.

4.3. Participatory Control

4.3.1. Exchange Structure

An Exchange Structure is a sequentially defined structure in which at least two interaction participants take turns filling in a structural slot of speaker turns. Here I have particularly in mind the Stubbs' (1983) concept of exchange structure developed from Sinclair and Coulthard (1975). As important are two additional structures widely acknowledged in face-to-face interaction, i.e., the turn-taking system and the adjacency pair.

According to Coulthard (1977:106), the exchange structure characteristically observed in the traditional teaching context consists of the classroom interaction structure in which moves and exchanges occur in a predictable order. Stubbs (1983:141) attempts an analysis of complete interchange by setting up categories such as I(nitiation), R(esponse), F(eedback), O(pening), Ir(Re-Initiation), and C(lose).

The exchange taking place in an interaction may also be broken down into smaller segments, for example, the speaker turns. As mentioned elsewhere (Maynard 1989: chapter 6), I recognize two approaches in the study of the turn-taking system. The first is the "rule-governed one-at-a-time approach" represented by Sacks, Schegloff and Jefferson (1974). The other is the "systems approach supported by a statistical analysis of signals" represented by Duncan and Fiske (1977, 1985). While their approaches differ, both recognize a structure or system in which participants identify the unit of the speaker turns, signal their boundaries, take and yield turns. Some functions of DM indicators are directly connected to the strategy of turn taking. For example, the modal adverb *yahari/yappari* functions as a filler and/or a planner during the turn-transition period.

From an even more local perspective, the concept of conditionally relevant adjacency pairs (Schegloff and Sacks, 1973) may operate in such a way as to encourage the speaker to respond to the speech action initiated by the coparticipant. A question is expected to be followed by an answer, and a greeting by a greeting. If the second-pair-part is missing, it is noticeably absent. If the second-pair-part is dispreferred, such a turn may be signaled by a type of Discourse Modality indicator, i.e., what Pomerantz (1984) calls "dispreference markers" or what Bilmes (1988) calls "reluctance markers."

While these three structures operate on different levels of discourse, each contextualizes each utterance, and thereby constrains the semantic interpretation of the relevant proposition. It is to our immediate interest to recognize these structures and use them as analytical resources. Through exchange structure, for example, I identify how a relevant proposition is contextualized to mean what it means. Among the DM indicators, the modal adverb *yahari/yappari* and the connective *datte* function as dispreference markers. The functions of the interactional particles *yo* and *ne* also can be characterized in terms of exchange structure. *Yo* and *ne* evoke different types and degrees of listener responses.

4.3.2. Designing Speaker Turns

Here I focus on the characteristics of the turn itself--particularly how an utterance is designed and shaped to meet the demand imposed by its discourse and interactional environment. A turn-initial utterance may be preceded by an expression that acknowledges the turn-transition period followed by an expression announcing that the turn is now taken. At the same time as I described elsewhere (Maynard 1989:94), each utterance is designed to realize broader social expectations. At the end of each utterance, a variety of utterance-final and/or turn-final signals may be added. For example, the connective *dakara* functions to mark turn-initial and turn-final positions. The phrase *to itta yoona* also function to design the speaker turns by presenting one's view in a less imposing way. These devices are DM indicators since their primary function lies in reflecting interactional attitude and showing emotional response to others, which in turn help define the overall atmosphere or the "tone" for each social encounter.

4.4. Interactional Appeal

4.4.1. Personal Emotion

Interactional Appeal is concerned with the interactant's feelings and attitudes toward the speaker. The aspect of the personal emotion refers to the speaker's emotional attitude toward the content and/or toward the partner. The term related to the personal emotion is "affect" discussed in Ochs and Schieffelin (1985) and Schieffelin and Ochs (1986). According to Ochs and Schieffelin (1985), "affect" refers to aspects of communication that express feelings, moods and attitudes and it employs a variety of verbal and nonverbal strategies. As will be shown in the course of this study, it is in this emotional aspect of modality that the Japanese modal adverb *doose* has the most prominent function.

4.4.2. Sociolinguistic Style

While sociolinguistic style refers to an array of stylistic features controlled by sociolinguistic factors--social register, speech genres, relative social status of the participants, and so forth--here I focus on what Leech (1983) refers to as the maxims of the Politeness Principle. Leech (1983:132) proposes six maxims of the Politeness Principle:

1. Tact Maxim: minimize cost to other, maximize benefit to other;
2. Generosity Maxim: minimize benefit to self, maximize cost to self;
3. Approbation Maxim: minimize dispraise of other, maximize praise of other;
4. Modesty Maxim: minimize praise of self, maximize dispraise of self;
5. Agreement Maxim: minimize disagreement between self and other, maximize agreement between self and other;
6. Sympathy Maxim: minimize antipathy between self and other, maximize sympathy between self and other.

These maxims serve as guidelines for a language producer to behave in a socially pleasant manner. In order to achieve this goal, the speaking self often uses DM indicators such as verb-final forms and interactional particles which contextualize the meanings of the proposition in such a way as to suit the social expectation.

5. Modal Contextualization: Its Process

Modal Contextualization is a process in which a D(iscourse) M(odality) indicator activates one or more aspects of Discourse Modality and consequently achieves some M(odal) C(ontextualization) effects which contribute to building a modal "scene." I propose that in contextualization, the following principles apply.

1. A set of propositional information (P) contextually implies information (MC(P)) if and only if the union of MC and P is semantically and pragmatically possible.

2. The semantic and/or pragmatic possibility of such union is judged upon socioculturally based knowledge in that the interpretation reached by the combination (MC(P)) is conventionally, or otherwise, mutually acknowledged as being meaningful to the participants.

3. Modal Contextualization qualifies, through Discourse Modality indicators, the meaning/function of (P) by:

   (1) Strengthening or weakening the speaker's commitment to (P), or altering the quality of (P) to the extent that the level of commitment required for the interpretation allows;

   (2) Identifying, qualifying and declaring speech action and consequently characterizing (P) as said speech action;

   (3) Signaling the interactional role of (P) within the participatory framework regulated by participants, and altering the meaning of (P) to suit the participatory demand characterized by that DM indicator or indicators;

   (4) Presenting (P) in reference to one's personal emotion toward (P) and/or the partner, and signaling the interpretation of (P) only to the extent that (P) is presented in accordance with said emotional characterization and such combination is socioculturally interpretable.

4. For some DM indicators one may identify "semantic source" which in a particular context is interpreted as achieving a certain MC effect. At the same time a DM indicator through the MC process contextualizes the meaning of (P).

5. Among various MC effects, a hierarchy exists in such a way that the more subjective the effect, the higher up it is in the hierarchy, and therefore the more effective. If two or more conflicting MC effects occur, the more subjective effect overrides the less subjective one. The distinction between the greater or lesser subjective effect generally corresponds to the location in which the DM indicator appears. The DM indicator increases in subjectivity the closer it is positioned to either the utterance beginning or end.

6. DM indicators not only define which aspects of DM are activated but may also intensify or weaken the MC effects already activated.

7. Paired or multiple DM indicators may function to increase the level of already activated DM aspects.

8. The more DM aspects are activated, the more the referential meaning of (P) is qualified and the more subjective and personal the meaning of the utterance becomes.

9. When conflict exists in the semantic and/or pragmatic meanings between activated DM aspects and the (P), the DM aspects override the (P).

10. The interpretation of an utterance is achieved within the DM "scene," which is defined by a combinatory whole of all relevant MC effects associated with the utterance, and which offers the overall tone and the mode of its Discourse Modality.

The process of Modal Contextualization is schematized in Figure 2.1.

Figure 2.1. *The Process of Modal Contextualization: A Case of* Yahari/Yappari *as an Example*

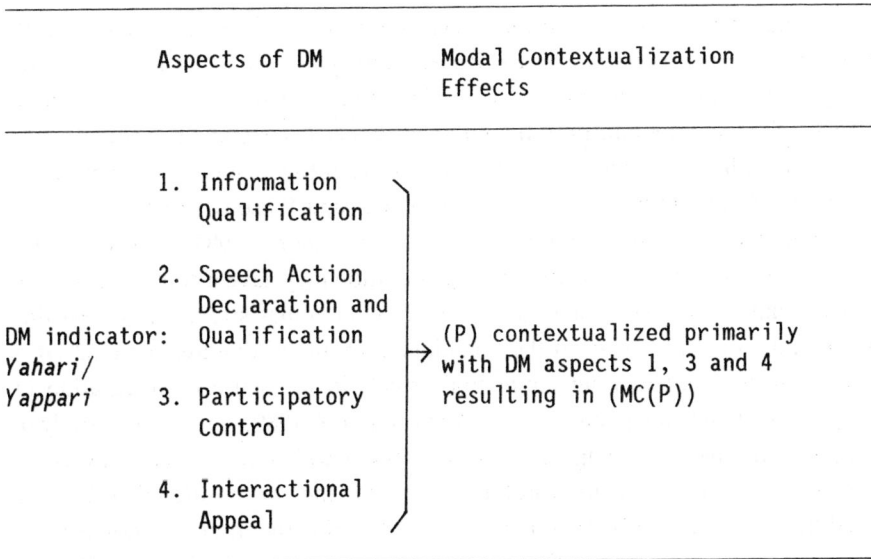

```
            Aspects of DM          Modal Contextualization
                                   Effects
_____

            1. Information
               Qualification

            2. Speech Action
               Declaration and
DM indicator:  Qualification       (P) contextualized primarily
Yahari/                            with DM aspects 1, 3 and 4
Yappari     3. Participatory       resulting in (MC(P))
               Control

            4. Interactional
               Appeal
_____
```

It should be reminded here that although the process of Modal Contextualization can be attributed to occurrences of DM indicators, their absence--in contrast with their existence--can also convey certain DM aspects.

As will be made explicit in chapter 5, the naked abrupt form of the verb can be attributed to some of the DM aspects. The process of how the effects of Modal Contextualization are integrated into the semantic interpretation of MC(P) is that of a gradual and accumulating specification of MC(P).

In understanding this mechanism of contextual specification, I find it useful to borrow from the concept of "relevance" developed by Sperber and Wilson (1986) and further explored by Blakemore (1987). According to Sperber and Wilson (1986:102), "the relevance of new information to an individual is to be assessed in terms of the improvements it brings to his representation of the world." In other words, relevance correlates with informativeness. In their words:

> ... a deduction based on the union of new information {P} and old information {C} is a contextualisation of {P} in {C}. Such a contextualisation may give rise to what we will call contextual effects. (1986:108)

Contextual effects result when the integration process of new information with old information occurs in various degrees and types, and such an integration brings about non-trivial contextual modification. That is to say, contextual effects arise from the interpretation of an utterance in context when they are not deducible either from the utterance alone or from the context alone but are "a synthesis of old and new information" (Sperber and Wilson 1986:108).

Following Sperber and Wilson (1986), Blakemore (1987:53) summarizes three ways in which a newly presented proposition may have a contextual effect: "it may lead to the formation of a new assumption; it may strengthen an existing assumption; or it may lead to the abandoning of an existing assumption." It is important here not to limit contextual effects in the sense of integration of propositional knowledge only. As Blakemore (1987, 1989) states in her study of conjunctions, there is a range of linguistic devices which the speaker may use to constrain the hearer's interpretation not in the propositional (or truth conditional) sense, but "their sole function is to guide the interpretation process by specifying certain properties of context and contextual effects" (1989:21). Consider that the DM indicators' informativeness cannot be defined in terms of logical semantic relations alone. Rather, a DM indicator, by evoking contextual knowledge and through the mediation of such knowledge, offers contextual effects which activate the resulting MC(P).

6. Methodological Issues

The study of Discourse Modality falls under the general field of discourse analysis. Although the term "discourse analysis" is somewhat ambiguous, in its most general sense it refers to the linguistic analysis of naturally occurring connected spoken or written discourse. While the scholars who work within discourse analysis agree that their main interests lie in the study of the organization of language above the sentence, and therefore to the study of larger linguistic and interactional units such as conversational moves and narrative structure, actual analytical methods chosen by these scholars vary. In the past, scholars have proposed a variety of theoretical concepts, models and principles by incorporating analytical characteristics of linguistics and related fields in an attempt to analyze select aspects of discourse.

In this study I will adopt a number of these analytical devices in my analysis of DM indicators. Particular problems raised by DM indicators necessitate a method of analysis which draws on the complementary strengths of several models and frameworks. These models and frameworks will be introduced wherever relevant in the course of this study. My immediate concern here is to present the overall research steps taken in this study, which is summarized below.

1. Select a linguistic sign for analysis:
    Based on a set of criteria, one must choose a linguistic sign for analysis. In this study I have chosen DM indicators (as defined earlier) as targets of analysis.
2. Select discourse genre/type for data collection:
    One must speculate on the type of genre/type of discourse in which appropriate tokens can be frequently found. In this study six different types of discourse are chosen as data source as was pointed out in chapter 1.
3. Collect all tokens:
    The researcher must collect all tokens of the linguistic sign(s) appearing in the identified corpus of data.
4. Discover distributional characteristics:
    All tokens must be examined in light of both syntactic and discourse distributional characteristics. This includes the data manipulation, including the creation of inappropriate utterances, and the semantic and

functional contrast of discourse segments with and without the linguistic signs under investigation.

5. Analyze tokens in reference to models and/or concepts:
    This step requires examination of the signs in reference to a select number of theoretical models and concepts.

6. Hypothesize meanings and functions based on steps 4 and 5:
    Based on the characteristics found through steps 4 and 5, the semantic source for the sign as well as its pragmatic and interactional functions are proposed.

7. Examine if proposed meanings and functions are appropriate in all cases by examining all tokens found in the corpus of data.

8. Alter if necessary the meanings and functions and repeat step 7 until reasonably convincing generalizations are made.

In my study, after following these steps, and as the results of analysis of DM indicators multiplied, I began to see common features among the indicators. In order to present these characteristics in a coherent manner, a new theoretical concept was needed. I searched for a coherent model/concept which would make it possible to incorporate the analytical models and frames deployed earlier. After an unsuccessful attempt to find a model/concept already available in the field, I came to the conclusion that I should propose my own model: the concept of Discourse Modality. Concurrently with this process, I searched for a philosophical basis for the idea that was forming. In the end, my study reached the final step in which I offer a new perspective toward the concept of language itself and some insight as to how language functions.

Hence, the concept of Discourse Modality as a scene builder, and its related concepts such as Modal Contextualization are largely an outcome of actual analysis of DM indicators. In fact I have gone through these steps not in a strictly chronological sequence nor in the exact order presented in this book; rather I have taken many detours and traced repeated paths before reaching the final step. In order to view DM indicators as having a function within the overall integration of meaning in language, repeated reexamination of data was necessary. The process I took in this research project resembles a spiral of repeated interaction amongst three different endeavors; (1) data analysis, (2) theory building and (3) discovering significance in the research process itself.

I am aware that a certain amount of circularity is involved in this method of analysis. Obviously in order to decide on the type of signs to be analyzed, i.e., DM indicators, some concept of Discourse Modality itself must have been recognized. After all, DM indicators are not concrete (physical) objects outside of the analytical framework of Discourse Modality. And as stated above, in order to build upon the concept of Discourse Modality, certain relevant signs needed to have been chosen among a vast number of possible signs based on some criteria. In other words, the data and the theoretical model mutually define each other, and therefore coexist in one way or another throughout the process of analysis. In this sense this research has followed both inductive and deductive processes.

Some readers may argue that the methodology adopted here lacks strong formal orientation. However, a simple adoption of and promotion of the formalism in linguistic analysis, by itself, is nothing but mere assumption. And however formalized the linguistic analysis may be, assumptions unsupported by data simply remain mere assumptions. I maintain that observation of data must be the starting point for linguistic research and its theoretical and analytical adequacy must ultimately be evaluated against the data. Provided that the observation is guided by some emerging analytical framework, and provided that such framework is answerable to data, the results are expected to be meaningful. Obviously, we must be cautioned not to indulge ourselves with observations unconnected to adequate integrating theory. Such observations are little more than a mass of unorganized facts, which contribute little, if any, to our understanding of language and communication.

Part 2

Analysis of DM Indicators

CHAPTER 3

Discourse Connectives <u>Dakara</u> and <u>Datte</u>

1. Introduction

In this and the following four chapters I analyze several of the Japanese DM indicators. Our first task is the analysis of two Japanese connectives *dakara* 'so, therefore' and *datte* 'but, because.'[1] Let us start by discussing the general background of connectives.

Connectives have received attention from scholars who have found it necessary to define the functions and meanings of these devices in a broader sense than they had been characterized in the past. Work by van Dijk (1979), for example, addresses the functions of connectives not only in semantic but pragmatic terms. Thus van Dijk (1979:447) states that semantic connectives "express relations between denoted facts," and pragmatic connectives "express relations between speech acts." Faced with a question of how the semantic and pragmatic connectives interact, van Dijk (1979:449) remains intentionally vague as to whether "we either have different uses of the same set of connectives, or else different connective meanings or functions which happen to be expressed by the same expression." Van Dijk (1979:449) continues, "even when they (connectives) are used as expressions for relations between speech acts, there may remain traces of their semantic meanings."

Connectives are also characterized as discourse markers by works along the lines of that proposed by Schourup (1985) and Schiffrin (1987).[2] Following Schiffrin's (1987:31) definition of discourse markers, i.e., "sequentially dependent elements which bracket units of talk," whereby brackets refer to "devices which are both cataphoric and anaphoric whether they are in initial or terminal position," connectives *dakara* and *datte* can also be categorized as discourse markers. Note that the connectives *dakara* and *datte* are expected to function in expressing a semantic and/or pragmatic connection existing between propositions, and also are expected to operate in bracketing further the units of conversational interaction. It is important to note here that, as mentioned earlier, discourse markers are also identified as DM indicators and therefore we investigate *dakara* and *datte* within the framework of Discourse Modality.

Closely associated with the issues at hand is a significant tradition in Japanese *kokugogaku*, which I find useful in my approach to the analysis of connectives *dakara* and *datte*. Tokieda (1950) characterizes Japanese conjunctions as *ji*, non-referential words whose primary role is to express speaker's attitude and feelings. Tokieda (1950:162) states that "although conjunctions are generally defined as words that connect words, phrases, and sentences, this definition is misleading because it encourages the interpretation that conjunctions function as if they are devices connecting one thing to another."[3] Let us follow Tokieda's discussion on data set (1).

     (1.1) Sore wa watashi mo   yonda.
              that T I   also read
              'I also read that one.'

     (1.2) Shikashi omoshiroi   hon dewa-nai.
              but   interesting book BE-NEG
              'But it isn't an interesting book.'

Tokieda (1950:162-164) cautions that the conjunction *shikashi* 'but' in (1.2) does not connect two statements per se. Rather, it expresses the speaker's position where he or she recognizes a contradictory relation between the facts represented by two statements. It looks as if *shikashi* connects one sentence to another, but its appearance results from the speaker's judgment of the existing relationship between two statements. Therefore, *shikashi* does not represent logical referential meaning; rather it expresses the speaker's subjective attitude, or, *kokoro no koe* 'voices from the heart,' an expression borrowed from Suzuki (1979/1824).

If we take this view to its extreme, we may conclude that conjunctions in general do not signal logical and factual relations--such as cause and result--but rather, they only represent the speaker's personal attitude. It is obvious, however, that some conjunctions appear in a context where recognized logical relations exist. Thus, avoiding an extreme interpretation of Tokieda's position, and following Ookubo's (1974) position, I pursue a more moderate path. I maintain that although connectives such as *dakara* and *datte* may occur where logical relations exist in terms of truth conditional semantics, their essential function is to express the speaker's personal voice as reflected in all aspects of communication including semantic and pragmatic as well as interpersonal aspects.

The discussion to follow in this chapter is based on the examination of tokens of connectives in two types of data, i.e., (1) transcribed casual conversations and (2) dialogue portions of fictional works as specified in chapter 1. I will also use some fabricated data to facilitate the discussion.

Among the many connectives in Japanese I selected *dakara* and *datte* as the targets of my analysis. The reasons for selecting them are threefold. First, both *dakara* and *datte* share an etymological connection in that both forms can be connected to the verb *da* 'be' and particles *kara* and *te* respectively. At the outset of the project I felt that this etymological commonality may offer some insight as to how to characterize these connectives in a consistent manner. Second, *dakara* 'so, therefore' and *datte* 'but, because' share both compatible and opposing semantic properties. In fact *dakara* can be sometimes translated as 'because' as well as 'so,' offering similarity and opposition to the "because" and "but" readings of *datte* respectively. Given this fact, I thought it interesting to investigate these two connectives in contrast to each other. Third, both *dakara* and *datte* appear fairly frequently in spoken Japanese. Based on these three characteristics, choosing *dakara* and *datte* was rendered appropriate. The choice of these two connectives does not mean that other connectives do not deserve analytical attention. Rather, I simply find that these connectives serve a good starting point for analyzing Japanese connectives within the Discourse Modality framework.

2. *Dakara*

The conjunction *dakara* 'so, therefore' in Japanese has traditionally been analyzed as a logical connector representing the relation of "cause-and-result," as shown in [2].[4]

```
[2.1]  Kodomo ga ookega        o shita.
       child  S  serious injury O did
       'The child was seriously injured.'
```

[2.2] <u>Dakara</u> hahaoya wa sugu   byooin   ni
      so   mother T   immediately hospital to
      tsurete-itta.
      took
      'So the mother took the child to the hospital immediately.'

In [2] the cause is stated in an independent sentence and the result follows in a
separate statement, the latter of which is initially marked by the conjunction
dakara.

   While this characterization applies to the aforementioned pair of sentences,
a cursory examination of Japanese conversational data reveals that *dakara*
frequently appears in a context where this "cause-result" relationship is not
obviously present. In an effort to achieve a more appropriate characterization
of *dakara*, I will first address the issue of causality, and then continue on to
examine the occurrences and distribution of *dakara* focusing on the sequential
and global contexts in which it appears.

2.1. Dakara *and the Concept of Causality*

The most widely recognized characterization of the conjunction *dakara* may be
represented by Martin's statement (1975:818); (*sore*) *da kara* is a "consequential
conjunction 'and so'." Kenkyuusha's *New Japanese-English Dictionary* lists a
group of English conjunctive expressions for the utterance-initial *dakara*; "so,
accordingly, therefore, consequently, for that reason, on that ground, that is why,
and so," and "so that." (1974:178).[5]   Many Japanese grammarians'
characterization of *dakara* (or, *kara* in some cases)--as given in Yamada (1922),
Tsukahara (1959), Ichikawa (1976) and others--is similar in that *dakara* is a
(conditional) conjunctive phrase used for logically connecting cause/reason with
the consequence/result.

   More recently Yokobayashi and Shimomura (1988:21) state that "*dakara* (or
its politer version *desukara*) expresses the speaker's judgment that the facts or
events occur as a natural result of the facts and events described in the
preceding position."[6] Although the characterizations mentioned above differ in
emphasis placed on the role the speaker's judgment plays in connecting two
events and facts in the cause-result relationship, they share the fundamental view

that *dakara* occurs following a cause-expressing proposition and preceding a result-presenting proposition.

Although so far I have used the term "cause-result" without qualification, further consideration of this concept is necessary. First, looking for some clues in formal semantics, we find that there are no logical connectives corresponding to the cause-result relationship. In natural language the causal relationship must be rather broadly interpreted. As stated by van Dijk (1977), an actual conditional (of which English conjunctions such as *so* and *therefore* are examples) is true/satisfied if both its connected propositions are true in a specific world. In characterizing connectives in natural language, van Dijk (1977:88) concludes;

1. Natural connectives are INTENSIONAL. They do not relate truth values but propositions and values of propositions in possible worlds: facts. (original emphasis)
2. Natural connectives presuppose that clauses and sentences express intensionally CONNECTED PROPOSITIONS. Propositions are connected if the facts denoted are related in some possible situation and if they are connected with the same TOPIC OF CONVERSATION. (original emphasis)

In regard to the natural language causal relationship, van Dijk (1977:69) assumes that "A is a cause of B, if A is a SUFFICIENT CONDITION of B, and B is a POSSIBLE (or probable) CONSEQUENCE of A" (original emphasis). I adopt van Dijk's view in this study in characterizing causal relations, although I continue to use the term "cause-result."

Let us return to our example [2] here.

```
The child was seriously injured.
dakara
The mother took the child to the hospital immediately.
```

In this situation, we recognize the probable sequence of events, the child's injury followed by the consequent visit to the hospital. That a child being seriously injured is sufficient condition for a possible consequence of the mother taking her child to the hospital.

Even with this extended understanding of the cause-result relationship, however, there are cases in Japanese conversation and dialogues from fiction where *dakara* does not occur in the appropriate sequential position where natural language causal connectives plausibly occur. This point is noted by Mizutani and Mizutani (1981:112) in which they report that there are some cases where *dakara* is used in interaction "when there seems to be no preceding indication of the reason." According to Mizutani and Mizutani (1981:113), *dakara* in *dakara itsumo no chiisai no desu yo* '(lit.) therefore, it's the small one we always use' said by a wife in response to her husband's question regarding the size for a tube of toothpaste he intended to purchase can be paraphrased as "you don't listen to me carefully, so I have to repeat my instruction" or "you always say smaller ones are better so I'm asking you to buy a smaller one." Mizutani and Mizutani (1981) conclude that *dakara* can be used when there is a situational context where some need for repetition is felt and the speaker is irritated about it. Similar use of *dakara* is also found in our data; we will pay special attention to this and other types of *dakara* which occur in the context where clearly marked causal relationship is absent.

2.2. Dakara *in Casual Conversation*

Let us first start our discussion by focusing on the usage of the connective *dakara* in data set (3).

(3) Speakers A and B are college seniors concerned about finding jobs. They are wondering whether other seniors have begun to actively seek employment. (Male Pair 3)

(3.1)A: [Demo naa itsumademo/ gakusei yatte-ru wake   ja-nai
        but uh forever   student do   reason BE-NEG-
        shi/]
        and
        'But, you know, it's not that we are students
        forever...'

(3.2)B: [Soo da ne./]
        so BE IP
        'Yeah, I guess so.'

(3.3)A: [Uun yatte-ru yatsu wa yatte-ru no ka na./]
        uh do   fellow T do   NOM Q IP
        'I wonder whether those who are active (in seeking jobs)
        are really doing that (seeking jobs).'

(3.4)B: [Un yatte-ru mitai./]
        yes do   seem
        'Yeah, they seem to be doing that.'

(3.5)A: [Hoomon?/]
        visit
        'You mean company visits?'

(3.6)B: [Un./]
        yes
        'Yeah.'

(3.7)A: [Kanzen   naru   hoomon?/]
        complete become visit
        'You mean formal (complete) visits?'

(3.8)B: [Un   dakara   zemi   no tomodachi ni kiite/
        yeah so/therefore seminar LK friend   IO ask
        'Yeah, so I asked a friend who is in the same seminar
        (about it),'

                                        (A: Un.)
                                        uh huh
                                        'Uh huh.'

(3.9)   kiite-mita   n   da yo ne konoaida/
        tried asking NOM BE IP IP the other day
        'I asked him the other day.'

(3.10) Soshitakke moo/   shigatsu no owari/ gogatsu no
        then   already April   LK end   May   LK
        hajime   kara moo/]
        beginning from already
        'Then (he said) already from the end of April, uh,
        beginning of May'

(3.11)A: [Gogatsu no hajime?/]
          May   LK beginning
          'Beginning of May?'

(3.12)B: [Un./
          yeah
          'Yeah.'

          (A: Kotoshi   kongetsu   ka.)
              this year this month Q
              'This month, this year, huh?'

(3.13)   Moo   itte-kita tte issha./]
          already went   QT one month
          'He said that he already went to one company.'

(3.14)A: [Issha?/]
          one company
          'One company?'

(3.15)B: [Issha   ka nisha./]
          one company Q two companies
          'One or two companies.'

(3.16)A: [Hee de nani shite-kita n   da tte?/]
          I see and what did   NOM BE QT
          'I see, and what did he say he did there?'

(3.17)B: [Shiranai,   sokorahen made hukaku   kiite-nai./]
          I don't know there   till in detail ask-NEG
          'I don't know, I haven't asked about that in detail.'

(3.18)A: [Sooyuu koto wakan-nai   jan ne./
          such   thing understand-NEG IP IP
          'We don't really know about it, do we?'

(3.19)   Iku tte yuu no wa sa./
          go QT say NOM T IP
          'I mean, what going to companies means.'

(3.20)   hoomon, kaisha hoomon da kara   hoomon sureba
          visit   company visit BE because visit do-COND

ii   na to omou kedo/
good IP QT think but
'Since it is a visit, a company visit, I think it is
fine to visit the companies, but'

        (B: Un)
        uh huh
        'Uh huh.'

(3.21)   it-te hatashite   nani shite-kuru n   daro   tte
         go-and in the world what do   NOM I wonder QT
         no wa.
         NOM T
         'when they get there what do they actually do?'

        (B: So   so   so)
        yeah yeah yeah
        'Yeah, yeah, yeah.'

(3.22)   Nee/   jinjika   no hito   ni toriaezu au
         you know personnel LK people IO at first meet
         desho?]
         IP
         'You know, you meet the personnel staff first, right?

(3.23)B: [so   so/ ore wakan-nai   n da yo ne./
         yeah yeah I   understand-NEG NOM BE IP IP
         'Right, (but) I don't really know.'

(3.24)   Dakara   kuwashiku kikitai   n   da kedo
         so/therefore in detail want to ask NOM BE but
         ne.]
         'So I would like to ask about it in detail, but...'

In this segment, we find two tokens of *dakara*, one in (3.8) and the other
in (3.24).[7] What are the discourse contexts relevant for interpreting these two
cases of *dakara*? If we express two utterances relevantly connected by *dakara*
as [X] and [Y], the [X. *dakara* Y] relationship in (3.24) may be illustrated as the
following.

Situation in (3.24); (B's utterance)

```
[X]:    I don't really know.
        dakara
[Y]:    I would like to ask about it in detail.
```

There is a causal connection identifiable in propositions [X] and [Y] in this situation.

In (3.8), however, the relationship between [X] and [Y] is different from what we can characterize as "cause-and-result." *Dakara* is used in the context where speaker B answers A's question; B utters *un* 'yeah' first, inserts *dakara* and then continues "I asked a friend who is in the same seminar," and so on.

Situation in (3.8); (B's utterance)

```
[X]:    Yeah, (it is a formal visit.)
        dakara
[Y]:    I asked a friend who is in the same seminar.
        [Then the friend said that he did actually go to visit
        companies since the beginning of May.]
```

In the situation depicted in (3.8), the [X. *dakara* Y] relationship in the sense we identified in (3.24) is not recognizable. The fact that B's friend made a formal visit to a company seeking employment is not the "cause" for B's asking the friend whether the friend went or not. The lack of cause-result relationship observed here holds true regardless of how extensively we interpret [Y], i.e., turns (3.8) and (3.9) only, or more extensively, turns (3.8) through (3.15)-- excluding A's (3.11) and (3.14).

Consider the discourse context in which (3.8) occurs. Earlier in (3.4), in response to A's question about other students making a move to actively look for jobs, B answers "yeah, they seem to be doing that." A challenges in (3.7) whether other students are formally visiting companies in a serious search for a job. It is in response to this question that B starts his turn. Having answered "yeah" at the beginning of his turn in (3.8), B already affirms by a statement that his friend did indeed go. What follows *dakara* is not, therefore, the "result" corresponding to the "cause"; rather, it is a piece of information added to further substantiate the claim that B has just made in his affirmation.

This point becomes clear when we observe what happens interactionally in data set (3). The information provided by B following *dakara* in his turns (3.8) through (3.10), (3.12), (3.13) and (3.15) provides additional support that can help substantiate the answer "yeah" given at the turn-initial position. A continues to send listener responses and interrupts B by asking questions, but it is only in (3.16) that A appreciates B's answer as a complete unit. In (3.16), A expresses "I see" and then advances the flow of conversation to conform with the current topic framework by seeking additional information, which is related to the now-substantiated answer given by B.

When *dakara* is used, it often points out that a relevant conversational move [X] is already made and that the speaker wishes to provide further information. In other words, what follows *dakara* is given as supporting evidence to the previous point when such additional elaboration is felt necessary.

A similar situation is observed in data set (4).

(4) Immediately preceding this segment, speakers A and B discuss a town called Kimitsu in Chiba Prefecture and B mentions that her grandmother often goes to Chiba. (Female Pair 1)

```
(4.1)B: [Yoku  Chiba iku n   da yo, ano  hito./]
         often Chiba go  NOM BE IP   that person
        'She goes to Chiba often.'

(4.2)A: [Aa/ ima wa/ Chiba ni sunde-ru n    ja-nai no   ka./]
         oh  now T   Chiba in live    NOM  BE-NEG NOM Q
        'Oh, doesn't she live in Chiba now?'

(4.3)B: [Iya dakara/      uchi to  ato   Chiba ni Narashino
         no  so/therefore home and other Chiba in Narashino
        tte tokoro ga atte/]
        QT  place  S  there is
        'No, so she's at our house and there's a place called
        Narashino in Chiba,'

              (A: Un   aru.)
              yeah there is
              'Yeah, there is.'

(4.4)    soko ni itoko ga sunde-n no ne./
         there in cousin S live    IP IP
        'and that's where my cousin lives.'
```

                                    (A: Hun.)
                                      uh huh
                                   `Uh huh.'

(4.5)   De nanka/ Chiba ni geetobooru tomodachi ga iru
         and like   Chiba in croquet   friend   S there is
         kara/
         because
         'And she has some friends to play Japanese croquet with
         in Chiba, so...'

              (A: Hun.)
                uh huh
             `Uh huh.'

(4.6)   tenki   no ii   hi wa/ LAUGH
         weather S good day T
         'on the days when the weather is good,'

                   (A: Ten...)
                      wea...
                    `Wea(ther)...'

(4.7)   Soo tenki   no ii   hi wa taitei   dakara
         yes weather S good day T   mostly   so/therefore
         itoko n chi itte   asonde-te./]
         cousin LK home go-and play-and
         'Yeah, when the weather's good, most of the time, so she
         goes to my cousin's place, and plays there.'

(4.8)A: [Soo ka un...Narashino/ Narashino tte ano yakyuu
          So Q uh...Narashino Narashino QT that baseball
         no Narashino kookoo   ga aru   toko?/]
         LK Narashino high school S there is place
         'I see...Narashino...You mean Narashino where that
         Narashino High School, which is famous for their
         baseball team, is located?'

In (4.3) speaker B inserts *dakara* immediately after her answer to the question
raised by A. Similarly to the case in data set (3), what follows *dakara* does not
constitute a "result" or natural consequence caused by any of the earlier

statements. The information associated with [X] and [Y] in (4) is described below.

Situation (4.3) through (4.7): (B's utterance)

[X]:   No, (my grandmother does not live in Chiba.)
       dakara

[Y]:   Grandmother lives at home.
       B's cousin lives in Narashino, Chiba.
       Grandmother has friends there with whom she plays Japanese
       croquet.
       On days when the weather is good, grandmother goes to the
       cousin's place and plays there.

In this segment speaker B's long turn provides supplementary explanatory information to substantiate the point, i.e., her grandmother does not live in Chiba. In fact *dakara* is used to mark the initial point of a unit of discourse which constitutes the second pair part of a question/answer adjacency pair (the first pair part being A's [4.2]). Here again as in the case of (3), the listener response 'I see' given by A in (4.8) provides evidence that the segment of discourse under (4.3) through (4.7) provides a unified block of information supporting the answer "no" given at the beginning of (4.3).

Dakara in (4.7) is inserted in the middle of a grammatical sentential unit. For interpreting the meaning of (4.7), there seems to be at least three possibilities depending on how the interpreter identifies the scope of *dakara*. To illustrate:

Interpretation 1: B's utterance (4.6) and (4.7)

[X]:   The weather is good.
       dakara

[Y]:   B's grandmother goes to B's cousin's place to play
       Japanese croquet with her friends.

Interpretation 2: Portion of B's utterance (4.3)--starting from *uchi to...*-- through (4.7)

[X]:   Grandmother is at home. B's cousin lives in Narashino,
       Chiba. Grandmother has friends there to play Japanese
       croquet with.
       dakara

[Y]:   On the days when the weather is good B's grandmother goes
       to B's cousin's place to play Japanese croquet with her
       friends.

Interpretation 3: B's utterances (4.3) through (4.7)

[X]:   No, (grandmother does not live in Chiba).
       dakara
[Y]:   Grandmother lives at home. B's cousin lives in Narashino,
       Chiba. Grandmother has friends there to play Japanese
       croquet with. On the days when the weather is good
       grandmother goes to the cousin's place and plays there.

In the first two interpretation, [X] provides sufficient condition for explaining
why [Y], the possible consequence of [X], may follow. Thus the [X. *dakara* Y]
as an expression of "cause-result" relationship is established. In the third
interpretation, however, the interpretation of *dakara* is identical to what we just
observed in (4.3). The fact that different scope relations are activated by *dakara*
implies that *dakara* can bracket different levels of discourse organization. If
dakara is taken to operate strictly within the statement in (4.7), the first
interpretation is realized; if *dakara* is interpreted to operate on the larger unit,
B's turn (utterances [4.3]--excluding *iya dakara*--through [4.5]) offers explanation
leading to the consequence expressed by [Y] above. Additionally, the third
interpretation is possible if *dakara* is taken to connect B's answer "no" with B's
subsequent explanation given in (4.3) through (4.7).

Of these three possible interpretations, the most plausible is perhaps the
third one. Note that in B's long turn (4.3) through (4.7) the information most
relevant to the previous move made by A in (4.2) is given in B's (4.7). B's
grandmother does not live in Chiba, but she goes and plays there. In other
words, it is not that she LIVES in Chiba; she GOES there to play. Information
B provides in (4.3)--excluding *iya dakara*--, (4.4), (4.5) and (4.6) provides
background information why in fact grandmother goes to Chiba, instead of living
there. Interactionally it seems to make most sense when we interpret B's long
turn as a unit of discourse directly related to B's initial answer *iya*, which in turn
constitutes an answer to A's question. *Dakara* in (4.7) may in fact partly
function to remind the listener that B's conversational move is to be interpreted
as an answer to A's previous move. Considering the type of discourse structure
observed in B's turn, it is also plausible to interpret *dakara* as a marker similar
to narrative coda.[8] B tells a casual narrative about the mother which ends in

(4.7). *Dakara* here is best understood to have multiple discourse functions simultaneously.

Let us examine another discourse segment in which *dakara* seems to operate similarly to the case as discussed for (3.8) and (4.3).

(5)   Speaker A, sensing that B did not know their mutual friends had part-time jobs, asks a question to confirm his suspicions. (Male Pair 10)

(5.1)A: [Jaa   kanojo-tachi ga baito   yatte-ru no
         then they   S part-time job do   NOM
         shira-nakatta?
         knew-NEG
         'Then you didn't know that they had part-time jobs?'

(5.2)B: [Zenzen shira-nakatta sore wa uun./]
         at all know-NEG   that T uh
         'I didn't know about that at all uh...'

(5.3)A: [Un/ dakara/   anoo/ gogakukenkyuujo
         yeah so/therefore uh   Language Research Institute
         de hanashishi-nakatta kke?/
         at talked-NEG   IP
         'Yeah, so uh, at the Language Research Institute, didn't
         I tell you about the story?'

(5.4)   issho   no yatsu ga ne/ Nishiyama tte yatsu na n
         together LK guy   S IP Nishiyama QT guy BE NOM
         da kedo/
         BE but
         'the guy there, his name is Nishiyama.'

(5.5)   soitsu   to shiriai   datta no./]
         that guy with acquaintance BE   IP
         'I was an acquaintance of his.'

In the immediately following discourse B continues to tell a conversational narrative in which he explains how mutual friends of A and B ended up with part-time jobs through A's acquaintance at the Language Research Institute. *Dakara* in (5.3) is inserted after *un*. Unlike situations discussed for data sets (3) and (4), there is no interactional environment where A's *un* is interpreted as an answer to a question. This *un* is a filler (or a back channel to B's back channel) which signals that A understands the situation and is ready to take a speaking turn. Unlike situations in data sets (3) and (4), in this case [X] cannot be found within his own turn; it must be sought elsewhere. A is not attempting to substantiate A's answer; rather A is responding to B's answer. A feels a need to elaborate on how their mutual friends ended up with part-time jobs, since A served as a contact for finding them jobs. *Dakara* here is used across speakers; it functions to provide explanation in response to the partner's move. The information associated with [X] and [Y] in (5) is described below.

> Situation in (5.3): B's turn, in response to A's move.
> [X]:   B: B does not know that their mutual friends have part-
>   time jobs.
>   <u>dakara</u>
> [Y]:   A: The guy A knows at the Language Research Institute
>   offered part-time job opportunities to their mutual
>   friends. This is how they got part-time jobs.

Dakara here functions to add information relevant to the current goings-on in conversation which the speaker feels necessary. As seen in (3.8) and (4.3) and now in (5.3), we identify an important function of *dakara*, i.e., to signal the starting point for additional explanatory information felt necessary and assumed relevant by the speaker in a single turn as well as across speaker turns.

2.3. Dakara *in Dialogues of Fiction*

As one can easily predict, what we found in conversational discourse is also observed in dialogues of fiction. For example, the following data provides support.

(6)   At this point in the novel, Akira (A), the protagonist, explains to Yoshikawa
      (B), his friend, the situation regarding the book publishing deal that Akira
      is preparing for a woman Akira is romantically attracted to.

      (6.1)A: "Shikashi, kanojo wa byoonin   o
              but   she   T a sick person O

kakaete-iratoo?"
has under her care
'But didn't she have a sick person at home to take care
of?'

(6.2)   Akira wa Yoshikawa ni kyonen   kure no koto o
        Akira T Yoshikawa IO last year end LK fact O
        hitotoori hanashita.
        most of   told
        'Akira told Yoshikawa most of what happened at the end
        of last year.'

(6.3)B: "Un, <u>dakara</u>   sa, sakunen   datta ka toobun
        yes so/therefore IP last year BE   Q for a while
        e   dokoro ja-nai, to yuu tokini, anta ni au
        painting matter BE-NEG QT say when   you IO see
        kikai   o tsukuroo ka, to itta ja-nai ka. ..."
        opportunity O make   Q QT said BE-NEG Q
        'Yeah, so didn't I suggest an opportunity to see you
        when she didn't have time for painting at all?'

--Miura 1985:171

In (6.3) Yoshikawa responds to Akira by revealing that he himself was once
interested in publishing the woman's work. In fact Yoshikawa suggested to meet
with Akira--possibly to discuss the publishing possibilities then. Here *dakara*
marks the beginning of the statement which provides a supplementary
explanation for how Yoshikawa intended to make a move which would support
Yoshikawa's present proposal. As in the cases discussed earlier, the function of
dakara here is to add information relevant to, and which the speaker feels
necessary for, the current direction the conversation is taking.

Another point of interest regarding *dakara* in fictional discourse is depicted
in (7).

(7)   At this point in the novel, Chief Detective Taguchi and his subordinate,
      Detective Suzuki, are on a stakeout of a murder suspect, Sakakibara.
      Sakakibara is standing in front of Shibuya Station selling copies of his
      poetry collection. Suzuki wonders if Sakakibara had a love affair with the
      victim. Taguchi believes that is not the case and continues:

(7.1) "... Sakakibara no yuu yooni, kare nitotte higaisha wa
          Sasakibara S say as   he   for   victim   T
        hukoo   da ga aisu beki onnanoko no hitori ni
        unfortunate BE but love should girl   LK one   IO
        sugi-nakatta n   daroo to omou.
        surpassed-NEG NOM BE   QT think
        'I think that, as Sakakibara himself says, the victim was
        for him no more than a girl who was unfortunate but who
        needed to be loved.'

(7.2) <u>Dakara</u>   kare wa dooki no nai   jiken da to,
       so/therefore he   T motive S BE-NEG case BE QT
       watashi ni mukatte usobuita no da. ..."
       I   IO toward play dumb NOM BE
       'So he played dumb and told me that the crime was without
       a motive.'

                                              --Nishimura 1986:94

Dakara in (7.2) connects more than the mere cause-result relationship. It is true
that (7.1) provides cause/reason for drawing a conclusion as stated in (7.2).
However, in this narrative context *dakara* also offers an anaphoric function by
bringing into the reader's consciousness an incident referred to in prior text.
The fact that "he told me that the crime was without a motive"--which
constitutes [Y] in this [X. *dakara* Y] structure--was mentioned earlier in the
novel (Nishimura 1986:71). Thus by presenting (7.2) with *dakara*, the author
encourages the reader to recall already activated information, giving (7.2) the
reading of "that's why..." This means that the [X. *dakara* Y] structure not only
signals the cause-result relationship and marks the point where relevant
explanation follows, but it also functions anaphorically to bring into the
interpreter's consciousness the relevant information from the prior text.
       Another related phenomenon noteworthy is that *dakara* can connect [X]
and [Y] across inserted utterances. See (8), for example.

(8) At this point in the novel, Mibu (A) visits Kurata (B) who had a love affair
     with Mibu's wife a long time ago and he asks Kurata for money.

       (8.1)A: "... Ima da kara   oshiete-oku ga, Shooko wa ano
                  now BE because tell   but Shooko T that

```
jibun omae o sasae    toshite ikite-ita tokoro ga
time  you  0 support as        lived    place  S
atta.
there was
```
'Now I can tell you that Shooko lived then with her
thoughts of you as (emotional) support for going on with
life.'

(8.2)B: {"Uso o yuu na!"
      lie 0 say don't
      'That's a lie!'

(8.3)A: "Uso o itte mo   hajimaru-mai.} <u>Dakara</u>,   mada
      lie 0 say even begin-NEG   so/therefore still
      juubun   nozomi wa aru. ..."
      sufficient hope T there is
      'There is no point in lying. So there is plenty of hope
      still. ...'

--Tachihara 1976:137

In (8) an exchange--marked by curly brackets--is inserted between relevant [X] and [Y] in the [X. *dakara* Y] structure, where [X] is "Shooko having held special feelings for you" and [Y] is "there still being plenty of hope." Mibu's response--that's a lie--and Kurata's response to this charge--there is no use in telling a lie--are embedded in the higher level exchange between [X] and [Y]. Jefferson (1972) identifies an exchange such as this one as a "side sequence." According to her (1972:315), a kind of conversational work may be in operation "which provides for side sequence closure so that the on-going sequence can 'resume.'" In case of (8), it is as if *dakara* expects the reader to search for [X] which can be related to [Y] in the way *dakara* encourages. In other words, *dakara* provides a clue to activate anaphoric relations between [Y] and [X] across another discourse segment. And *dakara* achieves this by necessitating [Y] to connect to its relevant [X] which operates on the same discourse organizational level within the structural hierarchy. In this sense *dakara* can assist participants' work of "resumption of an on-going sequence" across side sequencing.

So far we have observed related but differently identifiable kinds of functions that *dakara* provides. These include: (1) signaling the cause-result relationship, and (2) marking the point where relevant explanation follows. Closely associated with these functions is *dakara*'s third function, i.e., capacity to bring [X] which is identified in prior text into the interpreter's consciousness, and to isolate it by identifying the [X Y] relationship on the same discourse organizational level. Our next task then is to look for some basic semantic source of *dakara* which makes it possible to function in the way as suggested here.

2.4. The Semantic Source of Dakara: *Signaling Cause/Result and Explanation Sequences*

At this point it is useful to remind ourselves that *dakara* does not "determine" that two relevant statements are to be in the cause-result relationship. For example, going back to our data set (1), the [X. *dakara* Y] relationship remains intact whether *dakara* is inserted in that position or not. *Dakara* executed by the user is only a surface sign to overtly signal the relationship between [X] and [Y].

   Dakara, being a connective to overtly signal the natural language cause-result relationship as well as being a marker to signal the beginning of supplementary explanation, organizes the linear sequence for elements in discourse. It is well known that there are several types of sentence sequencing in Japanese. For example, Nagano (1972:94-98) lists the following nine connection types.

   1. *Tenkai-gata* 'expansion,'
   2. *Hantai-gata* 'opposition,'
   3. *Ruika-gata* 'addition,'
   4. *Dookaku-gata* 'apposition,'
   5. *Hosoku-gata* 'supplementary explanation,'
   6. *Taihi-gata* 'contrast,'
   7. *Tenkan-gata* 'topic shift,'
   8. *Tobiishi-gata* 'jumping expansion,'
   9. *Tsumiishi-gata* 'piling expansion.'

Of these nine types, two are relevant to the discourse operation in which *dakara* is directly involved, namely, *tenkai-gata* 'expansion' and *hosoku-gata* 'supplementary explanation.' Nagano (1972:92) identifies the connective *dakara* as a representative conjunction used for the purpose of "expansion," which is defined as "the relation of expanding in the statement that follows what is already mentioned in the preceding statement."[9] Although this use of *dakara* is observed in our data, the explanatory *dakara* occurring in (2.8), (3.3) and (4.3) belongs to the fifth sentence extension type "supplementary explanation." Nagano (1972:94) defines "supplementary explanation" as "the relation of providing supplementary explanation regarding the statement that precedes in the sentence that follows," and lists the connectives *nazenara* 'the reason being' and *toyuunowa* 'that is to say' as devices typical for this relationship.[10]

The sequencing of [X] and [Y] in these two different usages of *dakara* poses a curious question. Consider the fact that for the *dakara* occurring in (3.24) the direction of the information flow coincides with the order of [X] and [Y], i.e., [X. and so Y]. However, the sequencing of explanatory *dakara* in (3.8), (4.3) and (5.3), is reversed, i.e., [X. Y provides information relevant to preceding [X]. While the first usage of *dakara* is forward directing in that cause precedes result corresponding to a logical process, the second usage is backward directing in that the explanation follows the relevant point made earlier, thus information [Y] anaphorically is connected to [X]. In this sense two cases of *dakara* promote information flow into two opposite directions. Why are there these seemingly contradicting functions for *dakara*?[11]

In interpreting the functional characteristics of *dakara* observed here, I propose that we can find a common basis for the different usages by viewing the semantic source of *dakara* as follows.[12]

Dakara anaphorically refers to what precedes *da* in discourse in two different ways, namely, (1) on the semantic level, to the content of the preceding statement and (2) on the pragmatic level, to the preceding conversational move. In the first case, *dakara* functions on the semantic level to express the relationship in which the meaning [X] of the preceding proposition is followed by "and so [Y]." This provides the general meaning of "[X] is a sufficient cause for [Y], a possible result/consequence of [X]." In the second case, *da* plus *kara* functions on the interactional level to point out that a relevant conversational move [X] was already made and it is followed by "and so." This provides the general meaning of "[X] is already mentioned in the current discourse, so I add an explanatory statement relevant to [X]."[13]

One can explain the third function pointed out earlier, i.e., *dakara* reactivates relevant information in prior text--by understanding the two functions in the following manner. First, when [*dakara* Y] is used, the reader searches for and identifies [X] in prior text in such a way that [X] and [Y] are connected on the same level of discourse organization. On the semantic level, *dakara* expresses speaker's view in terms of whether a certain causal relationship exists in a course of events in a possible world. On the interactional level, a recognized connection must satisfy an interactionally meaningful matching of conversational moves.[14] This interpretation of [*dakara* Y] as 'that's why' is likely to occur when [X] is assumed to be established fairly clearly in the consciousness of the participants making it possible for them to successfully retrieve [X]. When using *dakara* as in (3.8), (4.3) and (5.3) the speaker has previous conversational move [X] in mind and refers to the partner's move in such a way as to intentionally coordinate conversational interaction. In both the first and second functional aspects, *dakara* can be concluded to operate fundamentally in signaling the sequencing of information and interaction in a meaningful order within a conversational discourse.

At this point I should mention that depending on the two different communication aspects, *dakara* falls under different distributional constraints. These include; (1) the explanatory *dakara* falls outside the scope of sentential anaphora while the cause-result *dakara* does not necessarily do so, (2) the explanatory *dakara* is epistemologically limited to the direct expression of the speaking self, while the cause/result *dakara* is not, (3) the explanatory *dakara* cannot fall under the scope of the relative clause, while the cause/result *dakara* can. For the argument of the first point, observe [9].

[9.1]A: <u>Dakara</u>   ikitaku-nai   n   da yo.
         so/therefore want to go-NEG NOM BE IP
         'So I don't want to go.'

[9.2]B: Sore wa komatta   naa.
         that T bothersome IP
         'That is a problem.'

If *dakara* in [9] is interpreted as a case of cause/result, *dakara* can be referred to by *sore* 'that.' However the explanatory *dakara* cannot be included within the anaphoric scope of *sore*. Obviously this is because the explanatory *dakara* is not a constituent of the propositional information to which sentential anaphora refers.

Data [10] serves to illustrate the second point.

[10]   Dakara   okane o hoshigatte-iru n   da yo.
       so/therefore money O want   NOM BE LP
       'So he wants money.'

Under the cause/result interpretation of *dakara*, it is possible to interpret [10] as someone desiring money due to some cause. However, the explanatory *dakara* can be interpreted only as a direct expression of the speaking self's voice.

For the third point, the constraint of relative clause construction, observe data [11].

[11]   Dakara   yomanakereba-naranai hon wa takusan
       so/therefore must read   book T many
       aru   n   da yo.
       there are NOM BE IP
       'So there are many books that you must read.'

Only the cause/result interpretation of *dakara* can be included within the scope of the relative clause. The explanatory *dakara* cannot be interpreted as a part of the relative clause.

These constraints clearly show that the discourse connective *dakara* when interpreted as an interactional sign can express speaker's subjectivity, personal voice as well as attitude. The distributional differences observed here provide evidence to support the claim that the cause/result *dakara* and the explanatory *dakara* function on different levels of communication.

Another noteworthy point in using *dakara* should be raised here. When *dakara* is uttered, the speaker signals that what follows is a thought-out line of reasoning (rather than a spontaneous exclamation) that has resulted from having given consideration to the sequencing and organization of information. See, for example, in [12] and [13], *dakara* cannot cooccur with expressions of immediate description, or, what Mio (1948:83-84) calls *genshoobun* 'sentences of immediate description.'[15]

[12]   *Dakara,   aa kaji da!
        so/therefore ah fire BE
        *'So, there's a fire!'

[13]   *<u>Dakara</u>   ohayoo gozaimasu.
       so/therefore good morning
       *'So, good morning.'

Connectives are reflections of the speaker's intentions to present information in a cohesive and interactionally meaningful way. It is likely that the speaker makes a conscious effort to create reasonable discourse organization, particularly when *dakara* is selected. *Dakara* is a sign of the speaker's intent to make conversation textually coherent and interactionally coordinated. Perhaps said more accurately, the speaker's choice of *dakara* signals to the addressee that the speaker has every intention of presenting information and of performing conversational acts in a coherent manner. The fact that *dakara* cannot cooccur with *genshoobun* provides clear evidence that one of the functions of *dakara* is based on the speaker's conscious, thought-out and willful effort to achieve discourse organization.

2.5. Interactional Functions of Dakara

We have already noted that the causal relationship observed in natural language is flexible as discussed by van Dijk (1977). The recognition of causal relationship is not entirely based on formal logic, but is achieved on the basis of sociocultural knowledge shared by the participants and on the basis of actual interactional context. Perhaps because of this, each of *dakara*'s extended functions is interaction-centered; each function has a direct bearing on how participants negotiate interactions within the conversational encounter itself. In addition to the semantic source of *dakara* discussed earlier, other related but separately identifiable functions of *dakara* are found in our data as discussed in the following.

Let us start with data set (14).

(14) A and B discuss their mutual acquaintance Mr. Kaku who, according to B, is soon going to resign from the company he works for. (Male Pair 6)

(14.1)A: [Kaku-san kaisha   yamete doo   sun no?]
           Mr. Kaku company leave   what do   IP
           'What is Mr. Kaku going to do after leaving the
           company?'

(14.2)B: [Dakara/   koomuin/   daisotsu
       so/therefore government employee college graduate
       de shiken   ukete/ koomuin.]
       as examination take   government employee
       'So (he'll be a) government employee. He will take an
       exam once he gets his college degree and will be a
       government employee.'

(14.3)A: [Shokyuu   ja saa/
       lowest rank T IP
       'But if it's the lowest rank,'

                       (B: Un.)
                       uh huh
                       'Uh huh.'

(14.4)   saitei   demo chuukyuu   ukara-nakya
       at least even middle rank pass-NEG
       hanashi ni naranai jan./]
       meaningless   IP
       'it will be meaningless unless he passes at least the
       middle rank exam, right?'

(14.5)B: [Un   ukaru desho?/]
       yeah pass BE
       'Yeah, I think he will pass.'

(14.6)A: [Kokka koomuin?/]
       federal government employee
       '(Will he be a) federal government employee?'

(14.7)B: [Un.]
       yeah
       'Yeah.'

(14.8)A: [Ano hito   yamete doo sun no jaa/]
       that person leave what do NOM then
       'What's he going to do after leaving (the company)
       then?'

(14.9)B: [Dakara   shiken uken da yo.']
       so/therefore exam   take BE IP
       'So he'll take the exam.'

In (14.2) and (14.9) speaker B inserts *dakara* where no textual cause-result relationship exists. In (14.9), *dakara* appears immediately before B repeats the answer already given in (14.2). There is a trace of irritation found in B's answer. *Dakara* in this interactional context signals that the speaker answers the question as if expecting the addressee to already know the answer; it conveys the meaning of "something related to [Y] is already mentioned elsewhere, so I am TELLING you [Y] (again)." This usage is similar to what Mizutani and Mizutani (1981) discuss as mentioned earlier. Interpretation of speaker's reluctance or irritation is possible simply because *dakara* conveys that the answer is already given in an earlier conversational move. It should be added that a related case was found where *dakara* is used as a paraphrasing device. This again is a case of *dakara* presupposing an earlier conversational move or that the information is self-evident.

Dakara in (14.2) is another extension of *dakara* used in reference to the conversational move, although there is no concrete move identifiable as [X]. In (14.2) B answers A's question by taking a speaking turn starting with *dakara*. B does not really add explanatory information, but rather answers a question as if claiming that his answer is somehow connected to the prior move. *Dakara* here marks the speaker's claim of turn.

Let us examine another data set where *dakara* is used in a similar manner.

(15) A and B discuss going to the beach; they are concerned about tomorrow's weather forecast. (Male Pair 4)

```
(15.1)B: [Kumori dattara ore ika-nai/ kumori ame  dattara./
          cloudy BE-COND I   go-NEG    cloudy rain BE-COND
          'If it's cloudy I won't go, (I mean) if it's cloudy
          and it rains.'

(15.2)   Datte  yaki      ni iku dake da-shi ore./]
          because get tanned to go  only BE-and I
          ''Cause I go there only to get tanned.'

(15.3)A: [Dakara/      ore nanka   kumottara/    umi e  wa
          so/therefore I   such as cloudy-BE-COND sea to T
          ika-nai to omou  kedo      sa./]
          go-NEG  QT think although  IP
          'So as for me, if it is cloudy, I don't think I will
          go to the shore.'
```

Dakara in (15.3) does not assume a clear cause-result relationship. There is no identifiable [X] that A offers explanatory information about. *Dakara* in this example is best understood as a signal to claim a speaking turn. Note that in (15.3) A repeats information he gave in his earlier turn (15.1). This is a case where overt repetition provides a context in which *dakara* claims a turn; here A offers information presumed to be already understood.

Let us now examine a case where *dakara* is used for a different interactional purpose. (Female Pair 7)

```
(16.1)A: [Soo na no./]
          so  BE IP
         'Is that right?'

(16.2)B: [Zutto  hora shigoto de kooyuu/ kore kurai no shisei
          always see  work    at this   this about LK posture
          ja-nai?/
          BE-NEG
         'You know, at her work always, this kind of'

(16.3)    Dakara           uun/]
          so/therefore uh
         'So, uh...'

                    (A: Soo ka soo ka.)
                        so  Q  so  Q
                        'I see, I see.'

                              (B: Un    huun/)
                                  yeah uh
                                  'Yeah...well...'
```

(Approximately 5 seconds lapse between A's *soo ka, soo ka* and the next turn taken by A.)

In this case, *dakara* in (16.3) is used at the end of the turn to signal that A is willing to yield the turn.[16] *Dakara* may be interpreted as "that's why" in this position, giving a conclusive tone to the turn. This interpretation is supported by A's listener response, "I see, I see" which expresses (the claim) that A understands the point B is making. A similar case is found in data set (17).

(17) Speaker A takes a long turn explaining how many university courses he is
     taking this year. He mentions that he is taking eight courses, but two are
     half courses--one meeting during the first part of the year and the other
     meeting during the second half. So in terms of credit hours he is taking
     seven full-year courses. (Male Pair 10)

```
(17.1)A:  [Sono uchi  hutatsu nee/ zenki       dake no  to/
           that among two      IP   first half only one  and
           kooki        dake no  to aru       wake   yo./
           second half only one and there are reason IP
           'It is...among them, two of them are courses for only
           half a year, one for the first and the other for the
           second semester.'

(17.2)    Ne/ dakara/
          IP  and/therefore
          'See, so...'

               (B: A   soo ka soo ka soo ka)
                   ah so  Q  so  Q  so  Q
                   'Ah, I see, I see, I see.'

          wakatta?/]
          understood
          'do you understand?'

(17.3)B:  [NODDING]
```

Dakara in (18.2) is uttered with falling tone implying the end of the turn.[17] B
sends a listener response that he understands the number of courses A is taking,
with the clarification now given. A continues to directly ask the question as to
whether B understands. B takes a turn and nonverbally answers affirmatively.

2.6. *Functions of* Dakara *and Discourse Types*

Given the two different functional orientations of *dakara*, a curious question
comes to my mind. That is, which function is primary in which types of
discourse genre? This section discusses frequencies of *dakara* based on the

different functional orientations in casual conversation as contrasted with that of dialogues of fiction.

In terms of frequency and discourse context in which *dakara* appeared in our data, the following results are obtained. In casual conversation data, the total number of tokens of *dakara* is 77. It should be noted that 6 cases are excluded from the analysis. These are the cases in which immediately after *dakara* is uttered, the listener interrupts and the current speaker's turn is yielded. In some cases *dakara* is overlapped by the listener's consequent turn-initial phrase. Since the speaker's intention is interrupted in these cases I excluded these interrupted *dakara*'s from the frequency tabulation. The discourse context of *dakara* in these cases does not reflect the speaker's intention; we have access only to what precedes, but not to what follows in speaker's action. The fact that the speaker is interrupted at the point where *dakara* is uttered six times suggests that *dakara* occurs at a moment in conversation where turn-taking is negotiable, i.e., an interactionally sensitive temporal space. This is reasonable when one recalls that, as discussed earlier, *dakara*'s fundamental discourse function is precisely that of signaling cohesion and coordination in conversational interaction--regardless of whether it is realized or merely intended. In establishing cohesion and coordination in interaction, the timing of turn-yielding and turn-taking becomes a main concern for participants.

Table 3.1. *Occurrences of Different Functions of Dakara in Two Discourse Types*

Primary Functions of *Dakara*	Casual Conversation		Dialogues of Fiction	
	Number of *Dakara*	Percentage of *Dakara*	Number of *Dakara*	Percentage of *Dakara*
Cause-result	41	57.75	301	86.25
Explanation	26	36.62	45	12.89
End of Turn	4	5.63	3	0.86
Total	71		349	

The frequency count for occurrences of *dakara*'s two types of functions observed in two different types of discourse is reported in Table 3.1. As shown in Table 3.1, out of 71 cases, the most frequently observed use of dakara is in the first category, the cause-result *dakara*, which occurred 41 times (or 57.75%). Cases of the second functional orientation, the explanatory *dakara*, occurred 26 times (or 36.62%). *Dakara* primarily used for the purpose of end-of-turn signal occurred 4 times. The use of *dakara* in discourse context where natural language cause-result relationship is not readily recognizable is indeed high, a total of 30 cases (or 42.25%). In short, in conversational discourse *dakara* has significant functions to bracket units of discourse not only on the textual semantic level but also on the level of interactional move, while coordinating textual meanings and interactional moves.

In our second type of data, dialogue portions of 28 fiction, *dakara* appeared 349 times. Again, the most frequently observed use of *dakara* is in the first category, 301 (86.25%) of the total. The second category totalled 45 cases (or 12.89%). *Dakara* primarily used for the purpose of end-of-turn signal was found in three instances. This statistical information shows that in dialogues of fiction, far more than in casual conversation, the primary function of *dakara* is the first cause/result category and the other uses are much more limited. This leads us to conclude that different genres encourage or discourage certain functions of *dakara*. While dialogues of fiction presumably reflect natural conversation, they are no more than a writer's creation, i.e., the "spoken" language embedded in written language. The more the genre is interaction-based, as readily expected, the more the use of *dakara* offers an interaction-based function.

Characteristics of *dakara* as observed here are perhaps best understood when we view language as a device for realizing the speaker's intentions to communicate. Linguistic sign is not a complete self-sufficient unit; it offers possibilities to mean what it means in an actual, realized interaction. It is because of this interactionally pragmatic aspect of language that linguistic signs behave differently in a variety of genres. In casual conversational discourse *dakara* bears responsibility for coordinating interactional strategies, whereas in written discourse the cause-and-result function assumes dominance.[18]

2.7. Dakara *as a Discourse Modality Indicator*

We have seen that a single linguistic sign, a Japanese connective *dakara* has multiple functions. One function is primarily semantic in that *dakara* expresses the culturally shared assumption that [X] is a sufficient cause/explanation for a possible (or plausible) result/consequence [Y]. Dakara's other functions

Figure 3.1. *Summary of Modal Contextualization Effects Realized by* Dakara

Semantic Source:	Context-bound Meaning Distribution:	Modal Contextualization, Aspects of Modality:
Dakara in [X. *dakara* Y] connects discourse segments [X] and [Y] in that [Y] provides semantic and/or interactional reason for [Y] to naturally follow.	1. Propositional Meaning: [X] is sufficient cause/ reason for [Y], a possible result/ consequence of [X]	1. Information Qualification: Discourse Cohesion (connecting discourse segments [X] and [Y] to indicate cause/result, *dakara* [Y] triggers anaphoric relation with appropriate [X])
	2. [X] is already mentioned and [Y] follows as an additional explanation of [X]	2. Speech Action Declaration and Qualification: (signaling that [Y] provides explanation related to [X])
		3. Participatory Control: Designing Speaker Turns (signaling the claim of turn and yielding of turn)
		4. Interactional Appeal: Personal Emotion (an expression of irritation --[X] already mentioned but repeated anyway)

contribute to several aspects of Discourse Modality. The explanatory *dakara* signals a point in discourse where relevant explanation will begin. It signals that [X is already mentioned in discourse, so I will now add an explanatory statement Y which is relevant to X]. This interpretation of *dakara* contributes to Speech Action Declaration and Qualification. *Dakara* signals the speaker's intention that the segment to follow will provide an explanation related to [X].

From an interactional perspective *dakara* expresses that [X is mentioned by self or by another speaker or is assumed to be understood or self-evident in the current discourse, so I add (reluctantly) an explanatory statement Y relevant to X]. Expression of reluctance is permitted only when one is allowed to express emotion whether it is guaranteed by the acceptance of the *amae* 'psychological and emotional dependence' relationship, or it appears in a disputing and/or argumentative discourse.[19] Using *dakara*, then, can signal the existence and/or continuation of the Personal Emotion aspect of Discourse Modality. *Dakara* may be further used as a signal to claim a speaking turn especially when the speaker expresses the intention of providing information as relevant to the prior discourse. *Dakara* appearing at the end of the turn or a narrative, without being followed by [Y], signals the end of the current turn, the speaker's wish to yield the turn, or to end the casual narrative framework in conversation. These functions contribute to the aspect of Designing Speaker Turns within the Participatory Control Discourse Modality. *Dakara*'s contributions to the aspects of Discourse Modality are summarized in Figure 3.1.

3. *Datte*

Let us now turn to our second discourse connective *datte*. Traditionally, the Japanese conjunction *datte* 'but, because' has been described as a logical connector with two distinguishable meanings. For example, according to Yokobayashi and Shimomura (1988:38), *datte* is categorized as "an expression used to logically connect two facts" and that "the connection is achieved in such a way that the conclusion is stated first and then the reason/cause is given as an added explanation."[20] More specifically, Yokobayashi and Shimomura (1988:38-39) state that *datte* has two functions; (1) "to provide a reason/cause for the preceding statement," and (2) "to express feelings of opposition toward one's partner's words or to offer excuses in conversation."[21] Likewise, Kenkyuusha's *New Japanese-English Dictionary* (1974:189), lists *datte* as a conjunction which has two semantic subcategories with the following list of English equivalents; (1) "but, yet, still" and "though," and (2) "well, because" and "for."

While the characterization above offers some explanation, important questions remain unanswered. For example, what is the difference between the "but" reading of *datte* and other Japanese conjunctions which express feelings of opposition, or, between the "because" reading of *datte* and other conjunctions which provides a reason/cause for the preceding statement? Does a commonality--semantic or otherwise--exist in the two listed semantic subcategories of *datte*? If it does, what is that property? What function does *datte* perform in the discourse organization? Why do conversation participants use *datte* in the first place? In this section I answer these and other related questions concerning the semantic and functional nature of *datte*. The data for *datte* consists of casual conversation and dialogues of fiction as described in chapter 1. I will also use examples I created to facilitate the discussion.

In this section I will propose that *datte*'s raison d'être lies in the speaker's intention to declare his or her own speech action in conversation, i.e., supporting the position the speaker is associated with, with the intention to justify one's own position. Unlike the case of *dakara* which partly has its prominent semantic source in the propositional content, *datte*'s semantic source is only limitedly connected to the propositionally characterizable function. Although *datte* functions to signal reason/cause, the dominant message lies elsewhere. By focusing on the pragmatics of speech actions in conversation, we are able to appreciate that some linguistic signs are fully understood only when we search for the "meaning" in the speaker's intention to communicate and in the process of interaction itself. The case of *datte* provides a basis to appreciate the essentially psycho-social nature of the DM indicators.

As described earlier, from the perspective of Discourse Modality I start with the assumption that (1) *datte* has its basic semantic source although it is defined primarily in pragmatic terms and (2) *datte*'s semantic source, in turn, can be further specified or extended into various pragmatic Discourse Modality aspects depending on its conversational context. Through the analysis of *datte*, I will illustrate that the relationship between the semantic and pragmatic aspects of DM indicators is that of reciprocal and symbiotic action, each influencing and being influenced simultaneously.

3.1. Distributional Characteristics of Datte

As a preliminary step for investigating the semantic source and functions of the DM indicator *datte*, I will concentrate on three discourse distributional characteristics, (1) *datte* is exempt from sentential anaphora, (2) the use of *datte* is constrained to direct discourse, and (3) *datte* assumes known or shared information.

For discussion of the first characteristic, observe [18].

```
[18.1]A:  Datte        ikitaku-nai    n   da yo.
          but/because want to go-NEG NOM BE IP
          'But I don't want to go.'

[18.2]B:  Sore wa komatta        naa.
          that T  is bothersome  IP
          'That's a problem.'
```

In [18.2], the pronoun *sore* refers to the semantic content of the preceding utterance, i.e., I don't want to go. Notice that *datte*'s meaning is excluded from what is anaphorically referred to by *sore* 'that.' This fact implies that *datte* is a residual of the propositional meaning; it falls outside the scope of truth conditional semantics.

The second point. In Japanese, as stated by Kuroda (1973), epistemology controls the lexical selection of emotional adjectives. For example, examine [19] and [20].

```
[19]  Datte        okane ga hoshii n   da mono.
      but/because money O  want    NOM BE since
      'But I want money, so...'

[20]  Datte        okane o hoshigatte-iru n   da mono.
      but/because money O want           NOM BE since
      'But he/she wants money, so...'
```

Utterance [19] describes the speaker's desire for money. When the speaker uses *datte* to reflect his or her own perspective, it poses no cooccurrence problem. In [20], the lexical choice, i.e., *hoshigatte-iru*, implies that the person who wants money is a third-person. Here if we interpret *datte* to reflect the speaker's perspective, and not the third-person's, there is no problem. However, if we attempt to interpret *datte* to reflect someone else's perspective as in [*datte okane o hoshigatte-iru*] *n da mono*--with *datte* being within the scope of *hoshigatte-iru*, as marked by the square brackets here--, the utterance becomes inappropriate. This is because two conflicting perspectives are reflected in the latter reading of *datte okane o hoshigatte-iru*, i.e., while *hoshigatte-iru* implies the third person's perspective (in indirect discourse), *datte* implies the speaker's perspective (in direct discourse), and yet both are assumed to be under the scope of *hoshigatte-iru*.

A similar point can be made by observing the following phenomenon.

[21]   <u>Datte</u>   [ikitai]   tokoro wa takusan aru   n
       but/because want to go place T many   there are NOM
       da kara.
       BE since
       'But there are many places I want to go, so...'

[22]   *[<u>Datte</u>   ikitai]   tokoro wa takusan aru   n
       but/because want to go place T many   there are NOM
       da kara.
       BE since
       'There are many places but/because I want to go, so...'

In the interpretation given in [21] in which *datte* is outside the scope of the relative clause, there is no problem. Here *datte* expresses the speaker's attitude. However, if *datte* is interpreted to be within the scope of the relative clause as in [22], a problem arises. *Datte* cannot be used in a descriptive embedded clause which does not construct the speaker's direct discourse.

These three constraints that *datte* falls under are identical with those discussed earlier for the explanatory (but not cause-result) use of *dakara*. As alluded to before, what we observe above suggests that *datte* brings with it a feeling of speakerhood. *Datte* attests to the fact that the utterance is personalized and the speaker is present. Like other discourse connectives, *datte* cannot escape the I-you relationship nor the sense of directness in communication. An objectively inclined descriptive statement from a faceless speaker does not readily take *datte*.

Datte further exhibits an interesting distributional behavior, which is our third point. When using *datte*, the speaker normally assumes information commonly shared among participants. Thus, in an utterance such as an answer providing new information, *datte* cannot usually occur as shown in [23].

> [23.1]A: Ima nanji?
> now what time
> 'What time is it now?'
>
> [23.2]B: *<u>Datte</u>   go-ji   da yo.
> but/because five o'clock BE IP
> 'But/because it's five o'clock.'

The utterance expected in answer to the question (assumedly) provides a new and/or surprising piece of information against the discourse background where such information is absent. *Datte* is not appropriate under such circumstances. When using *datte*, the speaker must be aware of a piece of information which is assumed or associated in some way. That is to say, *datte* expresses the speaker's personal attitude toward some shared information.[22]

3.2. The Semantic Source of Datte: Declaring Self-justification

The aforementioned three distributional characteristics of *datte* direct me to conclude that *datte* (1) has no referential function in its own right, (2) must be explained in terms of the speaking subject's attitude expressed in direct discourse, and (3) must relate the speaker's attitude with some (assumedly) shared knowledge. In order to explore the semantic sources of *datte*, let us examine the following sets of data.

> [24.1] Sukoshi kyuuka   o toroo to omotte-ru no.
> a little vacation O take QT think   IP
> 'I'm thinking about taking a small vacation.'
>
> [24.2] <u>Datte</u>   hataraki-sugiru no wa yoku-nai tte
> but/because work too hard   NOM T good-NEG QT
> minna   ga yuu no yo.
> everyone S say IP IP
> 'Because everyone tells me working too hard is not good.'

[25.1]   Sukoshi kyuuka   o toroo to omotte-ru no.
         a little vacation O take   QT think   IP
         'I'm thinking about taking a small vacation.'

[25.2]   *Datte   ryokoo demo   shite-miyoo ka na.
         but/because travel or something try doing   Q IP
         'But/because I may travel or something.'

For the convenience of discussion, as we did for *dakara*, let us use [X. *datte* Y] structure where [X] is the (assumedly) shared information suggested or mentioned in prior text, and [Y] is the statement following *datte*, and concentrate on the relationship between [X] and [Y]. Since [X] (I'm thinking about taking a small vacation) is identical in [24] and [25], the appropriateness of the use of *datte* in [24] versus the inappropriateness in [25] must stem from the relationship [Y] holds to [X]. In [24] [Y] provides a reasonable reason/cause for [X]. In [25], [Y] (I may travel or something) is a further development of the topic introduced in [X]; it is difficult to see that [Y] provides a reasonable reason/cause for [X]. In other words, as reviewed at the outset of this paper, one obvious semantic nature of *datte* is that [Y] offers a relevant reason/cause for [X].

In fact, even when a less obvious reason/cause is provided, if the speaker connects [X] with [Y] by *datte*, the implication is that there is a reason/cause relationship to the extent that reasonable interpretation is possible. Observe [26].

[26.1]   Sukoshi kyuuka   o toroo to omotte-ru no.
         a little vacation O take   QT think   IP
         'I'm thinking about taking a small vacation.'

[26.2]   Datte   sugoku   isogashii no yo.
         but/because extremely busy   IP IP
         'Because I'm extremely busy.'

Depending on the sociocultural environment [26] takes place, finding some reason/cause between [X] and [Y] may be more or less difficult. Some may hold the view that when the job demands more work than one thinks fair, one should naturally take a vacation to get away from it as a safety measure (avoiding overwork and burnout, for example). Therefore [26.2] offers reasonable cause for [26.1]. On the other hand if others hold the assumption

that one should not dare to take a vacation when there is much work to do--
which perhaps is the dominant view among Japanese--, then [26.2] may be
difficult to interpret. Even within this sociocultural environment, however,
although it may be difficult to immediately find a logical connection between [X]
and [Y] in [26], because the speaker chose *datte*, the implication is that [Y] does
offer some reason/cause for [X]. One may find the implication of this [X. *datte*
Y] relationship to be such that the speaker finds himself or herself overwhelmed
by work and for combatting this perceived unfair labor practice, he or she might
take a vacation (in protest). In other words, interpreting *datte*, one searches for
a relevant reason/cause connection between [X] and [Y], and when failing to do
so, the use of *datte* is considered inappropriate, as in the case of [25]. Although
[X] and [Y] in [25] are cohesive, [Y] does not relate to [X] in such a way as to
provide reason/cause for [X]. The distributional characteristics of *datte* as
shown in [23] through [26] provide enough evidence to claim that *datte* functions
to signal the speaker's view that [Y] offers reasonable reason/cause for [X].

   This function characterizes only one, if not minor, aspect of *datte*, however.
Let us look into the pragmatic nature of *datte* by focusing on the participants'
communicative acts as depicted in the following sets of data.

```
[27.1]A:  Sukoshi  kyuuka   o toroo to omotte-ru no.
          a little vacation O take  QT think      IP
          'I'm thinking about taking a small vacation.

[27.2]B:  *Datte        sore wa ii   ne.
          but/because that T  good IP
          'But/because that's nice.'

[28.1]A:  Sukoshi  kyuuka   o toroo to omotte-ru no.
          a little vacation O take  QT think      IP
          'I'm thinking about taking a small vacation.'

[28.2]B:  Datte        sugoku    isogashii n   deshoo?
          but/because extremely busy       NOM BE
          'But you are extremely busy, aren't you?'
```

Whereas in [27] speaker B agrees with A's idea of taking a vacation, in [28]
speaker B opposes A's idea. The distributional constraint evidenced in [27] and
[28] suggests that *datte* is appropriately used when the speaker opposes (or
challenges) the partner's position. Having said this, it is important to point out

that the nature of the opposition relevant here involves more than surface logical contradiction. Observe, [29], for example.

[29.1]A: Sukoshi kyuuka   o toroo ka naa.
          a little vacation 0 take QT IP
          'I'm wondering if I should take a small vacation.'

[29.2]B: <u>Datte</u>   zutto   totte-nai n   desho?
          but/because for a long time take-NEG NOM BE
          'But you haven't taken a vacation for a long time,
          have you?'

[29.3]A: Un.
          yes
          'That's right.'

[29.4]B: Sorenara tottara?
          then   how about taking
          'Then, why don't you take (the vacation)?'

The relationship between [X] and [Y] in [29] is not so obvious at first glance. Speaker B offers support--which can be interpreted to be reason/cause for A to take a vacation. At the same time B expresses an opposition (or challenge) to A's doubt (of perhaps not taking a vacation). Here the relationship between [X] and [Y] seems to result from the convergence of both "because" and "but" interpretations of *datte*. Let us observe another similar example.[23]

(30.1)A: "Kore datte zuibun   herashita no yo.
          this even considerably reduced   IP IP
          'Even this, I reduced a lot.'
          Sukaato, seetaa, wanpiisu, burausu, kutsu, keshoohin,
          skirt   sweater dress   blouse shoes cosmetics
          heaa-karaa, doraiya, denki   haburashi."
          hair color dryer   electric toothbrush
          'Skirts, sweaters, dresses, blouses, shoes, cosmetics,
          hair-color, (hair) dryer, and electric toothbrush.'

(30.2)B: "Sore minna motte-kita no?"
          that all   brought   IP
          'Did you bring all those?'

```
(30.2)A:  "Datte      doremo    hitsuyoo na no yo."
          but/because all of them necessary BE IP IP
          'But/because I need all of them'
```

--Akagawa 1983:241

Similar to the case in [29], [X. *datte* Y] in [30] can be interpreted by adopting either the "but" or "because" interpretation. While A opposes B's position, A simultaneously offers reason/cause for A's position [X] as expressed in (30.1). If "but" and "because" interpretations do, in fact, converge in the use of *datte* as [29] and (30) suggest, what commonality do they share?

Upon closer examination we note that in both [29] and (30), and in fact in all other examples examined so far, the speaker presents [*datte* Y] as he or she finds it necessary to justify his or her own position when faced with (a possibility) of a challenge. Regardless of whether the speaker provides a reason or opposes someone else's position, in all cases *datte* prefaces the statement which ultimately justifies the position the speaker has taken or is assumed to have taken in prior text. In fact even when [X] is not overtly mentioned, it is possible and reasonable to assume [X] which triggers B's self-justification in (29.2). B believes that people in general, which, of course includes A, should take vacations, particularly when the person has not had one for a long time.

When understanding the speaker's intentions and actions that *datte* implies as outlined above, I find it useful to use two speech action labels POSITION and SUPPORT. I adopt these two categories from Schiffrin (1987) in which three elements of argument, i.e., POSITION, DISPUTE, and SUPPORT, are introduced. According to Schiffrin (1987:18-19), POSITION is the speaker's commitment to an idea often expressed by assertion; DISPUTE expresses the opposition to position, as well as to any (or more) of its parts; and SUPPORT is realized by speech actions such as explanation, justification, and defense of the position that can be disputed. In the discourse context of *datte*, although DISPUTE exists as a part of context, two categories, POSITION and SUPPORT, are relevant.

Taking into consideration *datte*'s distributional constraints discussed above, I propose that what *datte* signals is best characterized when I view *datte* as a device to point out the pragmatically and semantically significant linkage the speaking self identifies between the (assumedly) shared knowledge and the upcoming discourse unit. In other words:

[X. *datte* Y] structure is used where:

[X] is a POSITION taken or suggested by a participant of conversation, and,

[Y] is information or action provided by the speaker himself or herself with the intention to SUPPORT the POSITION [X] through the speech act of justification, where [X] may be either given in prior text, or merely suggested or implied,

in the context of,

opposition/contrast against POSITION [X] about which the speaker finds himself or herself being challenged.

Note that this characterization satisfies three distributional characteristics discussed earlier as well as *datte*'s semantic nature discussed here. In actual conversation the speaking self declares through the use of *datte* that the upcoming segment is intended to perform the speech action of self-justification.

The two meanings that have been associated with *datte* can now be viewed as two conventionalized cases of semantic interpretations of the prefacing in two different contexts of speaker turn exchange, as depicted in Figure 3.2.

Figure 3.2. *The Use of* Datte *in the Same or Different Speaker Turn Context*

Speaker A	Speaker B
[X] *datte* [Y-1]	B takes a turn
[X] *datte* [Y-2]	

When [X] and [Y] associated with *datte* appear across speaker turns, since [Y] expresses self-justification, *datte* encourages the reading of "but,"--a case of [Y-1]. One is more likely to feel a need to self-justify by opposing the partner's opposition or challenge than otherwise--thus the "but" interpretation. When [X] is within the speaker's turn, *datte* encourages the reading of "because,"--a case of [Y-2]. One is more likely to add additional information such as cause in order to SUPPORT the position one has just taken.

This characterization does not mean all cases of datte fall into either one of the interpretations solely on the basis of the speaker turn context. Obviously as discussed earlier, data sets [29] and (30) demonstrate otherwise. Therefore the turn context does not by itself define the specific interpretation of *datte*, but this phenomenon provides a case where a conventionally acknowledged interactional context helps specify a likely interpretation.

3.3. Discourse Functions of Datte

So far we have characterized *datte* in terms of its discourse distributional constraints, and based on these and other characteristics, we identified what *datte* signals in broad semantic terms. In this and the next sections we focus on the additional discourse function of *datte*. First, in terms of discourse organization, *datte* enhances the segmentation of discourse unit [X] and [Y], and at the same time, it subordinates [Y] to [X]. Recall that [Y] is presented as information necessary to justify the speaker's position already identified. [Y] provides information to be interpreted within the same topic boundary and at the same time in such a way that [Y] provides background information to support [X]. This segmentation and subordination of discourse unit contributes to achieve cohesion in discourse. *Datte* prefaces what is going to be expressed, i.e., new information, with what is already shared, i.e., old information, serving as a clue to signal what Halliday and Hasan (1976) call textual "ties."

Second, in terms of the flow of local information, *datte* signals backward directing sequencing in that [Y] is interpreted only in relation to the item [X] mentioned or suggested in prior text. Regardless of whether *datte* expresses the relations of "but" or "because" or a combination of the two, it has a direct bearing on the linear order organization of elements in discourse. Of Nagano's (1972) types of sentence-sequencing, two are relevant to the discourse operation in which *datte* is directly involved. These are *hantai-gata* 'opposition' and *hosoku-gata* 'supplementary explanation.' What is unique about [X. *datte* Y] structure is that in both 'opposition' and 'supplementary explanation' sentence-sequencing types, [Y] must be integrated with [X], representing a backward directing information flow. This contrasts with the connective *dakara* which is both forward and backward directing as discussed earlier.

As we have seen, *datte* is a device for expressing the speaker's subjective attitude in organizing and connecting the events and states described. As evidenced by its discourse distributional constraints, *datte* is a device dedicated to operate in direct discourse. By declaring one's speech action, one appeals to the partner that one is making an effort to be fully involved in the conversational interaction itself. Here the speaker expresses that he or she is paying close attention to the current goings-on of the conversation not merely in semantic terms but also, if not more importantly, in terms of full engagement and commitment to one's speech participation. The significance of this characterization increases even more when we note that the two seemingly unrelated readings of *datte*, i.e., "but" and "because," are rooted in the contextualized interpretation of *datte* rather than in its referential and/or logical meaning.

3.4. Interactional Functions of Datte

As much as *datte* achieves the direct expression of the speaking self, it is also important to recognize that *datte* is a sign which assumes the "other." In fact in conversational discourse, *datte* often appears at interactionally significant points such as at the utterance- and/or turn-initial position, at the turn-transitional period, and at hesitation points.

Following Schiffrin (1987:24-25) I will incorporate two kinds of non-linguistic structures in conversation as a methodological framework for analysis. First is the "exchange structure" (specifically in reference to turns and other conditionally relevant adjacency-pair parts), and the second, speech "action structure."

As a first step, let us examine a conversational segment in (31).

(31) Speaker A and B discuss the current system of college entrance examinations in Japan. (Female Pair 4)

```
(31.1)A:  [Nihon no daigaku nyuushi   seido?/]
          Japan LK college entrance exam system
          'About Japanese college entrance exams?'

(31.2)B:  [Un./]
          yes
          'Yeah.'
```

(31.3)A: [Watashi wa ima no mama de ii   to omou n   da kedo
         I   T now LK as is BE good QT thing NOM BE but
         Iino-san wa?/]
         Ms. Iino T
         'I think (the system) as it is is fine; what do you
         think, Ms. Iino?'

(31.4)B: [Anmari   yoku-nai to wa omou n   da kedo./]
          not much good-NEG QT T think NOM BE though
          'I don't think it is too good...'

(31.5)A: [Tatoeba   doko ga?/]
          for example where S
          'For example, in what ways?'

(31.6)B: [Datte   saa, nanka   daigaku ni haitta hito
           but/because IP something college IO enter person
          mitemo   sa/
          even see IP
          'Well, because, even when you look at people who
          entered the university'

                    (A: Un)
                        uh-hun
                        'Uh-huh.'

          are ja-nai, tokuni   A-Daigaku   nan   te no
          that BE-NEG especially A University such as QT one
          wa hanbun un   de   haitte-ru yoona mon desho?/]
          T half   luck with enter   such fact BE
          'isn't it true, that especially at A University,
          people enter it half with luck (and half with merit),
          don't you think?'

(31.7)A: [Soo?/]
          so
          'Really?'

(31.8)B: [Soo yo./]
          so IP
          'Really.'

(31.9)A: [Soo demo-nai wa yo./]
          so BE-NEG   IP IP
          'That's not true.'

(31.10)B: [Soo yo./ <u>Datte</u>,   zettai   soo da to omou wa
           so IP   but/because absolutely so BE QT think IP
           <u>datte</u>./
           but/because

           (A: Soo?)
              so
              'Really?'

           Shakai   to eigo   to/ shakai   to
           social study and English and social study and
           eigo   to/ are
           English and that

              (A: Un.)
                 uh huh
                 'Uh-huh.'

           sae dekireba   kokugo   ka/ sae dekireba
           even if one is capable Japanese or only is capable
           hairu nante   sonna hooshin deshoo?/
           enter such as such policy BE
           'Sure, it's true. Because I absolutely think so,
           'cause--Isn't it the case that a person can enter
           (the university) if he or she is good in social
           studies and English, I mean social studies and
           English and that, I mean, Japanese.'

           <u>Datte</u>   soreni   itten   de sa/ itten
           but/because besides   one point BE IP   one point

              (A: Tatoeba?)
                 for example
                 'For example?'

           de nanbyakunin   mo kirarechau   wake
           BE several hundred people even cut-off-PASS reason
           desho?/]
           BE

'Because, besides, with one point, with just one
point of difference on the score, several hundred
applicants are cut off and fail the exam, right?'

(31.11)A: [Sono hen   ga ii   n   ja-nai, kibishikute./]
           that aspect S good NOM BE-NEG strict-and
           'Isn't that what's good about it, I mean, being
           strict?'

(31.12)B: [Kibishiku tte yuu ka saa./]
           strict   QT say Q IP
           'Well...I wonder if you can quite say "strict," but'

(31.13)A: [Datte,   yononaka tte sonna mon   yo./]
           but/because world   QT such thing IP
           'But that's how it is in life.'

(31.14)B: [Hontoo no, datte   saa, jitsuryoku o
           real   LK but/because IP   capacity   O
           hakatte-ru wake   ja-nai ja-nai?/]
           measure   reason BE-NEG BE-NEG
           'But the truth, the real ability, they never find
           out, right?'

(31.15)A: Tatoeba   donna toko   o mitai   no?/]
           for example what aspect O want to find out IP
           'For example, what sort of things do you want to
           find out?'

(31.16)B: Dakara   ne/ nyuushi   o shi-nai de, sukina,
           because IP entrance exam O do-NEG BE favorite
           uun,/
           uh

                    (A: Un.)
                    uh huh
                    'Uh-huh.'

           nan te yuu no/sukina   dake   daigaku ni
           what QT say IP favorite as much as college IP enter
           haireru   yooni shite/   sorede koo, anoo,
           can enter so that do-and   then   this uh

```
(A: Un.)
     uh huh
     'Uh-huh.'

sotsugyoo-suru toki ni/ muzukashii mitaina
graduate       when at  difficult  such    g
huuni-shite-oita hoo      ga ii   n  ja-nai
do so that       direction S good NOM BE-NEG
ka na to omou./]
Q IP QT think
'Well...what I mean is that without taking an entrance
exam, people can enter the university as easily as
they want, and then uh...before graduating, it gets
difficult; I kind of think that way is better..."
```

Note that *datte* appearing at the sentence and/or turn-initial position has a function of declaring the speech action of justifying one's position in an environment of actual or suggested challenge. *Datte* in (31.6) prefaces B's turn which provides SUPPORT for the position she takes in (31.4). Although (31.5) is a simple question, A takes it as a challenge; A feels that A must provide information necessary to justify her position. Likewise, B continues to justify her position in her next long turn in (31.10). Here again, B defends her POSITION facing the challenge from A, i.e., "that's not true." Note that the third *datte* B uses in (31.10) prefaces additional information which is used to further substantiate the SUPPORT, the point made in (31.10). This *datte* signals that the upcoming utterance still constitutes a part of the current speech action of self-justifying B's POSITION. Speaker A uses *datte* once in (31.13) when she finds herself being mildly questioned by B about her view. B's strategy is to insert *datte* again in (31.14) to continue supporting the position that she develops throughout this conversational exchange.

In terms of exchange structure, then, *datte* is a device for warning the listener that the upcoming turn contains self-justifying information in the context of opposition--a case of what Pomerantz (1984) calls "dispreference markers" or what Bilmes (1988) calls "reluctance markers." Here *datte* has the primary function of prefacing the speech action of opposing someone in conversation, of mitigating the opposition through this accommodating device. Because *datte* warns the listener, *datte* softens the point of difference and helps encourage rapport even in the face of apparent or perceived disagreement.

It is also important to observe that the POSITION/SUPPORT observed in (31) interact both linearly and hierarchically. Obviously using *datte* in and of itself does not mean the speech action will be structured in the way that I suggest. Semantically motivated segmentation and subordination of discourse units as discussed earlier also influence the action structure. Figure 3.3 shows how POSITION/SUPPORT speech actions signaled by *datte* interact in order to carry out the speaker's intention of self-justification as a goal.

Figure 3.3. *POSITION/SUPPORT Speech Actions Signaled by* Datte *in (31). (The arrow indicates the direction of SUPPORT toward the relevant POSITION.)*

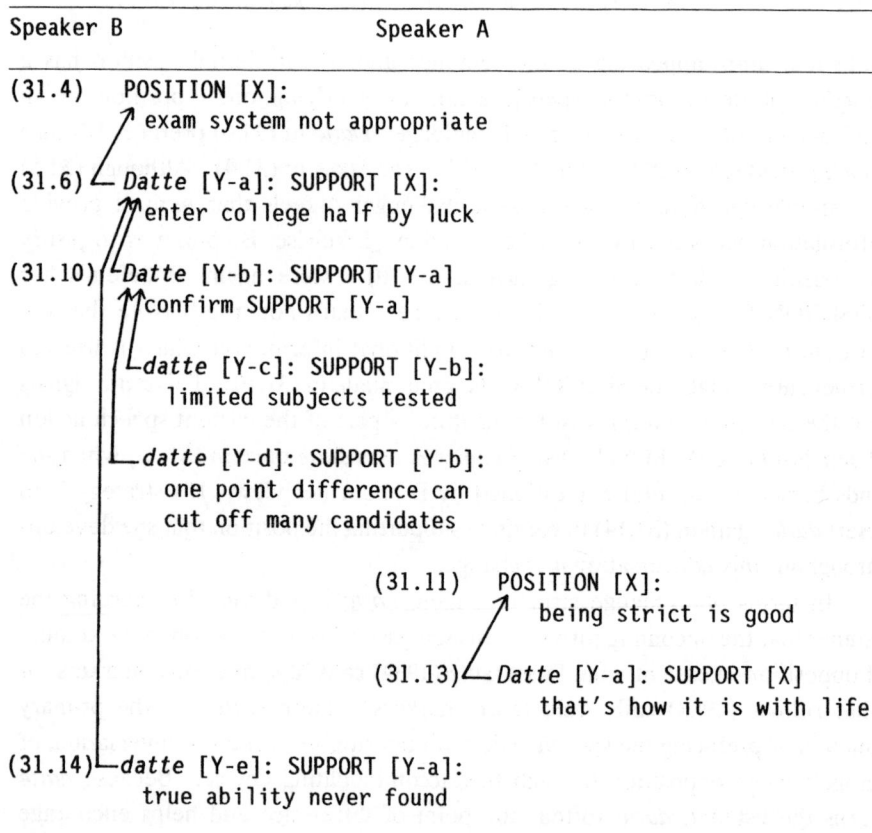

Speaker B	Speaker A

(31.4)   POSITION [X]:
↗ exam system not appropriate

(31.6) ∠ *Datte* [Y-a]: SUPPORT [X]:
↗ enter college half by luck

(31.10) ┌ *Datte* [Y-b]: SUPPORT [Y-a]
↗ confirm SUPPORT [Y-a]

└ *datte* [Y-c]: SUPPORT [Y-b]:
limited subjects tested

└ *datte* [Y-d]: SUPPORT [Y-b]:
one point difference can
cut off many candidates

(31.11)   POSITION [X]:
↗ being strict is good

(31.13) ∠ *Datte* [Y-a]: SUPPORT [X]
that's how it is with life

(31.14) └ *datte* [Y-e]: SUPPORT [Y-a]:
true ability never found

Note that SUPPORT can also function as POSITION when it is backed by another SUPPORT. Here, however, I maintain that lower level SUPPORT can add support to higher level SUPPORT (as illustrated in [31.10], for example), and they indirectly support POSITION [X].

In terms of action structure, then, *datte* is a surface signaling device for declaring speech actions of SUPPORT--which is motivated by the speaker's self-justification--both in the linear and hierarchical sense. *Datte* specifies a speech action overtly, thus contributing to the clarification of conversational action structure.

I should point out in passing here that *dakara* in (31.16) prefaces a long turn which answers A's question in (31.15) by providing explanation. Note that (31.16) does not appear in the context of opposition or contrast. It is also true that what follows *dakara* in (31.16) offers potential for a related but new topic, while the turns prefaced by *datte* do not. By using *datte*, the speaker expresses her intention of providing information to justify her POSITION, rather than neutrally providing explanatory information, as in the case of choosing *dakara*.

It is perhaps due to this function that *datte* by itself is sometimes used. See for example [32].

```
[32.1]A:  Dooshite tabe-nai no?
          why       eat-NEG  IP
          'Why don't you eat?'

[32.2]B:  Datte...
          but/because
          ''Cause...'
```

Although speaker B offers no specific reason, by choosing *datte* B attempts to offer some justification for not eating even though no identifiable reason/cause for his or her POSITION [X] is available. Yet this speaker's effort in attempting to justify [X] is what gives the partner a favorable impression. This *datte* is often used by a child in an interaction with parents or people with whom the *amae* 'psychological and emotional dependence' relationship is established.

3.5. Datte *as a Discourse Modality Indicator*

The process of Modal Contextualization that *datte* brings can be summarized in Figure 3.4.

Figure 3.4. *Summary of Modal Contextualization Effects Realized by Datte*

Semantic Source:	Context-bound Meaning Distribution:	Modal Contextualization, Aspects of Modality:
Datte in [X. *datte* Y] signals that the speaker intends to justifiy position [X] in the context of opposition/ contrast.	1. Propositional [Y] provides reason/cause for [X]. 2. If [X] is the position taken across turns, "but" reading. 3. If [X] is within the turn, "because" reading.	1. Information Qualification Discourse Cohesion (segmenting, subordinating and sequencing discourse segments) 2. Speech Action Declaration and Qualification: (declaring self-justification of position, marking hierarchical structure of speech actions) 3. Participatory Control: Exchange Structure (expressing dispreference or reluctance) 4. Interactional Appeal: Personal Emotion (expressing commitment to interaction, expressing *amae* 'dependence')

By using *datte* the speaker ultimately communicates to the partner how the information should be interpreted by contextualizing the information [Y]. First, *datte* prefaces SUPPORT for POSITION in conversation when one is challenged or when one challenges, and therefore [Y] should be interpreted as a speech action of self-justification, an aspect of Speech Action Declaration and Clarification. Second, *datte* provides discourse organizational information by segmenting and cohesively connecting discourse units contributing to the Discourse Cohesion aspect. Third, *datte* prefaces the dispreferred speech action which operates within the Exchange Structure aspect. Forth, *datte* conveys the speaker's emotional involvement in the conversation, often appealing to the psychology of *amae*.

I do not mean by the process of Modal Contextualization that *datte* merely contextualizes semantic interpretation, excluding the possibility that *datte* itself is also contextualized. In fact as shown in section 3.3, *datte*'s "but" and "because" interpretations are contextualized by the speaker turn exchange. The process in which language interacts with its context as well as the interpretive process in which its meaning integrates contextual effects simply reflect how language works. And obviously here by context I mean not merely the physical setting but the social, psychological and emotional world as well. Language reflects the context because it is only in its context that the full meaning is constructed. This context also influences the semantic interpretation because no meaning exists out of a context. Here we see that Discourse Modality offers a framework which allows us to focus on this fluid relationship binding between linguistic code and its physical as well as cognitive contexts.

4. *Dakara* and *Datte* in Contrast

The reader at this point may question the difference between *dakara* and *datte*, the two connectives at issue, particularly the explanatory use of *dakara*. Let us examine data set (33) which contains both *dakara* and *datte*.

(33) In this segment of the novel, the protagonist "I" asks the chauffeur the reasons why proper names are given to certain objects but not to some other objects. The chauffeur suggests that only objects that are considered to have "life" are perhaps deserving of being named. "I" responds...

```
(33.1)A:  "Naruhodo" to boku wa itta.
          I see      QT I    T  said
          '"I see," said I.'
```

(33.2)   "Shikashi sa moshi namae no konpon ga seimei no
           but   IP if   name LK source S   life   LK
           ishiki   kooryuu sayoo ni aru   to shitara
           consciousness exchange action at there is QT do-COND
           da yo. Dooshite eki   ya kooen ya yakyuujoo
           BE IP why   station and park and baseball field
           ni wa namae ga tsuite-iru n   daroo. Seimeitai
           IO T name S be attached NOM BE   life-form
           ja-nai noni   sa."
           BE-NEG despite IP
           'But if the sources for naming lie in the exchange
           process of life consciousness, why are there names for
           stations, parks and baseball fields? They are not
           life-forms, you know.'

(33.3)B: "<u>Datte</u>   eki   ni namae ga nakya
           but/because station IO name S unless there is
           komaru   ja-arimasen ka."
           bothersome BE-NEG   Q
           'But isn't it bothersome not to have station names?'

(33.4)A: "<u>Dakara</u>   mokutekiteki dewa-naku genritekini
           so/therefore functionally BE-NEG   in principle
           setsumeishite hoshii n   da.
           explain   want   NOM BE
           'So I want you to explain not in terms of its function
           but in principle.'

                                     --Murakami 1985:240

Datte in (33.3) is used to support a commonly accepted POSITION [X]--a sort of common sense knowledge--that people will be inconvenienced without names for stations. While POSITION [X] is not explicitly mentioned in the prior text, the use of *datte* implies acknowledgment of such a position. The interpreter is asked to search for the relevant POSITION. The information flow is backward directing in that SUPPORT [Y] must be traced back to the relative POSITION [X]. Contrast this with the use of *dakara* in (33.4). In (33.4) the protagonist "I" responds by saying that instead of a functional explanation, he wants to hear some explanation based on the principle of such a naming practice. By using *dakara*, the speaker suggests that he implied this earlier and he is now repeating it. Note that unlike *datte*, *dakara* pushes the information forward by making the relevant point [Y] more clearly by repeating it or presenting [Y] as if being repeated.

Based on similar examination of discourse segments where *datte* and *dakara* may be contrasted, I propose the following differences between the uses of *datte* and the explanatory *dakara*.

(1) [X. *dakara* Y]--only in reference to explanatory *dakara*:

  [X] POSITION

  [Y] additional information to provide explanatory information to SUPPORT [X] or to elaborate on the information given in [X]; the context may not necessarily be in an oppositional, contrastive or challenged environment; the information flow is forward directing.

(2) [X. *datte* Y]:

  [X] POSITION

  [Y] self-justification to SUPPORT [X]; the relationship between [Y] and [X] may be causal and/or explanatory; the context must provide or indicate oppositional, contrastive or challenged environment; the information flow is backward directing.

In this chapter I have analyzed two discourse connectives *dakara* and *datte* in Japanese. Unlike the traditional view that connectives (or conjunctions) operate primarily in the logical framework, we have observed that connectives exemplify linguistic signs which can be fully understood only when their functions are analyzed in the light of the relevant aspects of Discourse Modality. Although discourse connectives such as *dakara* and *datte* by themselves offer only limited meanings, they explain the very manner of how the speaking self perceives, characterizes and contextualizes what is described and what one is about to express. Through discourse connectives, the speaker directly reveals his or her personal position and attitude toward the facts, and the cognitive mode involved, as well as the way he or she declares the speech action in a particular interactional context. Consequently, one's verbal expression becomes, in essence, self-expression authorized by the speaking self and jointly legitimatized by the participants.

CHAPTER 4

Modal Adverbs <u>Yahari</u>/<u>Yappari</u> and <u>Doose</u>

1. Introduction

In this chapter I investigate two Japanese modal adverbs, *yahari* and its colloquial version *yappari* 'as expected, at any rate' and *doose* 'anyway, after all' within the proposed framework of Discourse Modality. While I could have chosen other modal adverbs, *yahari*/*yappari* and *doose* are quintessential modal adverbs in Japanese and even a cursory observation would reveal their significance in Japanese text and interaction. I do not mean by this choice, of course, that other modal adverbs are unimportant. On the contrary other modal adverbs--for example, *sasuga* 'as might be expected' and *semete* 'at least, at most, at best' come to mind--deserve researchers' attention and are expected to reveal the similar nature of Japanese modal adverbs. In this study I direct my attention only to *yahari*/*yappari* and *doose* with the expectation that their analyses will enable us to gain some insight into the workings of modal adverbs and DM indicators in general.

Modal adverbs are known to differ significantly from so-called manner adverbs. Unlike manner adverbs which have a direct bearing on the propositional content, modal adverbs reflect the very style of how the speaking self perceives, epistemologically characterizes, and contextualizes the propositional content. Let us start with a brief literature review of modal adverbs in Japanese and English. Then analyses of *yahari*/*yappari* in section 3 and *doose* in section 4 follow. The primary data consists of tokens of *yahari*/*yappari* and *doose* taken from both narrative and conversational segments of contemporary Japanese fiction as described in chapter 1. Additionally, where appropriate, I will discuss examples taken from other sources as well as some manipulated data to facilitate the discussion.

2. Background

The Japanese term meaning "modal adverbs," i.e., *chinjutsu hukushi* was introduced by Yamada (1922, 1936), and it is perhaps here that we should start our review of how adverbs have been described and analyzed in Japanese *kokugogaku* 'traditional Japanese language studies.' Yamada (1922:134-135) categorizes adverbial phrases into two major groups, one, *senkoo hukushi* 'preceding adverbs' and *setsuzoku hukushi* 'conjunctive adverbs.' Among 'preceding adverbs' are *go no hukushi* 'phrasal adverbs' and *kandoo hukushi* 'exclamatory adverbs.' Exclamatory adverbs include independent phrases often referred to as exclamatory expressions and interjections as well as interactional responses such as *yes* and *no*. Phrasal adverbs are divided into two further categories, one, attributive adverbs (*zokusei o arawasu hukushi*) which include manner adverbs and adverbs of degree; and two, modal adverbs (*chinjutsu hukushi*) which include adverbs for expressing strong assertion, doubt or condition. Although Yamada does not list *yahari/yappari* and *doose*, they fall into the category of modal adverb. According to Yamada (1922:134-135), "a modal adverb bears no relation at all with the (attributive) meaning of the verbal element; it explains (*sootei-suru*) the very manner of stating or predicating (*chinjutsu*).[1] The modal adverbs Yamada specifically had in mind have an overt syntactic feature, i.e., each requires certain predicate types in the sentence-final verbal forms. For example, as in [1], the modal adverb *kesshite* 'never' requires negation. *Kesshite iku* is unacceptable.

[1]   Kesshite ika-nai.
      never   go-NEG
      'I'll never go.'

More recently, in his study Watanabe (1971) broadens the concept of modal adverbs and includes in his extensive categories those adverbial phrases not overtly requiring certain predicate types. By introducing the concept of *yuudoo* 'guidance,' Watanabe captures the relationship of guidance (and response) as a major axis observed in Japanese language. For example, the primary function of *kesshite* 'never' is to provide some guidance and to issue warnings, so to speak, that what follows will be a negative predicate. Expressions such as *mochiron* 'of course, naturally' are also included in this category of *yuudoo hukushi* 'guidance adverbs.' *Mochiron* 'of course, naturally' provides speaker's evaluation and interpretation of what follows, a kind of guidance helpful for the interpretation of consequent statement and predication.[2]

In his work, Mikami (1972:304) divides modal adverbs into two main categories, i.e., *sakibure no hukushi*, and *yakusokuteki hukushi*. The *sakibure no hukushi* 'warning (or guiding) adverb' requires a predetermined predicate type-- as in *kesshite* 'never'--and it functions to emphasize the meaning of the predicate. Thus in case of *kesshite* 'never,' it emphasizes the meaning of the negation. The *yakusokuteki hukushi* 'commenting adverb' provides evaluation and interpretation related to the utterance, for example, *watashi ga yuu made mo naku* 'without my mentioning.'[3] *Yakusokuteki hukushi* is also called *hatsugen no hukushi* 'utterance-accompanying adverb' since it comments on the utterance itself. *Hatsugen no hukushi* is often accompanied by the verb *yuu* 'say' or verbs related to 'say.' This is similar to what Bellert (1977) calls 'pragmatic adverbs,' to be mentioned later.

Haga (1982:156-160) categorizes adverbs into five groups; manner, degree, correspondence (similar to Yamada's modal adverbs), evaluation/interpretation, and conjunctive. Haga's *chuushaku no hukushi* 'adverbs for evaluation and interpretation' include those similar to English sentence adverbs such as *mochiron* 'of course, naturally,' *saiwai* 'fortunately,' *ainiku* 'unfortunately,' and so on. The function of *chuushaku no hukushi*, according to Haga (1982:159), is "to add the speaker's thoughts to what is to be stated." Again since there is no mention of *yahari/yappari* and *doose* in his work, it is difficult to judge how Haga characterizes these two modal adverbs. However, it seems likely that Haga would associate *yahari/yappari* and *doose* with the adverb of evaluation/interpretation since they "add the speaker's thoughts to what is to be stated." Further categorization of Japanese "modal adverbs" was made by Kudo (1982). Kudo subcategorizes *chinjutsu hukushi* 'modal adverbs' into three sub-classes; *johoo hukushi* 'modal adverbs,' *toritate hukushi* 'focusing adverbs,' and *hyooka hukushi* 'evaluative adverbs.' Both *yahari/yappari* and *doose* fall into his sub-class of "modal adverbs."

The point common to all these precursors' works is that modal or evaluative/interpretive adverbs function outside the subject-predicate axis. These modal adverbs do not directly modify verbs, but rather, they express the speaking self's subjective, often emotional feelings and attitude toward and evaluation of what is to be stated.

Concerning English sentence adverbs, as Greenbaum's (1969) characterization of "attitudinal disjuncts" and Schreiber's (1971) "evaluative adverbs" suggest, it is generally accepted that sentence adverbs clearly constitute a class separate from manner (or predicate) adverbs. These are linguistic mechanisms that comment on the speaker's attitude or feelings during the speech acts themselves and these adverbs function essentially extra-grammatically. For example, according to Greenbaum (1969:94), "attitudinal disjuncts" express "the speaker's attitude to what he is saying, his evaluation of it, or shades of certainty or doubt about it." While many studies on English adverbs are concerned with how sentence adverbs behave syntactically, (see Michell 1974, Schreiber 1971, and Espinal 1987), some studies have explored adverbs within the framework of Speech Acts (see, for example, Sawada 1978).

In an attempt to clarify the general category of sentence adverbs, Bellert (1977) introduces the following five sub-categories:

1. Evaluative adverbs (*luckily*, *fortunately*, etc.),
2. Modal adverbs (*probably*, *possibly*, etc.).
3. Domain adverbs (*logically*, *mathematically*, etc.),
4. Conjunctive adverbs (*however*, *nevertheless*, etc.),
5. Pragmatic adverbs (*frankly*, *briefly*, etc.).

As evidenced above, the broad category of modal (or sentence) adverbs has been investigated both by Japanese and Western scholars. In semantic and functional terms, however, past efforts have been somewhat limited. Mostly scholars have concentrated on the categorization and subcategorization of modal adverbs and have not provided an answer as to what these modal adverbs do in defining the modality of an utterance. In what follows I will investigate two adverbs not with a direct intention to contribute to this commonly recognized effort, but rather, in an attempt to discover how modal adverbs help define the aspects of Discourse Modality.

3. *Yahari/Yappari*

Consider the following interaction in which the modal adverb *yappari* 'as expected, at any rate' appears.

```
(2.1)A:  "Ano  hito    jisatsu-shita      n    da tte..."
         that person committed suicide NOM BE I hear
         'I heard he committed suicide...'

(2.2)B:  "Yappari!"
         as expected
         'That figures!'

(2.3)C:  "Nani ga yappari      na no?"
         what S   as expected BE IP
         '(lit. What is so expected about it?)  What do you mean?
         How did you guess?'
```

--Fuji Sankei Television (New
York) drama: Ohima nara kite
ne, broadcast on March 30,
1989.

In this interaction it is evident that the last speaker has grasped the semantic content of *yappari* while simultaneously challenging its implication. It seems intuitively correct to assume that *yappari* implies something beyond the traditional sense of utterance content; but what does it imply?

Japanese scholars have long noticed this quality of *yahari/yappari*, and have provided some useful, if not ad hoc, explanations. For example, Itasaka (1971b) states that *yahari* expresses speaker's *shinteki taido* 'mental, psychological as well as emotional attitude' that conforms to the universal principle not on the basis of logical reasoning but on the basis of emotional and feeling-based judgment. By using *yappari* the speaker may convey that the choice he or she makes is something that was considered to be a better choice a long time ago. Itasaka also states that *yahari* expresses the speaker's attitude that avoids forcing one's opinion on others, and consequently it conveys the virtue of humbleness. Overall, Itasaka concludes that *yahari* represents a polar opposite of the attitude expressed by the English word *commit*. *Yahari* is used when one avoids "committing" oneself and avoids standing behind one's claim that what one says conforms to the universal truth and or objective fact.

More recently Nishihara (1988) offers the following three functions of *yahari/yappari*.

1. *Yahari* is used when adding to and emphasizing additional information and when the speaker confirms that such additional information is obtained as a result of appropriate logical reasoning of the speaker.
2. In conversational discourse, *yahari* is used a) when a speaker confirms the summary of the goings-on of conversation, and b) when a speaker decides to insist on and push through his or her own opposing view.
3. *Yahari* is used when the speaker wishes to point out that his or her reasoning agrees with what is the expected norm of society.

While these characterizations are insightful, they simply offer lists of functions with no reference to an overall theoretical framework or to other similar aspects of language. In fact in some cases the semantic characteristics attributed to *yahari/yappari* by different scholars seem almost contradictory; for example, while Itasaka (1971b) attributes non-logical nature to *yahari/yappari*, Nishihara (1988) claims *yahari/yappari* is supported by logical reasoning of the speaker. In what follows I will explore the semantic sources of *yahari/yappari* in order to clarify this seeming contradiction. In general terms, here, as throughout this book, I have three interrelated goals. First, I answer the specific question of what the distributional characteristics of *yahari/yappari* are. Second, I will inquire into the nature of their semantic sources as well as their functions. And third, I address the issue of to what aspects of Discourse Modality *yahari* and *yappari* contribute most effectively.

3.1. Distributional Characteristics of Yahari/Yappari

As a preliminary step in investigating the meaning and functions of *yahari/yappari*, I start with its distributional characteristics. Similarly to what I discussed earlier regarding the connective *datte*, *yahari/yappari* exhibits distributional characteristics including (1) *yahari/yappari* is exempt from sentential anaphora, (2) the use of *yahari/yappari* is constrained to direct discourse, and (3) *yahari/yappari* assumes known or shared information. In fact the three discourse distributional characteristics called upon here can be found across several types of DM indicators.

For discussion of the first characteristic, observe [3].

[3.1] <u>Yahari</u>   sono paatii wa hayaku owatta.
       as expected that party T early ended
       'As expected the party ended early.'

[3.2] Sore wa yoku aru   koto datta.
       that T often there are fact BE
       'That happened often.'

In [3.2], the pronoun *sore* refers to the semantic content of the preceding utterance, i.e., the party ended early. Notice that *yahari*'s meaning is excluded from what is anaphorically referred to by *sore* 'that.'

The second point. In Japanese, epistemology controls the lexical selection of emotional adjectives. For example, examine [4].

[4] Sasaki wa <u>yappari</u>   okane o hoshigatte-iru.
     Sasaki T   as expected money O want
     'Sasaki wants money after all.

Utterance [4] describes Sasaki's desire as reported by the speaker. When the speaker uses *yappari* to reflect his or her own perspective, it poses no cooccurrence problem. However, if we attempt to interpret *yappari* to reflect Sasaki's perspective, the utterance becomes inappropriate. This is because two conflicting perspectives are reflected in the latter reading of *yappari okane o hoshigatte-iru*.

A similar point can be made by observing the following phenomenon.

[5] *Chichi   wa imooto   ni [<u>yappari</u>
      my father T younger sister IO as expected
     denwa-suru yooni] to itta.
     make a phone call QT said
     *'My father told my younger sister to as expected make a
     phone call.'

[6] Chichi   wa imooto   ni <u>yappari</u>
     my father T younger sister IO as expected
     [denwa-suru yooni] to itta.
      make a phone call QT said
     'My father, as expected, told my younger sister to make a
     phone call.'

In the interpretation given in [5] in which *yappari* is assumed to reflect the younger sister's perspective, a problem arises. This is because *yappari* reflects the younger sister's view that there is a relationship which connects "to make a phone call" with what information she personally assumes. When the father tells his daughter to make a phone call, he cannot force her to view "making a phone call" in such a way as to show a semantically significant relationship to the situation surrounding her. When using *yappari*, one cannot force one's view on someone else; rather one can only describe one's own view in relation to an available fact. *Yappari* reflects the speaking self's personal epistemological positioning--an area sacred to each individual. If we interpret *yappari* as reflecting the speaking self's view as indicated by [6], it is appropriate. Here there is no forced choice of modality upon another individual. The speaker expresses his or her personal view toward the father's behavior, i.e., to tell the daughter to make a phone call.

Conversely, this evidence suggests that *yahari* brings with it a feeling of speakerhood, i.e., *yahari* attests to the fact that the utterance is personalized and the speaker is there. Like other modal adverbs (and DM indicators in general), an objectively inclined descriptive statement does not readily take *yahari/yappari*.

Yahari/yappari exhibits further distributional characteristics, which is our third point. When using *yahari/yappari*, the speaker normally assumes a critical mass of information commonly shared among participants. Thus, in an utterance such as "fire!" which makes an unexpected announcement, *yappari* cannot usually occur, as shown in [7].

[7] *Yappari   kaji da!
      as expected fire BE
     *'(As expected) fire!'

The utterance *kaji da!* 'fire!' provides a new and surprising piece of information against the discourse background where such information is least expected. *Yahari/yappari* is not appropriate under such circumstances. This is because when using *yahari/yappari*, a speaker must be aware of a piece of information which is assumed or associated in some way. A situation where *yahari/yappari* is appropriately used requires, for example, that the participants of the interaction have already suspected the possibility of a fire. Under such a circumstance, the speaker simply affirms--"as expected, it is indeed a fire." In

this situation *yahari/yappari* is appropriate because *kaji da* is used to confirm
one's thought, rather than to provide and focus on an unexpected new piece of
information. One utters "*yappari kaji da!*" almost self-confirmingly.

3.2. The Semantic Source of Yahari/Yappari: *Recognizing Realized Expectations*

Taking into consideration the distributional characteristics identified so far, let
us explore how *yahari/yappari* appears in discourse.

> (8.1) "Okusan, orusu desu yo.
>   wife   absent BE   IP
>   'The wife is not home.'

> (8.2) Ima, okusan ni denwa   ga arimashita ga, [amado   ga
>   now wife   IP phone call S there was but shutters S
>   shimatte-imasu] yo.
>   is closed   IP
>   'There was a phone call for her just now, but the shutters
>   are closed.'

> (8.3) Sakuya   mo   denwa   ga arimashita ga, <u>yahari</u>
>   last night also phone call S there was but as expected
>   [amado   ga shimatte-imashita. ...]"
>   shutters S was closed
>   'Last night also there was a call, but then the shutters
>   were also closed as expected.'

>   --Tachihara 1976:90-91

In discussing *yahari/yappari*, let us use the [X *yahari/yappari* Y] structure to
indicate two discourse segments significantly related to *yahari/yappari*. In (8)
yahari points out the sameness between two facts represented by [X] and [Y],
[X] in (8.2) and [Y] in (8.3) marked by square brackets. By using *yahari* the
speaker encourages the addressee to provoke just enough knowledge specified
by [X] so that such knowledge is relevantly connected with the proposition
expressed by [Y].

Unlike the case in (8), in (9) and (10) *yahari/yappari* triggers socioculturally shared information as knowledge which is relevantly associated with the proposition expressed in [Y].

(9.1) Sora wa nigotte-i-nakatta.
       sky T was cloudy-NEG
       'The sky was not cloudy.'

(9.2) Toomeina   koosen wa sora ippai o akarukushite-iru.
       transparent light T sky whole O lighten
       'Transparent lights lightened the whole sky.'

(9.3) Yahari   tori mo tonde-ita.
       as expected birds also were flying
       'As expected birds were flying.'

(9.4) Tori dake wa seikakuna shuukan de matte-ita.
       birds only T accurate   pattern in were flying
       'Only the birds were flying according to their accurate
       behavioral patterns.'

                                    --Matsumoto 1982:199

(10)   "Ima no yatsu wa okusan no ryooshin to   dookyo-
       now LK guy   T wife   LK parents with live
       shitete ne, yappari   kigane   na n da yo."
       together IP as expected constrained BE NOM BE IP
       'The fellow I just talked to lives with his in-laws and as
       expected he feels constrained.'

                                    Akagawa 1986:140

In (9), the writer describes the fact that the birds are flying in accordance with what is normally expected under such circumstance as a part of common knowledge; the sky was not cloudy, and the birds are expected to be flying in such a sky. *Yappari* in (10) evokes social knowledge that surrounds the relationships among in-laws; a married man feels less than totally relaxed because he lives with his in-laws.

A different kind of association between [X] and [Y] is observed in (11).

(11)   Shikashi <u>yahari</u>   shitsunai   ni kare no iru
        but   as expected inside the room in he   S exist
        kehai wa nakatta.
        sign T there was-NEG
        'But as expected, there was no sign of him being in the
        room.'

                                              --Morimura 1977:79

At this point in the novel, a conclusion is drawn based on thought presented or suggested earlier. The woman visits a man's apartment at a prearranged time but she cannot find him. She enters the apartment and discovers that he is not in the living room. She begins to suspect that the man is not home, i.e., [X]. By the time she reaches the bedroom she concludes he is not home at all as suspected. *Yahari* here is used in reference to the thought process which leads to the conclusion given in [Y].

When using *yahari*, one may present a piece of information as a choice among items of an identified or assumed set. The first type as exemplified by (12) is a selection of an item out of a pool of items.

(12)   "...Sorenishitemo, <u>yahari</u>   ichiban komatte-iru
            even so   as expected most   is troubled
        no wa keisatsu daroo na."
        one T police   BE   IP
        'After all, the one that is troubled most (out of all
        possible parties involved) must be the police.'

                                              --Hoshi 1976:259

Another related use is the choice of an item in contrast to other possibilities as shown by data set (13).

(13.1)   Kekkon-shite-kure to yuu tsumori   datta.
         get married   QT say intention BE
         'I intended to ask (her) to marry me.'

(13.2)   Daga <u>yahari</u>   moohitotsu no koto o yuu
         but as expected another   LK fact O say
         kotonishita.
         decided

'But nevertheless (lit. after all) I decided to talk
about another thing instead.'

--Komatsu 1980:48

Here the fact that the man decided to mention "another thing" is presented in contrast with something else, which is what he first intended to say, i.e., to ask her to marry him. Common to all cases presented in (8) through (13) is the strong position taken by the speaker, that is, recognition that what is expected or speculated to be expressed by [Y] is actually the case. In other words, by using different cognitive processes involving different types of relevant knowledge, the speaker ultimately expresses his or her comprehension that what is expected or speculated is realized.

Based on these observations I propose that the semantic source of *yahari/yappari* is best characterized when I view *yahari/yappari* as a device to signal the pragmatically and semantically significant linkage the speaking self identifies between the propositional content (P) expressed by [Y] and the relevant knowledge (K) provoked by [Y] in the [X *yahari/yappari* Y] structure. (K) may be specified in the prior text [X]. (K) may not appear in prior text; it may be only implied or it may be contextually or socially identifiable. *Yahari/yappari* conveys that a proposition (P) expressed by [Y] is most appropriately interpreted in the context of (K), relevant knowledge selected from a pool of general knowledge.

In *yahari/yappari* sentences, one does not necessarily present (P) to provide new information, but rather, often to confirm (P) through the mediation of (K) on the basis of identity, similarity or conformity. The semantic source of *yahari/yappari* is precisely this: to convey the speaker attitude to confirm a piece of propositional information (P) expressed by [Y] through the mediation of relevant knowledge (K) on the basis of similarity or conformity in both cognitive and social terms. When using *yahari/yappari*, the speaker affirms [Y] matter-of-factly as if he or she recognizes that the expectation/assumption is naturally realized. In fact the motivation for using [*yahari/yappari* Y] is not to present [Y], but to present the speaker's view that (P)'s legitimacy is established by calling in (K) as a piece of supporting evidence. In short, *yahari/yappari* signals that the speaker recognizes and confirms the reality of (P) as a part of universally accepted facts supported by commonly accepted knowledge (K). And the speaker's motivation for using *yahari/yappari* lies in his or her wish to signal a recognition that the expectation (P) expressed by [Y] is indeed the case.

When using *yahari/yappari* the speaker expects the partner to understand that (P) constitutes a phenomenon most aptly interpreted by integrating the information (K). In other words, by using *yahari/yappari*, the speaker signals his or her epistemological positioning toward and between two bodies of knowledge, i.e., (P) and (K). And more importantly, underlying this identification of the relationship between two pieces of information is the speaker's belief system or thought process which recognizes such a relationship. This belief system, being personal and not necessarily representing the world of universal logical belief, and consequently being argued on personal terms only, is indeed unchallengeable by others. One cannot argue logically unless participants agree on the same rules of logical thinking. Since the world occupied by *yahari/yappari* is a private world not easily violated by others, using *yahari/yappari* often gives the impression that participants are on the same wave-length, so to speak, sharing much of a common knowledge and attitude. This sense of shared identity evokes a feeling of "belongingness."

The relationship between (P) and (K) discussed above can be sorted out into four different types of knowledge associations as listed below. These association types operate on qualitatively different levels of language as indicated. One may think of these four epistemologically characterized association types as representing four different contexts relevantly activated for each use of *yahari/yappari*. The number of example data discussed earlier is assigned to each type as given in parentheses.

1. Textual Knowledge--textual level:
    (K) is information specifically provided in prior text, and (P) presents a case similar to (K)--(8),
2. Social Knowledge--pragmatics:
    (K) is information acknowledged as social knowledge, and (P) conforms to (K), (P) presents a case expected by (K)--(9), (10),
3. Knowledge for Conclusion--logical thought process:
    (P) is a logical conclusion expected to be drawn on the basis of specified or suggested evidence made available by (K)--(11),

4. Knowledge for Selection--confirmatory thought process:
   (K) conforms to the speaker's judgment against a pool of
   possibilities--(12), or, (P) conforms to speaker's judgment in contrast
   to (K)--(13).

These types are best understood as realizations of *yahari/yappari*'s
semantic source in that each represents specific cases of pragmatically and
semantically significant linkage between the propositional content and the body
of relevant knowledge (K). The seeming contradiction observed earlier between
Itasaka's (1971b) and Nishihara's (1988) characterizations of *yahari/yappari* can
now be seen as different realizations of the same semantic source. In both cases
the speaker's dependence on (K)--whether it is the logical thinking process or
illogical ways of thought--is the basic epistemological process triggered by
yahari/yappari.

3.3. Discourse Functions of Yahari/Yappari

We have identified the semantic source of *yahari/yappari* along with four
different types of knowledge association between (P) and (K). But we have not
yet asked the basic question: Why do speakers find it necessary to use
yahari/yappari in the first place? I propose that as in the case of discourse
connectives examined earlier, the essential function of *yahari/yappari* is to
express personal views and attitudes as characterized by aspects of Discourse
Modality.

Expressing one's perspective toward the very relationship one holds
between the statement and the knowledge base ultimately foregrounds the
speakerhood, and therefore, speaker subjectivity. Having stated this, I must
caution the reader that the personal voice expressed by *yahari/yappari* can
sometimes be disguised in the following sense. As suggested earlier, when
yahari/yappari is used, the relevant (K) reflects thought that the speaker holds
as a belief system or thought process. This personal voice often coincides with
what society conventionalizes as commonly accepted knowledge. Society's way
of thinking encourages one, at least in part, to hold similar or identical principles
of thought which one may fall back upon when making judgments. Or, more
accurately stated, when the speaker uses *yahari/yappari*, by virtue of the fact
that society's value is anaphorically evoked, the speaker expresses his or her

personal voice by appealing to (K) as a socially supported knowledge base that persuasively justifies the content of (P). In this sense the speaking self manages to avoid personally committing himself or herself overtly to the content of (P); rather, the speaking self sneaks in (P) through the backdoor, so to speak, as a widely held view that obviously should be accepted by all parties involved, including the addressee.

Clearly, *yahari/yappari* is a sign to signal the speaker's personal voice. Ironically, although *yahari/yappari* expresses subjectivity in a direct and dramatic way, it may also be used to escape the full responsibility of making the statement. In fact, as suggested by Itasaka (1971b), *yahari/yappari* often serves as a device for switching personal responsibility to that of society's (assumed) consensus. The strategy to use society's (assumed) consensus as a mediation of an individual's cognitive mode reflects what is widely discussed about the Japanese way of communicational strategies. For example, the often-cited characteristics of Japanese society by terms such as "group-oriented" or "frame-based" self-identification rather than attribute-based self-identification (see Nakane 1970), as well as the Japanese context-dependent nature of communication may serve as social motivation to support this communicational strategy. This point will be discussed further in chapter 8.

From the discourse organizational perspective, functions of *yahari/yappari* are two-fold; (1) as a cohesion marker and (2) as a cohesiveness marker. First, *yahari/yappari* points out the relationship between what is expressed in (P) and what is assumed, i.e., (K), through strategies of discourse anaphora. Obviously in the case of Textual Knowledge an item of prior mention serves as a surface trigger for the anaphoric relationship between (P) and (K). I use the term anaphora not in the narrow sense--a relationship realized by an antecedent and anaphor as reflected in the syntax of pronominalization or co-reference.[4] Rather, I am using discourse anaphora in a broader concept where a piece of information is presented as or as if it were semantically non-trivially linked to another piece of assumed and/or shared information. In my view anaphora addresses this discourse pragmatic relationship rather than the sentence-syntactic relationship, and actual existence of antecedent is not a necessary condition for, although it is a symptom of, anaphor. Thus the item to which the *yahari/yappari* statement relates may be given in prior text, or may be simply suggested in reference to socioculturally based knowledge, or *yahari/yappari* may merely trigger a presupposedly shared thought process, all cases being discourse anaphora.

I suspect that evoking (K) for the presentation and argumentation of (P) is cognitively motivated by the notion of foregrounding and backgrounding. The word "foregrounding" is an English translation of the word "*aktualisace*" in Mukařovský's work as given in Garvin (1964:65). According to Garvin's translation of Mukařovský, "foregrounding arises from the fact that a given component in some way, more or less conspicuously, deviates from current usage." However, more recently, the concept of foregrounding (along with backgrounding) has been broadened to include not only a deviation in linguistic form but also a semantic prominence (or focusing) in general. It is the latter sense of "foregrounding" that I adopt here. According to Hopper (1979:213), "foreground" refers to "the language of the actual story line" or "the parts of the narrative which relate events belonging to the skeletal structure of the discourse" in contrast with "the language of supportive material which does not itself narrate the main events," i.e., "background." It is Hopper's sense of foregrounding/backgrounding that seems to be useful here.

At the core of the foreground/background relationship lies a sense of connectedness by way of contrast. By placing (P) in the background of (K) which appears in the prior text, a textual tie is created and two divergent pieces of information become integrated. While this directly contributes to the discourse cohesion in the sense of Halliday and Hasan (1976), the relationship between (P) and (K) is not limited to the Hallidayan notion of cohesion. More importantly, *yahari/yappari* signals that cohesion exists by way of contrast between the linguistically coded information, (P), and the mentally recalled image, (K), which resides in the speaker's thought. This connectedness in the cognitive process ultimately makes it possible to interpret cohesive discourse as such.

The second discourse function, i.e., as a cohesiveness marker, is closely associated with cohesion, but it achieves a significantly different function, specifically in the case of Knowledge for Conclusion association type. When *yahari/yappari* evokes the assumed thought process--drawing (logical) conclusions on the basis of (K)--it functions to signal logical cohesiveness traceable in the speaker's thought process as discussed earlier in reference to data set (11).

Especially significant to both of the discourse functions discussed here is the notion of epistemic modality. And here I am using the term epistemic modality in a sense explored in chapter 2, i.e., to mean the degree of speaker confidence toward proposition. When *yahari/yappari* is used to evoke some commonly acknowledged information or the assumed thought process, the speaking self conveys to the addressee that the conclusion is based on logical or otherwise at least conscious thought process. This in turn expresses a high degree of speaker confidence in the content of (P).

3.4. Interactional Functions of Yahari/Yappari

While *yahari/yappari* pragmatically achieves the foregrounding of the speaking self, it is also important to acknowledge that, as in the cases of connectives discussed earlier, *yahari/yappari* is a sign which assumes the "other" and which aspires to share the identical epistemological position with the other. In what ways then is *yahari/yappari* interactionally functional? I propose the following.

1. The use of *yahari/yappari* is based on the assumption that knowledge (of either thought process or social convention) is assumed and/or shared by the communication participant(s). Regardless of whether this is true or not, the shared-knowledge-based identity enhances similarity among participants and therefore, encourages interpersonal rapport and empathy based on a shared sense of "belongingness." This feeling is likely to reach what I call "emotional resonance," i.e., a mutual acknowledgment of shared emotion.

2. Because *yahari/yappari* provides personal attitudes regarding some known fact, the use of *yahari/yappari* may give an impression that some thought process is involved on the speaker's part. The speaker maximizes this function of *yappari* when he or she needs to occupy an otherwise silent space in speech while planning speech (planner) and/or to warrant participation (filler) by signaling to the other participant that the speaker is involved in interaction (because he or she is thinking) and some utterance is anticipated.

3. The impression of the speaker's thoughtfulness also enhances a softening of awkward moments in interaction. Particularly when spoken slowly and with some hesitancy, *yahari/yappari* functions as a hesitation marker. Hesitation markers are particularly useful when a speaker wishes to make dispreferred statements such as opposing the partner's views--a case of "dispreference markers" or "reluctance markers."

Some examples follow.

```
[14.1]A:  Doo shiyoo ka naa...
          how do    Q   IP
          'What should I do...'
```

```
[14.2]B:  Sore wa yappari     mazui n   ja-nai?
          that T   as expected bad   NOM BE-NEG
          'Don't you think (lit. after all) that's bad, though?'
```

Yappari here shows that B thought about other possibilities, but chose a course of action that is expected and one that agrees with A's doubt, a piece of shared information. B's use of *yappari* enhances his or her agreement with A's doubt. In other words, one uses *yappari* by virtue of the fact that it normally assumes common knowledge, for manipulative purposes to show (as if) there were a common knowledge. The assumed sharing of common knowledge adds to sustain emotional resonance.

In (15) *yappari* may be interpreted as having different interactional functions.

```
(15.1)A:  [Doko  ga yuushoo-suru to omoimasu ka?/]
          where S  win            QT think    Q
          'Which team do you think will win?'
```

```
(15.2)B:  [Pa-riigu      wa yappari     Seibu deshoo./]
          Pacific League T  as expected Seibu BE
          'For the Pacific League, I think (lit. after all) it
          will be Seibu.'
```

> --Fuji Sankei Television (New York) news, broadcast on April 7, 1989

If the situation in which this exchange takes place is such that A and B are Seibu fans, then *yappari* may be understood to function as planner, filler or rapport seeker. On the other hand if the situation is such that A and B are fans of Seibu's rival team, and *yappari* is spoken hesitantly, then *yappari* may be interpreted as a case of "dispreference markers" or "reluctance markers." Consider another example, data set [16].

```
[16.1]A:  Sumimasen ga   sono kaigi,  shitsurei-shitemo
          excuse me but  that meeting be absent
          yoroshii  deshoo ka.
          all right BE     Q
          'Excuse me, but may I be absent from that meeting?'

[16.2]B:  Uun...yappari      mazui deshoo nee...
          uh   as expected bad    BE      IP
          'Well...I'm afraid (lit. as expected) that wouldn't be
          quite right...'

[16.3]C:  Ee, kamaimasen yo.
          yes no problem IP
          'Sure, no problem.'

[16.4]D:  *?Ee, yappari      kamaimasen yo.
           yes as expected no problem IP
          *?'Sure, (lit. as expected) no problem.'
```

Let us assume that in answer to [16.1], two possible responses are given. Speaker A requests permission, and B mildly refuses in [16.2], while C's intention is to grant the request in [16.3]. Since B's response involves negating the request, a case of dispreference, *yappari* may be inserted to express B's reluctance to respond negatively to A's request. If the response is favorable, however, *ee, kamaimasen yo* 'sure, no problem' or other expressions granting permission without *yappari* are most appropriate--as shown by the inappropriateness in [16.4]--, unless of course the situation is such that relevance to assumed knowledge exists and therefore *yappari* is primarily used for anaphoric purposes. *Yappari* serves to delay the dispreferred action, a device to soften the negative impact.

3.5. Yahari/Yappari *as a Discourse Modality Indicator*

Each function identified so far contributes to aspects of Discourse Modality through the process of Modal Contextualization. Regardless of the four knowledge association types I proposed earlier, *yahari/yappari* contributes to specifying several aspects of Discourse Modality; (1) it expresses a high degree of speaker confidence in that the speaker's expectation or assumption is considered indeed the case (Epistemic Modality), and (2) it signals textual anaphora (Discourse Cohesion). *Yahari/yappari* also functions as conversational fillers and planners (Exchange Structure) and as a dispreference marker (Exchange Structure) within the Participatory Control aspect. And ultimately *yahari/yappari* encourages personal rapport based on the shared knowledge (Personal Emotion).

The process of Modal Contextualization that *yahari/yappari* brings is summarized in Figure 4.1.

Figure 4.1. *Summary of Modal Contextualization Effects Realized by* Yahari/Yappari

Semantic Source:	Context-bound Meaning Distribution:	Modal Contextualization, Aspects of Modality:
Yahari/Yappari expresses speaker's recognition of realized expectations; (P) is confirmed through (K) on the basis of similarity or conformity.	1. Propositional meaning: (P) is logical conclusion. 2. (P) is similar to (K) in prior text. 3. (P) is similar to social knowledge (K). 4. (P) is one's strong belief.	1. Information Qualification: Epistemic Modality (expressing high degree of speaker confidence in recognition of realized expectations) Discourse Cohesion (achieving anaphora: foregrounding relevant information within discourse) 3. Participatory Control: Exchange Structure (fillers and planners; dispreference or reluctance markers) 4. Interactional Appeal: Personal Emotion (emotional resonance)

As illustrated in Figure 4.1, the Japanese modal adverb *yahari/yappari* operates on different levels and contexts of discourse with its meaning extending into epistemological and interactional aspects. The adverb *yahari/yappari* is characterized as a signaling device for the speaker's epistemological positioning toward the assumed or shared knowledge at whose core lies the speaking self's belief system and thought process. At the same time aspects of meaning realized by *yahari/yappari* become significant in reference to the other, the person addressed in an interaction. It is important to realize that *yahari/yappari* can be appreciated only as a bridge to connect, both epistemologically and interactionally, different ways of perception and thought advocated among communication participants.

4. *Doose*

Let us now examine the second modal adverb of our concern, *doose* 'anyway, anyhow, at best.'

Consider sentence [17].

>   [17]   Doose ashita   no paatii wa taikutsu daroo.
>   anyway tomorrow LK party   T boring   BE
>   'Tomorrow's party will be boring anyway.'

The interpretation process of this sentence requires evoking its appropriate situational context and its attitudinal meaning. By using *doose*, the speaker communicates his or her belief that what will happen at tomorrow's party is predetermined and therefore unavoidable. Additionally, *doose* expresses a certain personal attitude and feeling about this inevitability, often tinged with a negative sense of resignation. Given this intuitive interpretation, I will characterize *doose* by identifying the aspects of Discourse Modality it realizes.

4.1. Distributional Characteristics of Doose

As with other DM indicators, let us start our discussion by concentrating on syntactic and discourse distributional constraints. The three constraints we discussed for *yahari/yappari* also apply to *doose* as shown below. Regarding the first point, i.e., *doose* is exempt from sentential anaphora, examine data set [18].

[18.1]   <u>Doose</u> sono paatii wa hayaku owaru daroo.
         anyway that party T early end   BE
         'That party will end early.'

[18.2]   Sore wa yoku aru   koto de minna
         that T often there are fact BE everyone
         shoochi-shite-iru.
         is aware
         'That happens often and everybody knows it.'

In [18.2] the pronoun *sore* 'that' refers to the semantic content, the party will end early. Notice that *doose*'s meaning is excluded from what is anaphorically referred to by *sore*.

For the second point, i.e., *doose* assumes known or shared information, [19] is provided. When using *doose*, the speaker normally assumes some information commonly shared among the participants. In an utterance making an unexpected announcement, for example [19], *doose* cannot usually occur.

[19]   *<u>Doose</u> kaji da!
        anyway fire BE
       *'Anyway, fire!'

Doose exhibits an additional distributional behavior, which is our third point, i.e., *doose*'s use is limited to direct discourse. Observe [20].

[20]   Sasaki wa <u>doose</u> okane o hoshigatte-iru ni-chigainai.
       Sasaki T anyway money O want   must
       'Sasaki undoubtedly wants money anyway.'

When [20] is interpreted to describe Sasaki's desire as reported by the speaker, i.e., when the speaker uses *doose* to reflect his or her own perspective, it poses no cooccurrence problem. However, if we attempt to interpret *doose* to reflect Sasaki's perspective as in *Sasaki wa [doose okane o hoshigatte-iru] ni-chigainai--* with *doose*'s scope limited to the subordinate clause only--, the utterance becomes inappropriate. This is because two conflicting perspectives are reflected in the later reading of *doose okane o hoshigatte-iru ni chigainai*.

This point can be further illustrated by sentences [21] and [22] given below.

[21]   <u>Doose</u> paatii wa taikutsu daroo.
       anyway party T boring   BE
       'The party will be boring anyway.'

[22]   *Paatii ga taikutsu daroo to yuu koto wa <u>doose</u> da.
        party S boring   BE   QT say fact T anyway BE
       *'The fact that the party will be boring is anyway.'

In [21] the speaker expresses that--despite whatever wishes of people in general or of the speaker himself/herself--the party will end up being boring anyway. When [21] is expressed with the *koto* nominalization as in [22], however, *doose* cannot cooccur. This stems from the conflict between two contradictory forces, i.e., one, the more objective strategy of nominalization and two, the more direct and speaker subjective expression that *doose* implies.[5]

The three distributional characteristics pointed out here attest to *doose*'s inherent characteristic, i.e., a direct expression of personal feelings and attitude. As argued in all other cases of DM indicators discussed earlier, *doose* is an expression utmost and foremost attributed to the expression of the speaking self. And I propose that here lies the pragmatic motivation for using *doose*, i.e., to foreground the speaker's subjectivity, emotion and voice.

At this point I must discuss *doose*'s other distributional constraints. Observe the following.

[23]   *<u>Doose</u> Tookyoo e ikimasu ka.
        anyway Tokyo   to go   Q
       'Are you going to Tokyo anyway?'

[24]   *<u>Doose</u> Tookyoo e ikimashoo.
        anyway Tokyo   to let's go
       'Let's go to Tokyo anyway.'

[25]   *<u>Doose</u> ano hito wa Tookyoo e ikimashita.
        anyway that person T Tokyo   to went
       'That person went to Tokyo anyway.'

Sentences [23] through [25] are all inappropriate. The operating constraints seem to stem from the fact that *doose* cannot accompany utterances that straightforwardly ask the addressee's attitude or will as in [23] and [24], nor that strongly affirm one's attitude as in [25]. *Doose* in the [*doose* Y] structure seems to signal the speaker's speculative attitude that the propositional content (P) expressed by [Y] happened, happens, or will happen, as predetermined fate. Speaker is confident of (P) itself--yet speculates on the legitimacy of identifying (P) as a part of fate.

Interestingly, the constraints discussed here can serve as a device for understanding the differences between *doose* and another modal adverb we have discussed earlier, *yahari/yappari*. Observe [26] through [28], all of which are appropriate.

[26]   <u>Yappari</u>   Tookyoo e ikimasu ka.
       as expected Tokyo   to go   Q
       'Are you going to Tokyo after all?'

[27]   <u>Yappari</u>   Tookyoo e ikimashoo.
       as expected Tokyo   to let's go
       'Let's go to Tokyo after all.'

[28]   <u>Yappari</u>   ano hito   wa Tookyoo e ikimashita.
       as expected that person T Tokyo   to went
       'That person went to Tokyo after all.'

In case of *yahari/yappari*, the speaker simply recognizes and expresses his or her view that [Y] conforms to the relevant knowledge (K). Therefore [Y] can be a question, invitation, or affirmation. The speaker's attitude is successfully conveyed regardless of [Y]'s content. Given the observations so far we can conclude that while *yahari/yappari* expresses the speaker's "recognition" of expectation or assumption, *doose* signals the speaker's "speculation" of predetermined events.

4.2. The Semantic Source of Doose: Expressing a Fatalistic Speculation

So far we have noted *doose*'s distributional and pragmatic characteristics. But we have yet to answer the essential question: what does *doose* mean? How should we understand the cognitive processes involved for interpreting the expressions with *doose*? Based on the observation made so far, I propose that *doose* signals the pragmatically and semantically significant linkage between the propositional content (P) and the speaker's belief of the world that defines the possible world for (P), i.e., (P-W). More specifically, in *doose* sentences, a speaker speculates that (P) is certain to have existed, to exist or to have happened or to happen simply because (P) is part of the (P-W). In other words, the semantic source of *doose* lies in the speaker's epistemological positioning toward and between two manners of knowing (P) and (P-W), i.e., the possibility of (P) is undeniable and unavoidable because it is defined by (P-W). By using the expression [*doose* Y], the speaking self speculates on the unavoidable existence of the fact (P). When the speaker assumes that the addressee already shares this knowledge, the confirmatory action functions to encourage the increased level of the shared world view, which encourages emotional resonance. When the speaker assumes that the addressee does not know the unavoidable nature of the fact (P), he or she uses the expression [*doose* Y] to reveal--for the first time--the speaking self's personal attitude toward the fact (P), thereby exposing one's vulnerability. The speaking self hopes to strike an emotional chord with the communication partner and to achieve a sense of "emotional resonance."

In actual discourse, *doose* offers three related but distinguishable meaning types, all adding attitudinal information of confirmation. These three types, whose sample data are given in (29) through (31), are:

1. Surrendering unto Fate:

(29)   "Onaji koto da yo, <u>doose</u> ore wa wakai onna muki
         same thing BE IP anyway I   T young woman suitable
        ja-nai."
        BE-NEG
        'All the same, women don't see me as suitable, anyway.'

                                    --Morimura 1977:92

2. Facing Fate Bravely:

(30)   Sono hen o kokoroete-ite, <u>doose</u> nara   sunaoni
        that fact O realize   anyway BE-COND honestly
        shabette shinshoo   o yokushi, ikkokumo   hayaku
        say   impression O improve   one moment early

```
hoomen-shite-moraoo  to yuu shinsoko    ga mite-toreta.
have released         QT say bottom line S  could sense
```
'He seems to know this fact and one could sense his
bottom line--I have to confess anyway, so I might as
well tell the story honestly and give a good impression
(to the police officer) and get released as soon as
possible.'

--Natsuki 1981:261

3. Confirming Fate:

(31) "Moo _doose_ kaeru tokoro-datta" to yuu yoona koto o
      soon anyway return was about to QT say such fact 0
      itte chirarito udedokei   o kazashita.
      say quickly   wristwatch 0 held up
      'He said something like "I was about to leave anyway,"
      and he quickly held his wristwatch (to check the time).'

--Natsuki 1981:112

All three types express different speaker attitudes when faced with an undeniable and unavoidable fact which the speaking self feels is predetermined. For lack of a better term I use "fate" to mean this undeniable and unavoidable fact defined by (P-W) which the speaker faces. The term "fate" therefore implies more than a sense of destiny or doom. When faced with fate, one may respond in a variety of ways. The _doose_ appearing in the [_doose_ Y] utterance forces the interpreter to search for contextual cues which show a desire or wish other than (P), and/or cues which express the speaker's determination to change (P) as a positive condition to achieve further desire or wish. In the context of (1), the "Surrendering unto Fate" interpretation is reached; in context (2), one interprets _doose_ as an expression of "Facing Fate Bravely." If neither (1) or (2) is acknowledged in the context, interpretation (3) "Confirming Fate" is reached. In other words, _doose_ functions as a signal for making the interpreter search for contextual cues in order to find the appropriate interpretation. At the same time, _doose_ demands that the interpretation of (P) incorporate the process of Modal Contextualization as described below.

In "Surrendering unto Fate," the speaking self surrenders to (P-W) which he or she feels to be an overwhelming or overpowering fact. The speaker feels it is a fate simply impossible to avoid. Although the speaker's wish may be such that it is within the realm of possibility as defined by (P-W), often this reading assumes the speaker's wish to defy the (P-W). In the "Confirming Fate" category, the speaking self presents (P) as he or she concedes that (P) exists or is about to happen simply because (P) is a part of (P-W).

In "Facing Fate Bravely," the speaking self acknowledges the inevitability of (P); and then attempts to make the best of it, often turning the negative situation into a positive one. This type often occurs with the conditional *nara*. The clause, [X] *nara* 'if [X]' presents [X] as something that the speaker accepts [X] (as if) it were fact. Thus, there is a similarity in the speaker's judgment when using *nara* and when using *doose*. The pair *doose* [Y] *nara* 'if [Y] anyway' reinforces each other in what Halliday (1970:331) terms "concord," and both are cumulative in semantic effect. In language, devices representing different grammatical categories jointly realize the utterance-as-a-whole modal effect. Focusing on the concept of Discourse Modality enables us to unite seemingly unrelated linguistic devices in terms of combined effects.

The characteristics of *doose* proposed here all originate in the speaking self's view toward an event or state. By *doose* the speaker expresses his or her fatalistic speculation that something is certain to exist or happen regardless of his or her desire for it to be otherwise. *Doose* resides in the very relationship between (P) and (P-W), i.e., between the linguistically coded information and one's knowledge of the workings of the world. Through this personal evaluation mediated by the adverb *doose*, the *doose*-marked utterance succeeds in conveying a distinctive evaluative and emotional tone. In all interpretations of *doose*, by evoking (P-W), the speaker invites the addressee to share the same world view (P-W) which controls his or her cognitive process. The importance of this function seems even more revealing when we realize that the speaker's *doose* attitude toward (P) as well as the content of (P) may be already shared by the addressee. For example in all cases of *doose*, i.e., in (29), (30) and (31), the speaker may expect or at least suspect, that the addressees share the same attitude the speaker expresses by using *doose*. Uttering *doose* and emphasizing a shared world view reinforces and is reinforced by psychological and emotional identity. In *doose* one hears the inner voice of the speaking self that intends to communicate on an emotional level--the ultimate goal of which is to experience "emotional resonance."

Before concluding this section, I should briefly mention the difference between *doose* and its English translation 'anyway.' Let us reexamine [23] and

[20] reproduced here for convenience. For [20] we discuss the case where *doose*'s scope is limited to the subordinate clause only.

[23]   *Doose   Tookyoo e   ikimasu ka?
       anyway Tokyo   to go   Q
       'Are you going to Tokyo anyway?'

[20]   *Sasaki wa [doose   okane o hoshigatte-iru] ni-chigainai.
       Sasaki T   anyway money O want   must
       'Undoubtedly Sasaki wants money anyway.'

In [23], the use of *anyway* in English translation does not pose inappropriateness since *anyway* can express the attitude of either the speaker or the addressee. One can interpret *anyway* in [23] as expressing the attitude of the addressee, although it is impossible to do so in the Japanese use of *doose*. Similarly while in [20] we cannot interpret *doose* as expressing the attitude of Sasaki in Japanese, this interpretation is possible for *anyway* in the English translation. The use of the English adverb *anyway* not being limited to direct discourse in contrast to the limits imposed on the Japanese *doose* reflects the difference in epistemology between the two languages. While in English one uses the attitudinal adverbs to describe the world as well as the speaking self, Japanese modal adverbs are dedicated to describing the speaking self more than to describing the world. This difference reflects the basic structural difference between the two languages. While English is a subject-predicate prominent language with the dominant role of language being to describe the world in terms of proposition, the Japanese language is topic-comment prominent with the dominant role of language being not only to describe the world in terms of proposition but also to offer the speaking self's often personal comment about an identified set of topics. This point will be explored in detail in chapter 8.

4.3. Doose *as a Discourse Modality Indicator*

In conclusion I propose that the [*doose* Y] expression refers to the semantic source meaning "(P) expressed by [Y] will conform to the world defined by (P-W)." The semantic characterization here is attitudinal and general. In actual discourse one interprets the semantic source in three different meaning types; Surrendering unto Fate, Confirming Fate and Facing Fate Bravely. These are context-activated interpretations of *doose*, and yet each retains a general semantic source. The process of Modal Contextualization *doose* realizes is summarized in Figure 4.2.

Figure 4.2. *Summary of Modal Contextualization Effects Realized by* Doose

Semantic Sources:	Context-bound Meaning Distribution:	Modal Contextualization, Aspects of Modality:
Doose expresses speaker's fatalistic speculation that (P) will conform to the world defined by (P-W)	1. Surrendering unto Fate 2. Confirming Fate 3. Facing Fate Bravely	1. Information Qualification: Epistemic Modality (expressing high degree of speaker confidence in fatalistic speculation) 4. Interactional Appeal Personal Emotion (encouraging emotional resonance)

As shown above, in the case of *doose*, Personal Emotion is the primary Discourse Modality aspect. This attitudinal information adds to the contextual information to be integrated into the interpretation of (P) and therefore increases the level of Modal Contextualization. Since *doose* expresses a high degree of speaker confidence in speculating that (P) was, is or will be indeed the case, it also contributes to Epistemic Modality.

The study of *doose* reveals an interesting aspect of language. The meaning of *doose* lies not in referential semantics, but in the very manner of speculation that the speaking self experiences. Similarly to the case of *yahari/yappari*, *doose* signals how the speaking self expresses his or her subjective view when speculating on the course of events. Needless to say, the perceived fatalism is socioculturally bound, and therefore the meaning of the DM indicator *doose* can be appreciated only when we investigate its meaning from a broad perspective such as the one explored in this study.

In this chapter we have observed that modal adverbs serve to add to the building process of the modal scene by gradually characterizing aspects of

Discourse Modality and thereby contextualizing the propositional content. From the perspective of speaker motivation for using modal adverbs, we note that establishing the modal scene has very little to do with referential semantics. Instead the speaking self is engaged in presenting his or her subjective voice, ultimately making the verbal act a self-expression.

CHAPTER 5

Style as Discourse Modality:
<u>Da</u> and <u>Desu/Masu</u> Verb Forms

1. Introduction

In the preceding two chapters I investigated four separate independent DM indicators. In this chapter we shift our focus to cases of multi-phrase DM indicators--the DM manipulative devices of *da* and *desu/masu* verb-ending forms. Two dominant forms in verb morphology, *da* and *desu/masu* verb endings are widely recognized in Japanese. For convenience, let us call the *da*-ending forms "abrupt" and *desu/masu*-ending forms "formal" endings or styles. Traditionally, linguists have characterized these two forms as representing different "styles," for example, spoken versus written or informal versus formal. This chapter goes a step beyond this assumption and asks what motivates a speaker to choose these two types of verb-final forms in Japanese discourse. My intention here is, as in the previous two chapters, to investigate the verb-final forms from the perspective of Modal Contextualization within the Discourse Modality framework.

Consider the following example taken from contemporary Japanese fiction.[1]

(1.1)   "Hitori   <u>dete-kita</u>. (abrupt)
one person appeared
'A person is coming out.'

(1.2)   Ano ko   <u>desu</u> yo." (formal)
that child BE   IP
'That is the very girl.'

--Natsuki 1981:159

Notice that *dete-kita* in (1.1) is in *da* form while *desu* in (1.2) is in *desu* form. Both utterances are made by the same individual and constitute a single conversational turn in the fiction. Obviously (1.1) and (1.2) both exemplify spoken style, as evidenced by their appearance in direct quotation, and both are presumably on the same level of formality. It is difficult to imagine, at least in this situation, that the level of formality would change in the middle of the speaker's turn. Thus, one cannot persuasively argue that the speech producer (in this case the author) finds it necessary to mix *da* and *desu* forms on the two possible grounds mentioned earlier, i.e., spoken versus written or informal versus formal styles. This then suggests that one must seek out motivation for the style mixture elsewhere.

Specifically in this chapter, based on the discourse distributional characteristics of the *da* and *desu/masu* endings, I address the question--what are the specific textual and interactional effects of the verb morphology in Japanese? This in turn will lead us to discover the speaker's motivation for the choice and the mixture of *da* and *desu/masu* manipulation. We then ask the question: In what ways does the verb morphology contribute to the establishment of Discourse Modality? I will also inquire into the cognitive/social source which necessitates such manipulation in Japanese. In this regard, I once again return to the thoughts of modern Japanese philosophers, Watsuji and Mori mentioned in chapter 2, who provide the ontological background for the speaker's use of and mixture of two kinds of verb-final forms.

I have selected three different sources for the data : (1) transcribed casual conversation among friends, (2) dialogues appearing in modern fictional works, and (3) modern Japanese essays. The specific sources for each type of data are described in chapter 1. The rationale behind this selection is that at least one genre from both spoken and written discourse is necessary to investigate the phenomenon if I am interested in claiming that the "stylistic" difference--between spoken versus written style--does not alone motivate the selection between *da* and *desu/masu* forms. Consequently, casual conversation and essays are chosen. Additionally, dialogues in fictional works offer a unique data source since they represent a case of a spoken style (at least the author's intention being so) within a written text.

It should be pointed out that when examining abrupt verb endings, I chose only those without sentence-final particles and the like. This is because I am primarily interested in contrasting between (a) verb endings accompanied by some stylistic and/or interactional signals (one case of which is the *desu/masu* ending) and (b) abrupt verb endings with no further interactional devices attached. I suspect that abrupt endings which are accompanied by particles as well as other interactionally and discourse-organizationally motivated Discourse Modality indicators share modal characteristics similar to--or, at least which may be analyzed from a perspective similar to--*desu/masu* endings. Concentrating on the naked abrupt forms (i.e., *da* endings with no additional marker attached) allows us to limit the scope of our investigation, thus making it easier to concentrate on the pragmatic differences between the *da* and *desu/masu* verb morphology.

2. Background

Historically the issue of choice between *da* and *desu/masu* styles came into focus in the Meiji 20's (from 1887 to 1896) at the time of *genbun itchi undoo* 'the unification movement of the spoken and written language.' Some writers deliberately chose one style over the other at certain times of their careers. For example, Yamada Bimyoo adopted the *da* style in 1888 but changed to *desu/masu* style in 1889, and eventually came to be known as the author representing the *desu*-style writing. The *dearu* style which I categorize as a type of *da* style, was refined by Ozaki Kooyoo in 1897 and eventually became the common style in modern written Japanese.[2] In contemporary Japanese, *da*, *dearu* and *desu/masu* styles are used, sometimes mixed in a single text segment.

Among Japanese grammarians who have commented on the phenomenon of the style mixture, the following represents a generally accepted position. Most traditional prescriptivists recommend against mixing styles inadvertently. For example, Haga (1962:62) citing *danwatai* 'spoken style' and *bunshootai* 'written style'--similar to our abrupt and formal styles respectively--, suggests that mixture of these styles without reason should be avoided. Haga (1962) calls this rule *bunmatsu ikkan no gensoku* 'the principle of consistency in sentence-final forms.' Haga, however, points out several situations in which language users may purposefully mix *da*, *dearu* and *desu/masu* endings. First, in a discourse where *da* endings dominate with occurrences of sporadic *desu/masu* endings, the latter serves the following; (1) for expressing formality, (2) for expressing humor and for an insertion of personal comment, as well as for expressing sarcasm, and

(3) for expressing vocative and for directly addressing the listener. In a discourse segment where the *desu/masu* style dominates but where sporadic *da* endings appear, the latter expresses an interpersonal familiarity and closeness to the listener. In addition, Haga notes that sometimes the *da* and *desu/masu* mixture results from sociolinguistically uncertain circumstances--especially when the speaker fails to clearly assess the addressee's relative social status. Since the *desu/masu* style, in part, marks politeness, the participants' relative social status becomes a decisive factor in the style selection.

Kindaichi (1982) comments that the *da* style is used for self-addressed utterance or where brief pause in discourse exists, while the *desu* style is used when the speaker directly addresses the listener or where a major pause in discourse exists.[3] Kindaichi cites the writing style of Hukuda Kooson as a representative writer who effectively mixes abrupt and formal styles by offering the following example. (Glossing is mine.)

(2.1) Watashi wa higoro kara minoue   soodan   no inchikisei
       I   T always from personal advising LK phoniness
       ni wa goo-o-niyashite-imasu. (formal)
       IO T be quite irritated
       'I have always been quite irritated by the phoniness of
       advising on personal affairs.'

(2.2) Aite   to yohodo   hukaku tsukiatte-minai-koto-
       partner with considerable deep unless get to know
       ni-wa shinmina   kotae nado dekiru-mono-dewa-nai.
             considerate answer such can do-NEG
       'One cannot give considerate advice unless one has
       known the person well and for quite some time.'

(2.3) Okashii dewa-arimasen ka (formal), dono minoue
       strange isn't it   Q   any personal
       soodan   o mitemo, too honnin wa mina zendama no
       advising O see   very self   T all good   LK
       giseisha de, warui no wa haiguusha ka koibito ka
       victim   BE bad   one T spouse   or lover   or
       oya   ka motto daitan-hutekina no ni-naru to,
       parent or more bold   one become when
       shakai dano-nan-dano to yuu kumo-o-tsukamu-yoona
       society or something QT say vague

        mono o <u>uttaete-kuru</u>. (abrupt)
        thing 0 blame
        'Isn't it a bit strange to find that in every advising
        occasion, the person asking for advice is always a good
        person, while the one to be blamed is always this
        person's spouse, lover or parents? Or in some worse
        cases, one blames not easily definable things--
        including things such as society itself'

(2.4)   Totemo honkide kotaerareru <u>mono-dewa-arimasen</u>. (formal)
        at all truly   can answer   can do-NEG
        'One cannot easily respond to these personal questions
        if one takes these matters seriously.'

Examining this data, it is reasonable to interpret that the *desu/masu* style sentences are used when the author directly addresses the reader as evidenced in *okashii dewa-arimasen ka* 'isn't it a bit strange...' in (2.3) and *dewa-arimasen* 'one cannot easily respond...' in (2.4). It is unclear, however, what Kindaichi means by a "brief pause" and "a major pause" in discourse. I will explore this observation in more detail in the course of this chapter.

Mio (1942:192-197) in his study of spoken Japanese points out that the *da* style is generally used in the following three situations, although he acknowledges (1942:197) other factors involved--such as local and individual differences, including family practice and the social status of the speaker.

1.   When speaking in monologue;
2.   When speaking toward persons who hold relatively lower social status;
3.   When conversing among familiar and close friends.

More recently, Makino (1983, 1990) examines the formality/informality marking (identical to our abrupt/formal ending) in his proposed theory of the speaker-orientation. According to Makino's (1983:143) Principles of Speaker-Orientation, "a target element in a relevant domain cannot be marked formal if the particular domain is highly speaker-oriented; if it is not, it can be marked formal" and by "a relevant domain" he means "either a clause or a sentence." Makino defines the state of speaker-orientation as the state where we witness "the speaker's communicative motivation to express some highly subjective and presuppositional information by inwardly looking at himself." In addition, he (1983:139) states that "the listener-orientation is defined negatively as non-speaker orientation." As I will argue, although the concept of speaker-orientation identifies the basic premise regarding communication participants, it is not sufficient by itself to explain the *da* and *desu/masu* verb morphology. Makino (1990) proposes another principle regarding the formality/informality marking: "If Formality-Switching occurs, it normally takes place intra-paragraphically. Formality-Switching tends to create an intra-paragraphic writer-oriented island of cohesion." According to Makino (1990), the basic function of informality is to mark the speaker-orientation, and the informality represents a psychological inner space which can be reached only by penetrating through a psychological outer space marked by formality. Thus the switching normally occurs from formal-into-informal within a paragraph.

While studies briefly reviewed above offer helpful hints in understanding the choice of verb endings in Japanese, they fall short of answering the question posed at the outset of this chapter in reference to data set (1)--the speaker's motivation for the style mixture. Although Makino (1990) offers some answers, he leaves other questions unanswered. For example, Makino (1990) does not fully address discourse organizational functions nor the cognitive and social sources for the suggested usage of the style mixture. I find it both important and interesting to ask what underlies the seemingly unrelated lists of reasons for the style mixture suggested by various scholars. An answer to this question will provide the reason for the *da* and *desu/masu* morphological manipulation and thereby provide us with a more cohesive view of the pragmatics of the style. In the following sections I explore these and other possibilities to explain the reasons for the stylistic choice in Japanese in terms of sociolinguistic, ontological, interactional and discourse-organizational motivations within the framework of Discourse Modality.

3. The *Da* and *Desu/Masu* Mixture in Casual Conversation

In casual conversation among friends of equal or similar status, the normal speech style is abrupt. Formal styles do occur but only when specific need arises, for example, when directly quoting someone who spoke in the formal style.[4] The choice of style, at least in part, is without doubt sociolinguistically and interactionally motivated. For example, Hori (1985) states that speakers use *desu/masu* style to maintain personal distance. In this case the *desu/masu* style functions to maintain the invisible bubble of space surrounding every individual.

In casual conversation among friends, individuals tend to be encouraged to invade each other's personal space and therefore they avoid using *desu/masu* endings.[5]

Conversational utterances, however, rarely end with abrupt forms without final particle or the like attached. When do speakers use naked abrupt ending? In our data there are two possible sources for this choice. First, a speaker expresses surprise, abrupt remembrance or sudden emotional surge, as shown in data set (3), (Female Pair 9). Second, the speaker is in the narrative setting right there and then, i.e., the speaker takes a point of view internal to the world under discussion, as is the case in data set (4), (Female Pair 8).

(3.1)A: [Dooshiyoo,   Kimi-chan tachi nani hanashita n
          what should do Kimi and others what discussed NOM
          da./ (abrupt)
          BE
          'What should we do, what did Kimi and others talk
          about?' (abrupt)

(3.2)   Aa wakatta./ (abrupt)
          ah understood
          'Oh I remember it now.'

(3.3)   Kyooshoku no hanashi da./] (abrupt)
          teaching LK talk   BE
          'It's about teaching.'

(4.1)A: [Uchi no chichioya soo da yo./ (abrupt with IP)
          home LK father   so BE IP
          'My dad is like that, you know.'

(4.2)   Soide norikomu to   nee/
          then get on   when IP
          'When he gets on (the train),'

(4.3)   kutsu o nuide   nee/
          shoes O take off IP
          'he takes off his shoes,'

(4.4)   biiru o katte nomi-hajimeru./ (abrupt)
          beer O buy   begins to drink
          'he buys beer and begins to drink.'

(4.5)   Shinbunshi <u>shiku</u> no./] (abrupt with IP)
          newspaper   spread IP
          'He spreads the newspaper.'

In data set (3), the speaker wonders about her friend's conversation topic, but suddenly recalls it, and reports that it was about teaching. In utterances (3.2) and (3.3), the speaker does not design the utterance in a sociolinguistically and interactionally sensitive manner, for example, by adding interpersonal particles. Notice that although (3.1) ends with an abrupt form, the verbal *hanashita* appears with the so-called extended predicate (i.e., the *no da* construction) and therefore it is not in the naked abrupt form.[6] (3.2) and (3.3) are in naked abrupt style simply because the speaker uttered them at the instant the thought entered into consciousness.

In data set (4), the speaker utters (4.4) in naked abrupt form. As evidenced by the imperfective tense of the verb *nomi-hajimeru*, the speaker assumes a point of view internal to the conversational narrative setting where the incident takes place. It is as if she were there to directly witness her father drinking beer. She thereby describes the action dramatically and vividly and she places herself internal to the narrative scene. The internal (versus external) positioning of the speaking self (in relation to the event described) constitutes an aspect of narrative manipulation, the so-called point of view. As explained in chapter 2, I use the term point of view in a rather limited as well as practical way, that is, to mean the speaking self's viewpoint that is expressed through and reflected in various positionings that he or she takes toward the narrative event.

At this point it is useful to explore two further notions "perceptual point of view" and "conceptual point of view" proposed by Chatman (1978:152). In characterizing "point of view" Chatman identifies "perceptual point of view" as the manner of description that reports as actually seen. Conceptual point of view is identified as the case where "there is no reference to the writer's actual physical situation in the real world but to his attitudes or conceptual apparatus, his way of thinking and how facts and impressions are strained through it" (Chatman 1978:152). Chatman's conceptual and perceptual points of view involve broader literary phenomena and also seem too clear-cut as notions. Perhaps it is advisable to comprehend these notions only in terms of degree rather than in terms of being two distinct categories.

What is significant to our concern is that we can characterize the naked versus non-naked abrupt style, i.e., naked abrupt style on one hand and non-naked abrupt as well as formal styles on the other--, in terms of the narrator's perceptual versus conceptual point of view respectively. We can identify naked abrupt forms expressing the speaker's immediate report (perceptual view) as opposed to other styles expressing the speaker's second-order conceptualization about the narrative event. When the language producer places himself or herself in the location of the event, as if witnessing the very event, he or she is most likely to take the perceptual point of view, while when he or she exists external to the scene, it is more likely that the conceptual view is taken. At least in the latter case, it seems that there is more room for conceptual view to play a dominant role. This internal versus external distinction of narrative point of view appears to be one of the decisive factors in stylistic choice.

We have observed that the choice of the naked *da* style in predominantly non-naked *da* style achieves (1) immediacy and directness in expression, and (2) a narrative internal perspective. Notice that when interactional particles mark the utterances, by virtue of the fact that the speaker selects appropriate interactional particles, these utterances reflect a point of view external to the narrative setting. That is, speakers directly address the listener by taking the point of view of deliberately talking to the audience.

One also finds the naked abrupt endings in echo responses and questions as shown in (5)--(Female Pair 7), and (6)--(Female Pair 10).

(5.1)A: [Tsuisuto no Tame-chan tte <u>shitte-ru</u>?/] (abrupt)
          "Twist" LK Tame   QT do you know
          'Do you know Tame of the group "Twist"?'

(5.2)B: [<u>Shitte-ru</u>./] (abrupt)
          know
          'Yes, I do.'

(6.1)A: [Ashita   wa jikken   repooto ga/
          tomorrow T experiment report S
          'Tomorrow an experiment report,'

(6.2)B: [<u>Aru</u>./] (abrupt)
          there is
          'There is.'

(6.3)A: [Un, <u>aru</u>./] (abrupt)
           yes there is
           'Yes, there is.'

In these paired abrupt expressions where two participants exchange identical phrases, the rhythmicity of the language seems, in part, to motivate them. Notice that in (5), speaker B completes the utterance that A initiates by inserting an abrupt form of the verb *aru*. Here A and B jointly create the utterance. In this situation neither speaker consciously addresses the other; rather, they both address the information being jointly formed. In our data, naked abrupt forms appear in all three cases of jointly created utterances.

What is common in the observation made regarding conversational data-- i.e., *da* endings appear (1) for abrupt remembrance or sudden emotional surge, (2) for expressing narrative-internal point of view, and (3) for echo questions and for jointly created utterances--is that all three expressions are the kind not deliberately addressed to the communication partner. Rather, these *da*-ending utterances are made without going through the designing process that interactionally accommodates the addressee.

4. The *Da* and *Desu/Masu* Mixture in Dialogues of Fiction

In our second type of data taken from dialogue portions of modern fiction, the abrupt endings appear in similar situations. For example, let us examine our data set (1) again, reproduced here for convenience.

(1.1)   "Hitori   <u>dete-kita</u>. (abrupt)
          one person appeared
          'A person is coming out.'

(1.2)   Ano ko   <u>desu</u> yo." (formal)
          that child BE   IP
          'This is the very girl.'

                                    --Natsuki 1981:159

At this point in the novel, the author creates the following narrative setting.

Two police officers--Officers Tadokoro and Oono--are on duty secretly observing female high school students--suspected of prostitution--coming out of a local bar. Of particular interest to these men hiding behind the billboard across the bar is Kimie, the daughter of the couple who interact with the protagonists of the mystery novel. Tadokoro notices a girl coming out of the bar; he pokes at his partner and utters (1).

Tadokoro utters (1.1) as he immediately describes the incident of a girl coming out of a bar. (1.2), on the other hand, has a distinct explanatory tone in that it provides information as to who that girl is. The style chosen for (1.2) results from the speaker's effort to design an utterance appropriate to and appealing to the partner in that context. In the novel, Tadokoro consistently and primarily speaks in *desu/masu* form. Therefore, utterance (1.2) maintains the expected and sociolinguistically more appropriate style. Notice that the mixture of *da* and *desu/masu* verb endings observed in (1) results from factors beyond merely sociolinguistic. The style mixture is a manipulation device for the speaking self (in this case the author) to signal different sentence types within a single speaking turn.

If we manipulate (1) in such a way as to alter the *da* and *desu/masu* choice as given in [7], we observe a different effect.

[7.1]   "Hitori   dete-kimashita. (formal)
          one person appeared
          'A person came out.'

[7.2]   Ano ko   da." (abrupt)
          that child BE
          'That's the girl.'

Although the (logical) semantic content is identical in both (1) and [7], the effect is different. One may consider the following likely narrative setting for [7].[7]

Tadokoro describes to Oono that a girl is coming out of the bar; he calmly describes the situation in the style that he uses most often, i.e, [7.1]. Then all of a sudden he realizes that the girl he has just described is the one that he and Oono have been looking for. At this point Tadokoro exclaims [7.2].

Obviously the effect discussed here does not depend solely on the *da* and *desu/masu* manipulation. The underlying *ga* and *wa* markings and the verb tense, for example, play major roles in creating the said effect. Nonetheless, it is true that *da* and *desu/masu* verb morphology enhances, together with other strategies, the different utterance effect pointed out above.

Consider another similar case in which both of the relevant verb endings take the non-past tense.

```
(8.1)A:   "Aru oyashiki  no hanare         o karite-iru Mibu
           one residence LK detached room 0 rent        Mibu
           Shichiroo to yuu n   desu ga..." (formal)
           Shichiroo QT say NOM BE    but
           'His name is Mibu Shichiroo and he rents a detached
           room in someone's residence...'

(8.2)B:   "Aa, Mibu-san, Mibu-san nara     kono hen  no
            ah  Mr. Mibu  Mr. Mibu BE-COND this area LK
           meishi              da. (abrupt)
           prominent figure BE
           'Oh, Mr. Mibu, Mr. Mibu is a prominent figure in this
           neighborhood.'

(8.3)     Kono ushiro no uchi  no hanare   desu yo." (formal)
          this behind LK house LK detached BE   IP
          'He lives in the detached room in the residence behind
          here.'
```

--Tachihara 1976:23

At this point in the novel speaker A, Mibu's wife, is looking for the whereabouts of her husband and asks B, a young butcher at the meat shop, if he knows about Mibu. Notice that in B's single turn, B uses both *da* and *desu* endings. In (8.2), B says that Mr. Mibu is a prominent figure, not so much in answer to the question posed by (8.1), but rather, B utters this almost self-confirmingly. In this sense the utterance takes on the nature of a monologue. On the other hand (8.3) is an answer directed to the question from Mibu's wife. Since the social situation is such that A and B have not met before and the situation calls for formality and politeness, both take the *desu/masu* style. The *da* ending in (8.2) offers a sense of immediacy; B recalls Mr. Mibu and immediately identifies him as he almost self-convincingly defines him. Yet in uttering (8.3), the formal style

appears precisely because B realizes the current question-answer mode and
performs the speech act of answering the question.

The manipulation discussed above, however, is not the only motivational
source for the *da* and *desu/masu* verb morphology in the dialogues of fiction.
Let us observe another example taken from fiction.

(9)   At this point in the novel, Yazu, a secretary for the public prosecutor's
       office, reports to Akiko, a district public prosecutor, how Harue, a
       neighbor of a crime suspect, commented about the suspect. The discussion
       surrounds why Harue maintains an unfriendly attitude toward the suspect.

(9.1)   "Kore to itte gen'in ni naru   yoona   dekigoto ga
          this QT say cause   IO become such as incident S
          atta   wake   dewa-nai to omoimasu ne. (formal)
          there was reason BE-NEG   QT think   IP
          'I don't think there was a specific reason that caused
          the incident.'

(9.2)   Moshi omotedatta kenka demo   shiteireba, kitto
          if   apparent   fight such as do-COND   certainly
          Harue no kuchi kara kinjo   ni hiromatte-iru
          Harue LK mouth from neighbor IO spread
          hazu   desu kara. (formal)
          should BE   since
          'If they actually had a fight, that is sure to be known
          by the neighbors since Harue is certain to have spread
          that.'

(9.3)   Tabun,   Harue ni-shitemireba, jibun to doonenpai no
          perhaps Harue for   self as same age   LK
          onna ga hitoride shareta uchi ni sunde, akanuketa
          woman S alone   stylish house in live   fashionable
          minari de tsuukinshite-iru. (abrupt)
          clothes in commute
          'Perhaps for Harue, (it was upsetting to see that) a
          woman about the same age as herself lives in a stylish
          house and goes to work wearing fashionable clothes.'

(9.4)   Tokitama   gaisha   de okurarete
          sometimes foreign car by drive-PASS

kaette-kuru. (abrupt)
return
'And sometimes the woman is driven back home in a
foreign car.'

(9.5) Sooyuu hadena kurashi   ga netamashikatta to yuu koto
such   showy life style O was jealous   QT say fact
ja-nai n <u>deshoo</u> ka. (formal)
BE-NEG NOM BE   Q
'Isn't it that Harue was jealous of such a showy life
style?'

--Natsuki 1981:75

Utterances (9.3) and (9.4)--which, unlike (9.1), (9.2) and (9.5), take *da* endings--describe the kind of life style the suspect leads. It is as if (9.3) and (9.4) form a two-item list that describes the suspect's life style. Notice that *sooyuu* 'such' in (9.5) represents a case of sentential anaphora whose anaphoric scope includes both (9.3) and (9.4). In this discourse segment then, utterances (9.3) and (9.4) provide subordinate information that modifies *sooyuu hadena kurashi* 'such a showy life style.' Because of this, it is not necessary to design these utterances to conform to the expected speech style, i.e., the *desu/masu* style. This phenomenon corresponds to the sentence-internal situation in which subordinate clauses normally do not carry interpersonal features while the main clauses do.[8]

This interpretation clarifies the somewhat vague statement made by Kindaichi (1982) quoted earlier. In fact in the discourse segment presented as data by Kindaichi--our data set (2)--, sentences with abrupt endings simply describe Hukuda's own observation on advising in personal affairs. As suggested by Kindaichi himself, these utterances are given almost self-addressed, providing information that supports the argumentation, which in turn constitutes its major points. In other words, the *dewa-nai* utterance (2.2) and the *kuru* utterance in (2.3) offer information subordinate within the overall discourse organization. In this sense, when Kindaichi says (2.2) and (2.3) signal a "brief pause" and (2.1) and (2.4) signal a "major pause," the briefness of the pause reflects the close connection between the subordinate and main information. Subordinate information must be integrated into the main line of argument addressed directly to the reader. Points between two main pieces of information mark "major

pauses" because they are more autonomous than discourse subordinate
information marked by the *da* style.

As we have just observed, verb morphology in Japanese is functional for
distinguishing different statuses and types of information within a larger
discourse unit. In understanding this operation, the concept of "foregrounding"
is helpful. As mentioned earlier in chapter 4, I adopt Hopper's characterization
of "foregrounding" in the narrative discourse. What is significant here is that in
conversational discourse, information may be "foregrounded" in an additional
manner.   As we discussed in reference to data set (8), for example, in
conversation, a speaker "foregrounds" information that directly satisfies the
significant speech act of answering the question. When answering a question as
in (8), the answer (8.2) is foregrounded, while the speaker's monologic utterance
(8.1) is not. Thus foregrounding involves at least three elements; (1) deviation
in form, (2) information describing the skeletal structure of the narrative, and
(3) information interactionally relevant.

I conclude here that in dialogues taken from fiction one may use the
abrupt style (within predominantly formal style) when the content of the
utterance constitutes background information, while one may use formal style
to mark foregrounded information. This distinction between foregrounded and
backgrounded information in sentence and in discourse is useful not only for
understanding the verb morphology in fictional dialogues but also in prose as
well, as will be explained later.

In order to see whether or not our characterization applies to more
complex cases, let us examine another longer dialogue taken from fiction.

(10) At this point in the novel, Takeoka, a hired private investigator, tells
      Uchibori, the protagonist, how he found out Uchibori's secret.

```
(10.1)  "...Sorekara      daijina   koto wa ohutari      tomo
            additionally important fact T   two persons both
        kanari ookii shikin   de    sore o hajimeta koto ga
        fairly large capital with  that O started    fact O
        wakarimashita. (formal)
        understood
        'Additionally, an important point was revealed--that
        both of you started your business with a fairly large
        amount of capital.'
```

(10.2) Doko kara mo   kane o karizuni
        where from even money O without borrowing
        dokuryokude.
        on one's own
        'With your own financial resources, without borrowing
        any money from anywhere.'

(10.3) Amari itchishi-sugimasu. (formal)
        too   match excessively
        'Your cases resemble each other too much.'

(10.4) Dokoka   okashii. (abrupt)
        somewhere strange
        'There is something suspicious about this.'

(10.5) Nanika   arimasu. (formal)
        something there is
        'There must be something (going on here).'

(10.6) Nanika   hutari   no aidani wa, kyootsuuni
        something two persons LK between T   common
        kakusareta mono ga arimasu. (formal)
        hide-PASS thing S there is
        'You two share some common secret.'

(10.7) Shikamo anata wa watashi o Machida-shi no mihariyaku
        besides you   T I   O Mr. Machida LK watch
        ni yatotte-iru (abrupt)
        as employ
        'Besides you hired me to spy on Mr. Machida.'

(10.8) Soshite Machida-shi no yukue   o hisshini
        and   Mr. Machida LK whereabouts O desperately
        owasete-iru. (abrupt)
        make me follow
        'And you have ordered me to desperately follow
        Machida's whereabouts.'

(10.9) Anata ga Machida-shi o osorete-iru rashii koto ga,
        you   S Mr. Machida O fear   seem   fact O
        sorede wakatta. (abrupt)
        thus   understood

'From this fact, I sensed that you are afraid of
Machida.'

(10.10) Anata wa kare no kyoohaku o osorete-iru to watashi
         you   T he   LK blackmail O fear   QT I
         wa sasshimashita. (formal)
         T sensed
         'I knew that you were afraid of being blackmailed.'

(10.11) Watashi no soozoo   ni kurui   wa nakatta. (abrupt)
         I   LK suspicion at mistake T there were-NEG
         'My suspicion turned out to be reality.'

(10.12) Watashi wa Chiba kara Ogura ni suttonde-kite, basho
         I   T Chiba from Ogura to rushed   place
         no junbi   o kanryoo-shi, anata ni Machida-shi
         LK preparation O complete   you   IO Mr. Machida
         ga Ogura no kooyuu tokoro ni iru to yuu tegami o
         S Ogura Lk such   place at stay QT say letter O
         dashita. (abrupt)
         mailed
         'I came to Ogura from Chiba right away and prepared
         the place and wrote to you that Machida was going to
         be at a certain place in Ogura.'

(10.13) Anata o matsu tame datta no desu. (formal)
         you   O wait for BE   NOM BE
         'I did all this to wait for you here.'

(10.14) Ano tegami no keshiin o chuuishite mitara,
         that letter LK postmark O carefully look-COND
         Chibakyoku   de-naku Ogurakyoku   desu
         Chiba Post Office BE-NEG Ogura Post Office BE
         yo. (formal)
         IP
         'If you examined the postmark of that letter
         carefully, you would have known that it was not
         postmarked in Chiba but in Ogura.'

(10.15) Anata wa kanarazu Machida-shi ni ai ni koko ni
         you   T certainly Mr. Machida IO see for here to
         arawarerudaroo to neratte yatta koto desu. (formal)
         will appear   QT aim   did   fact BE

'I did all this thinking that you would certainly come here to kill Machida.'

(10.16) Anata wa Machida-shi ga osoroshikute-shikataganai no
         you   T Mr. Machida O fear extremely   NOM
         <u>da</u>. (abrupt with *no da*)
         BE
         'You are extremely afraid of Machida.'

(10.17) Sore wa hutari   no aida   dake no himitsu kara
         that T two people LK between only LK secret from
         <u>kite-iru</u>. (abrupt)
         come
         'That fear comes from the secret only you two share.'

(10.18) Dekireba, anata wa kare o koroshitai   no
         can-COND you   T he   O want to kill NOM
         <u>kamoshirenai</u>. (abrupt)
         may
         'Perhaps you want to kill him, if you can...'

(10.19) Soo omotta   kara, sooyuu jootai   o watashi ga
         so thought since such condition O I   S
         koshiraete anata o matte-ita no <u>desu</u>. (formal)
         make   you   O waited   NOM BE
         'Because I thought so, I made conditions suitable for
         that and was waiting for you.'

                              --Matsumoto 1980:32

The long speaking turn Takeoka takes at this point in the narrative consists of 31 utterances divided into four paragraphs. Data (1) is a reproduction of the second and the third paragraphs--whose boundary is located between (10.11) and (10.12)--consisting of 19 utterances. Although the first and last paragraphs contain utterances in formal style only, the segment presented as (10) contains a mixture of abrupt and formal endings. While the same speaker speaks predominantly here and elsewhere in formal endings, we find eight cases of naked abrupt style, (10.4), (10.7), (10.8), (10.9), (10.11), (10.12), (10.17) and (10.18).[9]

Why the mixture of styles? The motivation for choosing the abrupt style here seems to be multifold. First, as discussed earlier, the backgrounded nature of some of the utterances is at work. Notice that abrupt verb endings in (10.7) and (10.8) appear in utterances which are anaphorically referred to (*sorede* 'due to these facts') in (10.9). Likewise, *soo* 'so' in (10.19) anaphorically refers to utterances (10.17) and (10.18). These utterances represent the content of what Takeoka thought. This means that utterances (10.7), (10.8) as well as (10.17) and (10.18) are not directly addressed to the listener; rather the listener integrates information into other foregrounded utterances that maintain the thread of discourse. Utterances (10.4), (10.9) and (10.11) express what Takeoka felt; Takeoka directly expresses the feeling with a somewhat weaker intention of addressing Uchibori. The reader perceives these utterances to be almost self-addressed.

Second, utterances ending with *da* style give the impression that the speaker was present there and then at the scene of the event and has the immediacy of spontaneous expression. Recall that in the conversational data the abrupt style without interpersonal particles and the like often occur when the speaker vividly describes events as if he or she stays internal to the narrative scene and takes a narrative internal perspective. This interpretation is also applicable in the dialogues in fiction, as shown in (10).

Let us now consider utterance (10.12) which ends in abrupt verb form. Notice that it is possible to add *sore wa* 'it is' in (10.13) as in *sore wa anata o matsu tame datta no desu* 'it was to wait for you here,' which is in fact the English translation given earlier. This seems to indicate that the abrupt ending in (10.12) signals the subordinate nature of the utterance. Since no interpersonally motivated linguistic form marks (10.12), the listener searches for another utterance which is fully marked for interpersonal appeal. In this sense the choice between *da* and *desu/masu* forms functions to present information in accordance with the speaker's desire to qualify it--whether it is sometimes self-addressed subordinate backgrounded information or it is fully addressed foregrounded information that constructs the main thread of discourse. In short, the style mixture in casual conversation and dialogue in fiction reflects the speaker's intention of how to present that bit of information. Moreover, the mixture of these styles signals how and on what level of discourse each utterance places itself within a framework of the larger discourse unit.[10]

The backgrounding of information in dialogue through the use of the *da* ending proves useful in a situation where the author needs to make a clear distinction between backgrounded and foregrounded information. See, for example, data set (11).

(11) At this point in the novel, Yamamoto, a newspaper reporter who regularly
writes horse racing articles in a sports newspaper, tells his story to a police
inspector, Nakatsugawa. Yamamoto reports on a discussion he had with
a young man who works at a race track.

(11.1) "Boku wa hokani mo   yaochoo   o yatte-iru kishu
         I   T other   also fixed game O do   jockey
         o shitte-iru-shi, sono renraku   hoohoo mo,   ima
         O know   that communication method also now
         made no aidani shirabete shitta   ga, sore wa kondo
         until LK while   check   found out but that T this
         no jiken to wa kankei   nai   kara
         LK case QT T relation there is-NEG since
         hanashimasen. (formal)
         talk-NEG
         'I know other jockeys who participate in fixed races
         and I have found out the method of communication, but
         since that is unrelated to the present case, I won't
         talk about it.'

(11.2) Wakai torakkuman to   no hanashi desu ga, sono toki,
         young track-man with LK talk   BE but that time
         boku wa, ima made no yaochoo   wa, subete, go,
         I   T   now until LK fixed game T   all   five
         roku-too date   no chiisana reesu de
         six   pulled LK small   race BE
         okonawarete-kita. (abrupt)
         conducted-PASS
         'It's a discussion I had with a young track man--I said
         then that all the fixed races up to now have happened
         in small races with only five or six horses.'

(11.3) Yaochoo   ga yari-yasui kara   desu. (formal)
         fixed game S easy to do since BE
         'It is because it's easier to fix (small) races.'

(11.4) Shikashi, ugoku kane ga sukunai kara   mooke mo
         but   move money S small   since profit also
         kagirarete-iru. (abrupt)
         limit-PASS
         'But since the controllable sum of money is limited,
         the profit is also limited.'

(11.5)　Moshi, daabii no yoona ookina reesu de, yaochoo
　　　　if　　Derby LK such　large race BE　fixed game
　　　　ga yaretara,　soshite, sore ga seikoo-shitara,
　　　　S　can do-COND and　　　that S　success-COND
　　　　bakudaina kingaku ga te-ni-hairu-daroo to
　　　　huge　　　amount O will obtain　　　QT
　　　　hanashiatte-ta n　desu yo." (formal)
　　　　talked　　　NOM BE　IP
　　　　'If one can fix races in large races like the Derby,
　　　　and if that succeeds, one can obtain a huge amount of
　　　　money--so was I talking with this young track man.'

--Nishimura 1981:60-61

Here Yamamoto provides the content of the discussion in (11.2), continues on in (11.4) and a portion of (11.5). In (11.3), however, Yamamoto addresses Nakatsugawa directly as he comments that it is easier to fix small races. Note that utterance (11.3) takes a formal verb ending. Note, however, unlike the formal style which Yamamoto consistently uses in addressing Nakatsugawa, utterances (11.2) and (11.4) take abrupt endings. Utterances marked with abrupt endings semantically correspond to the content of the discussion between Yamamoto and the track man. Similarly the portion of (11.5) preceding the quotative *to* utterances marked with abrupt endings fall within the scope of the quotation. In other words, the author uses abrupt endings to mark the discourse subordinate nature of utterances (11.2) and (11.4) across the sentence boundary, thereby succeeding in backgrounding its content.

5. The *Da* and *Desu/Masu* Mixture in Literary Essay

In our data of twenty volumes of essay anthology containing 709 entries, 30 were written in predominantly *desu/masu* style, and all others were in *da* style. Out of 30 incidents of *desu/masu*-style essays, 18 entries contained the mixed style in which the *da* form appeared. The discussion to follow is based on these examples. Additionally I will discuss two cases of *desu/masu* forms which appeared in predominantly *da*-style essay.

In general, as expected from our earlier discussion, we find phenomena similar to those already observed in other genres of discourse. Abrupt endings within essays containing predominantly formal endings mark subordinate

information. For example, observe (12), in which the content of the thought--
(12.2) through (12.5)--appears in abrupt style.

(12.1)   Watashi wa kokoro ni <u>tsubuyakimashita</u>. (formal)
         I   T   mind   in muttered
         'I muttered in my mind.'

(12.2)   ---Dareka <u>i-nai</u>   no   ka. (abrupt with *no da*)
            anyone stay-NEG NOM Q
         'Isn't there anyone here?'

(12.3)   Dareka tasuke ni <u>ko-nai</u>   no   ka. (abrupt with *no da*)
         anyone help   to come-NEG NOM Q
         'Isn't anyone coming to help me?'

(12.4)   Konna hiroi tokoro ni, boku to   kono uma   dake
         such   vast   place   in   I   and this horse only
         <u>da</u>. (abrupt)
         BE
         'In such a vast place, only two of us are here, I and
         the horse.'

(12.5)   Boku wa darenimo shirarezuni   hidoi
         I   T   no one   without being known terrible
         me   ni <u>aooto-shite-iru</u>. (abrupt)
         experience at be about to meet
         'I am going to go through a terrible experience with no
         one knowing about it.'

(12.6)   Watashi wa moo   uma   no me   o miru koto ga
         I   T   anymore horse LK eye O see   fact O
         <u>dekimasen-deshita</u>. (formal)
         could not do
         'I could not look into the eyes of the horse any more.'

                                --Ogawa 1984:83

Notice in (12.1) the author clearly signals by implicit cataphoric expression that
what follows are his inner thoughts--what he muttered in his mind. Utterances
(12.1) and (12.6), however, create the effect of the writer actually recollecting
the story. It should be added that the tense marking in (12) also adds to the

interpretation depicted here. Notice that *desu/masu* ending verbs in (12.1) and (12.6) are in past tense, maintaining the narrative tense. Whereas the content of thought which appear in the *da* style in (12.4) and (12.5) are in non-past tense reflecting the internal thought as being thought by the author right there and then.[11]

We find a similar case in (13) in which utterances in abrupt endings--(13.1) and (13.2), as well as (13.4) and (13.5)--are anaphorically referred to by *sore* 'it' in (13.3) and in (13.6), both of which appear in formal style. This is precisely because these two utterances are directly addressed to the reader; they maintain the tone of the speaker telling the reader partly because they maintain the dominant formal style of that prose.

```
(13.1)  Hontoo no jihi        to wa, koko ni hontoooni mono
        true  LK compassion QT T    here at really      thing
        o ataeru ni  tekitoona    jijoo    o motsu   hito
        O give   for appropriate condition O possess person
        ga aru. (abrupt)
        S  there is
        'As for true compassion, let's assume that there is a
        person who deserves to receive things because of his or
        her misfortune.'
```

```
(13.2)  Sono toki, sono hito  ni tekitoona    hodo   no mono
        that time  that person IO appropriate degree of thing
        o ataeru. (abrupt)
        O give
        'At that moment, one gives something appropriate to
        that person.'
```

```
(13.3)  Sore ga hontoo no jihi       dearimasu. (formal)
        that S  real   LK compassion BE
        'That is true compassion.'
```

```
(13.4)  Koko ni hitori      no namakemono ga atte,    sore
        here at one person LK lazy person S  there is that
        ga kuchi-o-joozuni-shite sugatte-kita  to
        S  convincingly          beg for mercy QT
        suru. (abrupt)
        do
```

'Let's assume another situation where there is a lazy person here, and he or she asks for compassion with convincing excuses.'

(13.5) Sono kuchijoozu ni joozerare,   mono o yatta to
        that glibness   by deceive-PASS thing O gave QT
        <u>suru</u>. (abrupt)
        do
        'Let's assume that one is deceived by the glibness of the explanation and gives something.'

(13.6) Sore wa jihi   ni nite   hi   naru   mono
        that T compassion to resemble wrong become thing
        <u>dearimasu</u>. (formal)
        BE
        'That may have the appearance of compassion but it is not.'

(13.7) Odate-ni-notta,   ukatsumono no orokana
        deceived by false praise fool   LK foolish
        shogyoo <u>desu</u>. (formal)
        deed   BE
        'It is a deed of a fool who is easily deceived by false praise.'

(13.8) Sonna toki, mono o yaru kawarini, sono namakemono
        such time thing O give instead   that lazy person
        no ojoozumono   no hoo ni hirate no hitotsu mo
        LK cunning person LK cheek IO slap   LK one   even
        <u>mimatte-yaru</u>. (abrupt)
        give
        'At that moment, instead of giving something, one may slap this lazy phony person on his or her cheek.'

(13.9) Imashime   ni nari happunzai   ni naru
        discipline IO become source of inspiration IO become
        <u>kamoshiremasen</u>. (formal)
        may
        'This may serve as discipline and may become a source of inspiration.'

(13.10)   Sono hoo   ga hontoo no jihi   <u>desu</u>. (formal)
          that direction S real   LK compassion BE
          'That, more than anything else, is true compassion.'

                                        --Okamoto 1983:142

Upon closer examination of (13) we can find how the choice of *da* and *desu/masu* style functions as a surface-signaling device for the discourse organization. Note that the topic of segment (13) surrounds the issue of true compassion, which is signaled by the initial noun phrase marked by *wa* in (13.1). The discourse semantic structure of (13) is schematized in Figure 5.1.

There are three items of comment semantically linked to the topic; comment 1 and 2 represent true and false compassion each accompanied by an example, and comment 3 describes the recommended response to a case of false compassion, which in turn becomes an example of true compassion. In each underlined utterance marked by *desu/masu* style in the text, the author offers his own comment. In offering his comment, the author is more aware of the reader and takes the stance of author speaking to reader. In all other sentences marked by *da* endings, the author provides background information that leads to his comment; examples that must be incorporated into his line of argument. We find further evidence to support this view in that surface anaphoric devices *sore* in (13.3), *sore* in (13.6) and *sono hoo* in (13.10) all refer to the immediately prior described situation, which is enclosed by square brackets in Figure 5.1. This clearly shows that the *da* and *desu/masu* mixture corresponds to the author's discourse organization, specifically distinguishing between backgrounded versus foregrounded information. Utterance (13.8) resembles that of (10.12) discussed earlier. Here again, the content of (13.8) may be anaphorically referred to by adding *sore wa* to (13.8), i.e., *sore wa imashime ni nari happunzai ni naru kamoshiremasen*.

In the essay data examined I found two pieces in which the *da* style dominates and which contain *desu/masu* endings. Two kinds of motivations seem to exist for this stylistic mixture. First, as shown in (14), when the author addresses the reader as if talking to the reader right there and then, the style may change to formal.

Figure 5.1. *Discourse Structure of Data (13)*

(Underlined utterances appear in *desu/masu* form in text; single arrows semantically connect topic with comment; double arrows indicate information flow from support to argument.)

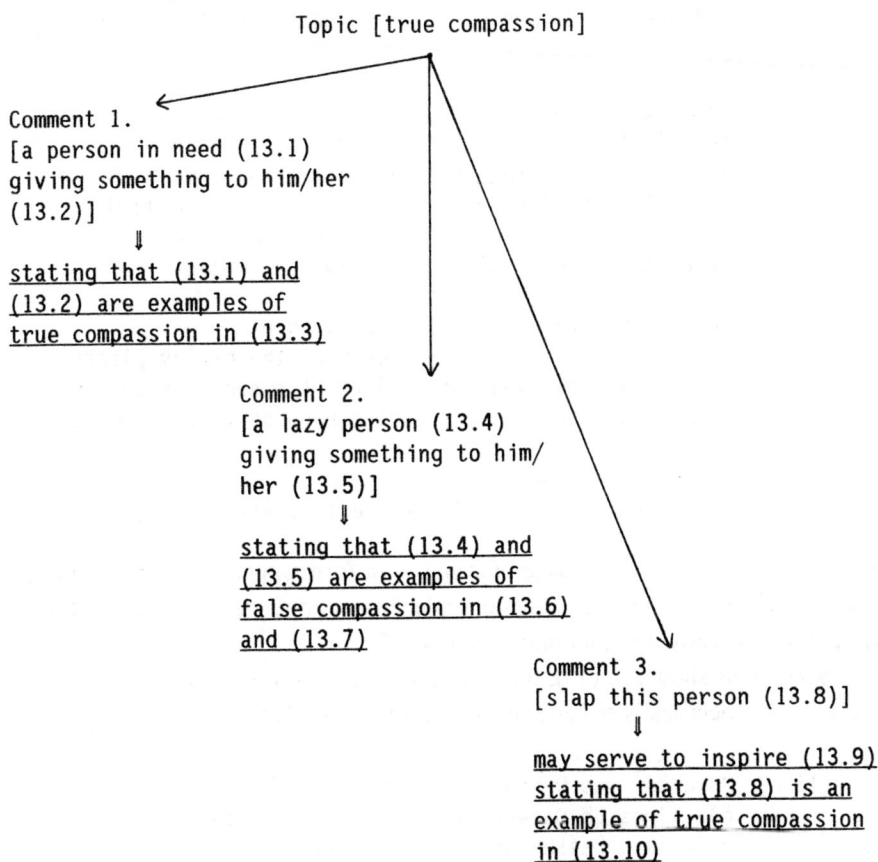

Topic [true compassion]

Comment 1.
[a person in need (13.1)
giving something to him/her
(13.2)]

stating that (13.1) and
(13.2) are examples of
true compassion in (13.3)

Comment 2.
[a lazy person (13.4)
giving something to him/
her (13.5)]

stating that (13.4) and
(13.5) are examples of
false compassion in (13.6)
and (13.7)

Comment 3.
[slap this person (13.8)]

may serve to inspire (13.9)
stating that (13.8) is an
example of true compassion
in (13.10)

(14.1) Haru   ga kite yuki ga kieru   to, mura no
        spring S come snow S disappear when villue LK
        hatake de wa mugihumi   ga
        fields at T treading on barley plants S
        hajimaru.
        begin
        'When spring comes and the snow disappears, in the
        village fields, people begin treading on the wheat
        plants.'

(14.2) Kimi wa mugihumi   no kokoroyoi
        you T treading on barley plants LK pleasant
        ashizawari   o shitte-imasu ka (formal), mono o
        touch to feet 0 know   Q   thing 0
        humu   to yuu, mashite   yawarakana shokubutsu
        tread on QT say still more tender   plant
        no ha o humu   kokoroyosa   o.
        LK leaf 0 tread on pleasant feeling 0
        'Do you know the pleasant touch of the barley plants on
        your feet, the pleasant feeling of treading upon
        something, especially treading upon soft leaves of the
        plants?'

                              --Maeda 1984:165

In the entire essay the only usage of *desu/masu* form appears in the postposed
sentence (14.2). The author asks the reader in a manner resembling the direct
quote, "do you know the pleasant touch of...?"

Second, as shown in (15), the *desu/masu* style is used to segment a piece
of discourse, specifically to label it as a narrative discourse.

(15.1) Mukashi   no Oriento Ekusupuresu wa tashikani
        old times LK Orient Express   T indeed
        gookana   ressha deshita. (formal)
        luxurious train BE
        'The Orient Express of long ago was indeed a luxurious
        train.'

(15.2) Shijin mo ongakuka mo, Yooroppa no hushoo,
        poet   and musician and Europe   LK rich merchant
        gaikookan, koozoku   ya ohimesama, minna ga
        diplomat   aristocrat and princess all   S

```
ooa          renraku   no ano  kokusai
Europe-Asia connection LK that international
shindai  ressha ni akogarete      Isutanbuuru e  no
sleeping train  IO be fascinated Istanbul     to LK
tabi   o shimashita. (formal)
travel O did
```
'Poets, musicians, rich European merchants, diplomats, aristocrats, princesses, all were fascinated by that international train with sleeping compartments, and they all took the trip to Istanbul.'

(15.3) Bungaku   ni mo   eiga ni mo   toriagerarete sekai
        literature in also movie in also cite-PASS   world
        ni sono nagatakai n   da kedo... (abrupt with *no da*)
        in that famous   NOM BE but
        'The train was cited in literature and appeared in the movies and it is quite well-known, but'

                        --Agawa 1983:26

Sentences (15.1) and (15.2) are the only two that take *desu/masu* endings in the entire prose, except, of course, direct quotations in which people may choose the *desu/masu* style for sociolinguistic reasons. This particular paragraph's effect is that it constitutes a different segment in which the author narrates a story with an awareness of the audience. This segment tells the story of the long faded glory of the Orient Express, with vocabulary (such as *mukashi* 'old times,' and *ohimesama* 'princess') typical in and therefore reminiscent of the Japanese folk narrative.[12] In such cases, the reader may have an impression that the author is performing an oral narrative. Again, similar to the case of (14), the awareness of the addressee seems to affect the choice of the *desu/masu* style in the sea of *da* endings.

6. Ontological Basis for the Verb Morphology

Observations made so far all point to the distinction between two types of utterances: (1) foregrounded utterances directly addressing the listener with full awareness of the listener, and (2) backgrounded utterances which provide subordinate information and that do not directly address the listener, but are rather almost self-addressed. The awareness of the addressee plays an important role in the production and comprehension of not only the verb morphology but also of the Japanese language in general. In Japanese communication, an awareness of others--or more generally the contextualization of the self in the scene of communication--forces one to choose different linguistic devices more demandingly than many of the Western communities.[13]

In this regard it is useful to inquire into how the Japanese mind constructs the speaker-listener relationship. As reviewed earlier, the philosophical thoughts of Watsuji and Mori are significant in that they recognize the importance of "thou" for the realization of "self" among Japanese. The speaking self's motivation for the *da* and *desu/masu* verb morphology is in fact founded in the Japanese speaker's sensitivity toward "thou." It is only when the awareness of the other momentarily lapses that naked abrupt utterances are made. Likewise all other abrupt forms offer subordinate information not directly addressed to "thou" and consequently do not require the designing of utterances for the purpose of interpersonal appeal.

The availability of the naked abrupt style makes it possible for a Japanese speaker to shun, if merely for a brief moment, the awareness of "thou." Historically it may be said that when the *genbun itchi undoo* 'the unification movement of the spoken and written language' made it available for writers of the Meiji period to use "spoken" language in writing, these writers' use of *da* style encouraged them to discover and re-create the inner self in a way different from the previous era. It is ironical that the abrupt style--often identified as spoken style--can function not only to encourage closeness to "thou" but also to distance oneself from "thou."

I noted earlier that speakers choose abrupt forms in casual conversation among friends. This fact can now be viewed from the concept of "thou" awareness. When an interpersonal relationship is such that the sense of *amae* 'psychological and emotional dependence' is allowed and the human relationship reaches a point of utmost closeness, the distinction between "thou" and "thy thou" becomes less distinct. As a result, the speaking self finds less need to address "thou" as a completely separate and distinct entity. Under this circumstance the speaker does not find "thou" as opposed to self, that is, "thou" as opposed to "thy thou." It is as if the speaker feels "thou" to be almost nondistinct from self and therefore the speech style chosen among close friends in casual situations becomes the same as the style in which one addresses oneself, i.e., abrupt.

One may understand the relation between the self and the other and how this relationship influences the choice of verb morphology in the following framework. The more the speaking self is aware of "thou" as a separate and potentially opposing entity, the more elaborate the markers for discourse modality become, one of which is the *desu/masu* ending. Thus we can identify the contextual circumstances where the level of "thou" awareness varies from lower to higher as shown below:

A: Low Awareness Situation--the *da* style is most likely:
1. When the speaker exclaims or suddenly recalls something;
2. When the speaker vividly expresses events scene-internally as if the speaker is right there and then;
3. When the speaker expresses internal thought self-reflectingly, including almost self-addressed utterance and monologues, making it possible to shun oneself from the addressee;
4. When the speaker jointly creates utterances whose ownership is shared;
5. When the speaker presents information semantically subordinate in nature i.e., backgrounded information;
6. When the speaker is in an intimate relationship with "thou" where the speaker does not consider "thou" as opposed to self; expresses social familiarity and closeness.

B: High Awareness Situation--the *desu/masu* style is more likely:
1. When the speaker expresses thought which directly addresses the partner perceived as "thou" with expressions appropriate in terms of sociolinguistics variables, a marker for social relationship; expresses formality;
2. When the speaker communicates main information directly addressed to the listener--especially when the *desu/masu* ending appears in the *da* style discourse.

In short, one chooses the *da* and *desu/masu* style as a result of a filtering process during which one recognizes the differing levels of the "thou" awareness as well as the distance between "thou" and "thy thou." The mixed style reflects the speaking self's choice as to how the utterance is located in the low and high points within the scale mentioned above. It should also be mentioned that there may be cases when the low and high awareness situation has yet to be defined among speech participants--specifically in cases under A:6 and B:1 above. Under such circumstances the social situation is yet undefined by the participants, and one may choose a mixed style until the participants decide on the most appropriate verb-final forms, as stated by Haga reviewed in section 2.

It is interesting at this point to recall that in traditional Japanese language studies Tokieda (1941, 1950) treats abrupt verb form as a case of zero-form of *ji*. This morphologically less committed form, i.e., absence of DM indicators, emerges precisely because there is a need for a form to express a low awareness of "thou." As mentioned before, when contrasted with formal verb endings, all functions attributed to the *da* style in low awareness situations--including those not discussed in this work such as exclamation, strong affirmation, command and so forth--represent less other-accommodating speech style. In this sense, the *da* style, although no DM indicator is attached to itself, contributes to aspects of Discourse Modality.[14]

7. Style as Discourse Modality

The alternation of *da* and *desu/masu* styles contributes to aspects of Discourse Modality as summarized in Figure 5.2. By manipulating the use of *da* and *desu/masu* the speaking self contributes to several aspects of Discourse Modality. First, in terms of perspective, the *da* ending represents the speaker's perspective internal to the narrative setting. The speaker "is there and then" and expresses inner feelings and makes comments directly and immediately. The *desu/masu* ending takes the speaker's perspective not necessarily internal to the narrative scene; but rather, it takes the position of self-awareness of talking to "thou." In terms of Discourse Organization, in predominantly *desu/masu* discourse, the *da* ending often marks backgrounded information subordinate to the overall structure of discourse. In terms of Interactional Appeal, when the awareness of "thou" is such that "thou" is understood to be emotionally close, *da* is often chosen. The *da* style is a style for casual and less formal interaction. When the speaker is aware of "thou," and the sociolinguistic situation calls for politeness, *desu/masu* endings are preferred. When *da* style is mutually permitted and encouraged, what is achieved interactionally is a sense of *amae*, closeness and a general feeling of belongingness.

Figure 5.2. *Summary of Modal Contextualization Effects Realized by the* Da *and* Desu/Masu *Manipulation*

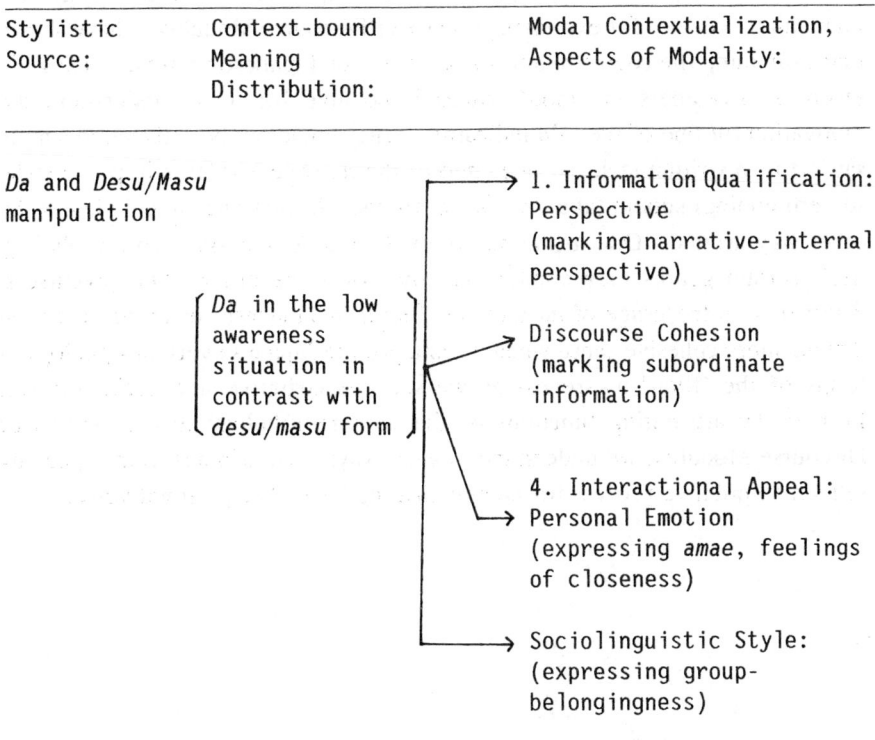

Stylistic Source:	Context-bound Meaning Distribution:	Modal Contextualization, Aspects of Modality:

Da and *Desu/Masu* manipulation

⌠ *Da* in the low
| awareness
| situation in
| contrast with
⌡ *desu/masu* form

→ 1. Information Qualification: Perspective (marking narrative-internal perspective)

→ Discourse Cohesion (marking subordinate information)

4. Interactional Appeal:
→ Personal Emotion (expressing *amae*, feelings of closeness)

→ Sociolinguistic Style: (expressing group-belongingness)

Before I conclude, I should mention a theoretical issue which has become self-evident in the course of the study on *da* and *desu/masu* verb morphology. The concept of "sentence" has plagued linguists for decades. Particularly in Japanese, syntactic definitions of sentence--for example, existence of subject and predicate--has been less attractive, since subjects are often absent in the surface form. One might recall here Mikami's (1972:88) point that the grammatical notion of "subject" does not exist in Japanese. Considering the fact that some individual sentences show syntactic and semantic features parallel to subordinate clauses, re-examining a definition of sentence from a discourse perspective seems prudent. Or, at least, it is important to understand that a sentence functions differently in terms of its discourse organizational role, and in terms of its "thou"-addressing quality.

In this chapter I have argued that the Japanese verb morphology is a manipulative device for expressing aspects of Discourse Modality. I have shown that examining the cognitive and social source of Japanese verb morphology in terms of awareness of "thou" makes it possible for us to understand the motivation for one of the DM indicators. One should not be satisfied to simply say, "It is in written style, so one chooses the *da* style," or "It is in polite style, so verb endings should take *desu/masu* forms." In fact one should view it the other way around. Due to the nature of *da* and *desu/masu* verb morphology itself certain genres may employ one style over the other. Our precursors' comments on the usage of *da* and *desu/masu* in Japanese reviewed in section 2 make more cohesive sense when we analyze the Japanese verb morphology in terms of the "thou" awareness as we seek its cognitive and social sources. Further, by attributing functions of the verb morphology to the aspects of Discourse Modality, we understand in what ways it contributes to the speaking self's manipulative process for communicating his or her personal voice.

CHAPTER 6

Interactional Particles <u>Yo</u> and <u>Ne</u>

1. Introduction

Japanese final particles--normally referred to as *shuujoshi* 'final particles' by Japanese grammarians--have been the focus of linguists' attention both in Japan and the United States. Incorporating some of the earlier findings, in this chapter I will examine two specific final particles *yo* and *ne*, from the perspective of Discourse Modality as proposed in this study. Due to their prominent interactional nature the particles *yo* and *ne* share which will be characterized in what follows, I will refer to them as "interactional particles."

The data for the analysis of *yo* and *ne* consists of two types; the three-minute segments of 20 casual conversations and dialogue portions of fiction as described in chapter 1. Since *yo* and *ne* appear predominantly in informal spoken discourse and their usage is severely limited in formal speech and written discourse, I examine tokens of *yo* and *ne* taken from two possible sources--one, actual casual conversation, and the other, dialogues in fiction--with the hope that this combination is likely to yield broad-based results.

Out of a large selection of final particles in Modern Japanese, this study examines only *yo* and *ne*. I made this decision based on the relative high frequency of these two particles. In casual conversational data under investigation, 863 tokens of what are normally identified as interactional particles were observed. These particles include, *ne(e)* with or without combination with other particles, *sa(a)*, *no*, *ka na*, and *yo na*, *yo* with or without other particles preceding, *ka*, *wa*, and *ze*. The frequency of these particles is given in Table 6.1.

Although frequently appearing, since in some cases the particle *no* functions to enhance the interrogative nature of utterances and directly involves the semantic interpretation rather than being primarily interactional, *no* is excluded from the study.[1]

Table 6.1. *Frequency of Interactional Particles in 3-Minute Segments of Conversation Among 20 Pairs*

Types of Interactional Particles	Number of Interactional Particles	Percentage of Interactional Particles
Ne	364	42.17
Sa	148	17.15
No	138	15.99
Yo	128	14.83
Na	49	5.68
Others	38	4.17
Total	863	

At this point we must note that interactional particles may or may not appear sentence-finally. In fact the term *shuujoshi* 'final particle' is used in a strict sense to refer to the particles appearing sentence-finally only, while those that appear intrasententially are often referred to as *kantoojoshi* 'insertion particle.' Although depending on the context certain interactional particles operate sometimes as *shuujoshi* and sometimes as *kantoojoshi*, some are strictly *shuujoshi*. Making a clear distinction between insertion and final particles is especially important when examining *yo* and *ne*. Although both particles can be used as insertion as well as final particles, the use of *yo* as an insertion particle is stylistically severely limited. Only in the most blunt and casual male conversation between social equals can *yo* be used as an insertion particle. So that this stylistic restriction does not possibly mislead us in our examination of and the consequent contrast between *yo* and *ne*, I focus my analysis on *yo* and *ne* occurring only at the sentence-final position. I do not mean by this decision, however, that there are two separate particles--for example *yo* being an insertion particle and another *yo*, a final particle. Obviously some semantic and pragmatic properties are shared by all occurrences of *yo*. Still, since specific functions realized by *yo* can differ significantly depending on its location--syntactic and otherwise--I find it important to make distinctions based on its locational context.

In fact an examination of the position of the particles identified in our casual conversation data reveals that *ne* appears frequently as an insertion particle (232 times), and less frequently, but still substantially at the sentence-final position (132 times). The particle *sa* shows a similar tendency, appearing at insertion points 102 times and at sentence-final position 46 times. Contrary to this tendency, *yo* appears more frequently in the sentence-final position (87 times) and only 41 times as an insertion particle. For this reason I chose the two most frequently occurring interactional particles at the sentence-final position, i.e., *ne* and *yo* as the target of this study. I should also add that in our second type of data, dialogues of fiction, sentence-final *yo* and *ne* appeared frequently while the occurrence of *sa* was significantly low.

2. Background

Before we begin our discussion, a review of some earlier works on particles in general and especially on *yo* and *ne* is in order. The work of Uyeno (1971), perhaps the most well-known study of Japanese final particles in English, can serve as our starting point. Based on Saji's (1956) classification of final particles--to be reviewed later--she examines *wa, zo, ze, sa, yo, ne(e)* and *na(a)* from the framework of performative analysis. In essence Uyeno claims that final particles are derived from presupposed performative verbs--including STATE, ASK, ORDER, and SUGGEST--, and she (1971:140) classifies the set of particles into two groups. These are:

1. Those which express the speaker's insistence on forcing the given information on the addressee;
2. Those which express a request for compliance with the given information leaving the option of confirmation to the addressee.

Uyeno categorizes *yo*--along with *wa, zo, ze* and *sa*--into the first group, and *ne*--along with *nee, na(a)*--into the second group.

These two features represent the interpersonal nature of final particles which until then were available primarily in Japanese literature alone. Further, Uyeno's detailed characterization of each final particle incorporates sociolinguistic variables, such as gender of the speaker, the relative social status of the speaker and addressee, and most importantly, the interpersonal relationship such as rapport that the use of some of the final particles realize.

Of course in Japanese traditional *kokugogaku*, as mentioned many times in this work, scholars acknowledged much earlier the importance of the interpersonal nature of final particles. Starting from the work of Suzuki (1979/1824) which categorizes the particle as expressing "voices from the heart," it was Tokieda's (1951) work which forcefully advanced the idea that the fundamental function of sentence-final particles is *"taijinkankei o koosei suru"* 'to form an interpersonal relationship.' Among his examples are particles *ne, zo* and *yo*. In Tokieda's view, *ne* represents a subjective expression which seeks to make the addressee a sympathizer, while *zo* and *yo* are expressions to force upon the addressee the speaker's will and judgment.[2]

In his 1956 article Saji pursues this direction further and proposes to distinguish two types of final particles; those that operate not only as utterance- (or, sentence-) final particles but insertion particles as well, and those that operate only as final particles. Noting that the particles in the first group--*ne, na, yo, ya, e, i,* and *sa*--can appear even at the utterance-initial position, Saji claims that these final particles are the only kind that directly express the speaker's attitude toward the addressee. The particles in the second group--*wa, tomo, zo, ze* and *ka*--do not directly achieve interpersonal relations, but rather express the speaker's attitude toward the content of the statement, specifically the variant degree of certainty (and uncertainty) the speaker feels toward the content. Although I take the position that Discourse Modality covers epistemic modality encompassing a varying degree of certainty, in this chapter, we focus on the interactional aspect of modality and we concern ourselves with Saji's first group of particles, limiting our analysis only to *yo* and *ne*.

Watanabe (1968) characterizes the distinction between *yo* and *ne* as follows. *Yo* operates within the territory of the vocative expression where speaker's judgment process is not involved and where a direct relationship exists between the speaker and the object called out for. *Ne* operates within the territory where only a direct relationship toward the addressee--and not toward the objects-- remains. While it is true--and as Watanabe himself acknowledges--that *yo* may be used as an insertion particle which functions similarly to *ne*, Watanabe's distinction essentially identifies, if merely intuitively, the fundamental differences between *yo* and *ne*.

Similar to Watanabe's characterization is Kitagawa's (1984) view. According to Kitagawa, *ne* marks the fact that the utterance is related to the second person--as opposed to *na* which is related to the first person, and *yo* marks the new information--as opposed to *sa* which marks old information. Although scholars agree that both *yo* and *ne* function primarily in terms of interaction, they also agree that a qualitative difference exists between *yo* and *ne*. I will follow this clue--especially Watanabe's (1968) and Kitagawa's (1984) remarks--and examine *yo* and *ne* from two aspects of communication--broadly stated, object-information-oriented versus person-interaction-oriented.

Tsuchihashi (1983) takes a different approach, that of the notion of a speech act continuum, in discussing several sentence final particles and auxiliary predicate expressions such as *kashira* 'I wonder.' Based on data consisting of conversation exchange taken from nine Japanese novels--but written by five novelists, five of the novels being written by one author--she concludes that sentence-final particles may be placed on a continuum of several variables. These variables--including (1) the speaker's confidence in his or her knowledge or information, (2) the speaker's willingness to admit challenge to his or her knowledge, and (3) the speaker's solicitation of confirmatory or corrective responses--are empirically examined by statistical analysis of the cooccurrence ratings of (1) subject of the sentence with a particular particle, and (2) types of responses observed in the speaker-hearer interaction when a particular particle is used.

Oishi (1985) describes Japanese final particles from the view of linguistics of particularity. Oishi's data consists of interviews with participants of conversation as they view video recordings of their earlier interaction and discuss what happened in conversation. Oishi concludes (1985:195) that final particles function to "(1) make conversation go ahead--by advancing from one topic to another, and moreover, (2) not merely go ahead, but toward a speaker's goals, safely--through considering the constraint from behind and flexibly,--by looking at a hearer's reactions."

Cook (1988) analyzes particles from the framework of indexicality. According to her, the sentential particles *yo* and *ne* are used to establish certain affective relationships between the speaker and the addressee. According to Cook,

...the particle *yo* draws the addressee's attention to the speaker's utterance. It is comparable to the gesture of pointing. If we want the addressee to notice some entity in the speech context, we typically point to that entity. In a similar manner, in order to draw attention to his or her own utterance, the speaker uses *yo*. Pointing to the speaker's own utterance is the direct indexical meaning of *yo*. (1988:126)

On the other hand, regarding the particle *ne*, Cook continues (1988:152) that "the particle *ne* directly indexes the speaker's and addressee's general attitude of mutual agreement but not necessarily agreement with any particular content of the utterance."

Cook (1988) further lists indirect meanings for these two particles. *Yo* functions to express assertive attitude, a variety of speech acts--including warning, advice, instructions, announcements, explanation, report, request/command, insistence and contradiction--and indexing social relations of "higher status" and "knowing party." *Ne* provides various speech functions such as initiating interaction, and introducing a new topic as well as displaying and seeking agreement, confirmation, cooperation, and mitigating FTA's.[3]

As summarized above, although previous works offer insights, I find several unresolved issues concerning final particles. First, the types and the quality of data examined in these works are questionable, if not problematic in most cases. In traditional *kokugogaku* studies and in Uyeno's (1971) study, the data source is obscure. Example sentences seem to be a collection of expressions gathered from all sources, including some created by the researcher. In Tsuchihashi (1983), the conversational exchanges are extracted from contemporary Japanese novels which must be treated as such, and they do not necessarily reflect how natural language operates. The issue of unnaturalness of data is solved in Oishi (1985). Oishi, however, studies one specific conversation and an ensuing interview with one of the participants. Although in the ethnomethodological framework of his linguistics of particularity this point remains irrelevant, I take the position that generalization reached by analyzing broad based data is not only possible but necessary in order to understand the interactional nature of particles. While Cook (1988) uses several cases of naturally-occurring conversations, 14 out of 15 hours of conversational data represent adult-child interaction. This results in a somewhat limited understanding of particles as will be discussed later. One possible solution to the difficulty in obtaining reliable data is to examine two types of data as I do here and to evaluate the results in relation to each other. This method enables us to understand the functions of final particles on a broader and more general basis.

Another drawback of previous studies lies in its relative isolation. Although studying a certain aspect of language without regard for the other aspects of language may be useful and convenient, it is important to examine the language phenomenon within a broader theoretical and philosophical framework as advocated in this work.

Except Tsuchihashi (1983), Oishi (1985) and Cook (1988), most previous works examine final particles as they are used in isolated individual sentences. Even when the data consists of conversational fragments as in the cases of Tsuchihashi and Oishi, neither author examines final particles against the mechanism of conversational exchange. It is true that Tsuchihashi (1983) examines listener's response following various expressions of final particles and auxiliary predicate expressions. The types of response she examines, however, are based on the semantic content of the listener's comments--whether they represent No Change, Challenged (including Insistence/No Insistence by the speaker), Clarification Requested by the Hearer, or No Response Allowed. One must note that listener responses are expected to be semantically responsive to the previous speaker turns. While the speaker turns are marked by varying particles to elicit different listener reactions, the semantic content of the resultant listener responses is not necessarily motivated by these particles alone. In fact it is likely that the semantic content of the preceding turn motivates more prominently the type of listener responses that Tsuchihashi examines. To discover a direct interactional control of *yo* and *ne*, for example, an additional method for examining primarily interactional aspects of listener response--such as listener back channels--becomes necessary.

Cook's (1988) study incorporates interactional structures and offers much insight. However, her analysis of particles can benefit from a broader data base, especially data consisting of longer speaking turns. Obviously the lack of long speaker turns in Cook's data stems from her choice of data, predominantly adult-child interaction, which tends to contain short exchanges. My present interest lies in examining sentence-final particles *yo* and *ne* in extended discourse, which requires adult conversational data. Note that in her analysis, Cook (1988) ignores different syntactic and stylistic constraints under which *yo* and *ne* are placed, and this seems to cause some misleading conclusions. Further, where *yo* and *ne* are syntactically and stylistically interchangeable, one must account for the different effect such an interchange may bring, for which Cook (1988) does not account. My primary goal is to examine *yo* and *ne* within a single speaker turn and to inquire into how *yo* and *ne* function differently--each bringing a complimentary effect to conversational interaction. Above all I will examine these particles on the level of conversation exchange and from the perspective of discourse organization of which they are a part and of which they assist in the creation.

3. Distributional Characteristics of *Yo* and *Ne* and Relative Information Accessibility and/or Possessorship

As has been pointed out by others, the particles *yo* and *ne* exhibit fundamentally similar yet somewhat different distributional characteristics. First, obviously both particles *yo* and *ne* appear in direct discourse only as in the case of DM indicators such as modal adverbs. In fact if and when these particles appear in indirect discourse such as reported speech, one is normally forced to interpret the content of the report as being direct and consequently such utterances result in awkwardness. Thus, [1a] and [1b] are not appropriate.

```
[1]  Sasaki-san ga ashita   kuru | a. *yo  | to yuu nyuusu
     Ms. Sasaki S  tomorrow come |    IP   | QT say news
                                 | b. *ne  |
                                 |    IP   |
     o kikimashita ka?
     0 heard        Q
     'Did you hear the news that Ms. Sasaki is coming
     tomorrow?'
```

It is also known that since interactional particles directly express personal attitude, they cannot occur within an idiomatic or formulaic expression. Thus, *yo* and *ne* can not occur as a part of a proverb as shown by (2).

```
(2)  Hito o omou wa mi  o omou | a. *yo  |, hito o
     other 0 think T  self 0 think |    IP   |  other 0
                                 | b. *ne  |
                                 |    IP   |
```

```
nikumu wa mi   o nikumu.
hate    T  self O hate
```
'If you are considerate to others, it will benefit you in
the end; if you trouble others, it will result in trouble
for you.'

--Ikeda and Keene 1982:113

Syntactically it is possible to place *yo* or *ne* at the sentence-final position in (2).
Note, however, that being a proverb, (2) represents a conventionalized utterance
unit that functions only as a complete unit and does not allow for the insertion
of one's personal view. *Yo* and *ne* cannot invade the conventionalized semantic
world; the speaking self cannot personalize such a discourse.

Although *yo* and *ne* share similar distributional constraints, they,
nonetheless, behave differently. For example, it is known that *yo* cannot
cooccur with Yes/No or WH questions as shown in [3a] and [4a], while *ne* can
as shown in [3b] and [4b].

```
[3]  Tanaka-san wa ikimasu ka  | a. *yo  |
     Ms. Tanaka  T  go     Q    |    IP   |
                                 | b. ne   |
                                 |    IP   |
     'I wonder if Tanaka is going.'

[4]  Dare ga ikimasu ka  | a. *yo  |
     who  S  go     Q    |    IP   |
                          | b. ne   |
                          |    IP   |
     'I wonder who is going.'
```

Note also that *ne* cannot cooccur with WH questions without *ka*, i.e., **dare ga
ikimasu ne*. This seems to be due to the often observed tendency for *ne* to focus
on the interactional emotion of soliciting the addressee's recognition and/or
approval. *Ne* by itself cannot convey speaker's intention of straightforward
interrogative which WH questions require.

Additionally, *ne* cannot cooccur with abrupt command form as shown in [5]
while it can with the less abrupt command form as shown in [6]. *Yo* can cooccur
with both forms.

[5]   Ike | a. yo |
      go | IP |
           | b. *ne |
           | IP |
      'Go.'

[6]   Ikinasai | a. yo |
      go | IP |
                | b. ne |
                | IP |
      'Go.'

The observations made above indicate that while *ne* can accompany question and request forms through which the speaker solicits a response, it cannot accompany the speech act which does not allow room for the partner to potentially dispute--as in the case of abrupt command. On the other hand, *yo* cannot accompany an utterance which solicits the addressee's response when the addressee has full control--as in the case of a question. Notably here, the functions of *yo* and *ne* seem to be complementary when insisting on one's view and soliciting other's view.

Yo and *ne* also exhibit different constraints regarding the type of information which they can mark. Observe [7] in which the speaker expresses his or her own wish.

[7]   Raishuu   wa Oosaka e ikitai   n   desu
      next week T Osaka to want to go NOM BE
      | a. yo. |
      | IP |
      | b. *ne |
      | IP |
      'I want to go to Osaka next week.'

Since the speaking self has absolute and exclusive access to his or her own personal desire, adding *ne* which solicits other's opinion regarding his or her own state of mind, results in awkwardness.[4] It is possible to do so, however, if one distances oneself and describes one's own desire from another person's view-- which can be translated into English as "I guess I am experiencing a desire that I want to go to Osaka next week." In this case the other person does not have exclusive access to one's feelings and therefore *ne* can be used to solicit a response. It should be added that [7b] is perfectly acceptable if the person wanting to go to Osaka is other than the speaking self. Here the speaker does not have exclusive access to the desire expressed, and therefore it makes sense to solicit confirmation from someone else. We observe here that *ne* cannot mark the utterance which focuses on speaker exclusive information while *yo* can.

Constraints discussed for data (2) through [7] can be generalized when viewed from the concept which I call Relative Information Accessibility and/or Possessorship. For convenience let us use both [X *yo*] and [X *ne*] structures to represent the sentential unit [X] followed by sentence-final *yo* or *ne*. Let's assume that in the [X *yo*] and [X *ne*] structures, the information base for [X] is obtained through a varying degree of accessibility and/or possessorship. And let us also assume that the decision regarding the degree of accessibility and/or possessorship is made personally by the speaker, based on how the speaker assesses the addressee's assumed state of mind. As shown in Table 6.2, information on which the proposition [X] is based can be exclusively accessible to and/or possessed by the speaker, i.e., [Sp-E], or exclusively accessible to and/or possessed by the addressee, i.e., [Ad-E]. In the former the information is inaccessible and/or unavailable to the addressee; in the latter case the same is true for the speaker. Information may be partially accessible to and/or possessed by both the speaker and the addressee, but to a relatively different degree; the speaker may have more accessibility to and/or possessorship of the information, i.e., [Sp-M]; or, so may the addressee, i.e., [Ad-M]. There are also cases in which the speaker assumes that the addressee shares just about the same quality and quantity of relevant information, i.e., [Sp/Ad-same]. The choice between *yo* and *ne* is made depending on the situation; [Sp-E] can take *yo*, but not *ne* and [Ad-E] can take *ne*, but not *yo*. In situations of [Sp-M] and [Ad-M], the most likely choice is *yo* and *ne* respectively unless some other factors exist in which case *ne* may be used in the [Sp-M] case as will be explained later. In [Sp/Ad-same] situations, the speaker is most likely to take *ne*, instead of *yo*. The relationship between the choice of particles and Relative Information Accessibility and/or Possessorship is summarized in Figure 6.1.

What we observe in [3] and [4] can be explained as the case of [Ad-E] or [Ad-M]. Since [3] and [4] are questions, the speaker assumes (correctly or incorrectly) that the addressee has either exclusive, or at least more, information. Thus the choice of *ne* is appropriate while *yo* is not with the restriction that WH

194 DISCOURSE MODALITY

Figure 6.1. *Choice of* Yo *and* Ne *Based on Relative Information Accessibility and/or Possessorship, i.e.,* Sp(eaker)-E(xclusive), Ad(dressee)-E(xclusive), Sp(eaker)-M(ore), Ad(dressee)-M(ore) and Sp(eaker)/Ad(dressee)-Same

Situation Label:	Relative Information Accessibility/Possessorship		Speaker's Choice of Particles
	Speaker	Addressee	
Sp-E	Exclusive	None	X *yo*
Ad-E	None	Exclusive	X *ne*
Sp-M	Partial-More	No/Partial-Less	X *yo*, (X *ne*)
Ad-M	No/Partial-Less	Partial-More	X *ne*
Sp/Ad-Same	Same	Same	X *ne*

questions require the *ka ne* combination. In case of data [5] and [6], if the command is abrupt as in [5] and the speaker denies any negotiating room for the addressee, the right to the information is exclusively given to the speaker, a case of [Sp-E]; if the command is less abrupt as in [6], there remains some potential power to challenge information on the part of the addressee, a case of [Sp-M] which encourages the choice of *yo*. Utterance [6b], *ikinasai ne*, is also possible. This is because this less abrupt command is not absolute and can leave room for interactional solicitation, precisely that which *ne* conveys.

To illustrate this mechanism, further examples are given below.

[8] Oosaka e ikitai n desu | a. <u>yo</u> |
Osaka to want to go NOM BE | IP |
| b. *<u>ne</u> |
| IP |

'I want to go to Osaka.'

[9] Anata wa nihonjin desu | a. *<u>yo</u> |
you T Japanese IP | IP |
| b. <u>ne</u> |
| IP |

'You are a Japanese, aren't you?'

[10] Ano hito   nihonjin desu | a. <u>yo</u> |
     that person Japanese BE | IP |
                                 | b. <u>ne</u> |
                                 | IP |
     'That person is a Japanese, isn't he/she?'

Since [8] expresses the speaker's personal desire to go to Osaka, the speaker has exclusive access to the information--[Sp-E]; thus *yo* is appropriate while *ne* is not. If [8] is used to confirm the desire of the addressee, i.e., "you want to go to Osaka, don't you?"--a case of [Ad-E]--, *ne*, but not *yo*, is appropriate. Since [9] confirms the addressee's nationality--a case of [Ad-E]--*ne* is appropriate but not *yo*. However, *yo* is not impossible given some circumstances. For example, one can easily imagine a situation where the addressee suffers from amnesia and the speaker informs the addressee of his or her nationality. Or, one can also imagine a situation where the addressee behaves as if he or she is not aware of being Japanese and he or she needs to be reminded of that fact. In these situations, since the speaker assumes to have more accessibility to and/or possessorship of the information, *yo* is appropriate. In case of [10], depending on Relative Information Accessibility and/or Possessorship, either *yo* or *ne* can occur. If the speaker thinks that he or she has more information regarding the third party's nationality, i.e., a case of [Sp-M], the choice of *yo* is appropriate, if not, i.e., a case of [Ad-M], *ne* is appropriate.

In fact the choice of *yo* and *ne* can reveal the speaker's assumption on the level of the addressee's knowledge and consequently it can imply crucial social meaning. For example, a teacher visiting his student's father may say either [11a] or [11b] depending on how the teacher views the student-father relationship.

[11] Ojoosan   wa Tookyoo no daigaku e ikitagatte-
     your daughter T Tokyo   LK university to want to go
     imasu | a. <u>yo</u> |
           | IP |
           | b. <u>ne</u> |
           | IP |
     'Your daughter wants to go to a university in Tokyo.'

If the teacher assumes that the father doesn't know his daughter's wish, *yo* is selected because the teacher assumes that he has more accessibility to and/or possessorship of information than the addressee. If the teacher's assumption is reversed, *ne* is appropriate since the addressee is assumed to have more information.

In fact because the accessibility to and/or possessorship of information is directly linked to the relative right to interactional and social power, display of [Sp-M] information toward one's social superior often results in a face-threatening act. Given this special factor, one chooses *ne* instead of the normally predicted particle, *yo*. For example, the social subordinate will choose *ne* even when he or she assumes to have more availability of the relevant information as shown in [12].

```
[12] Buchoo,  ja    kaigi   wa sanji            to yuu koto
     manager then meeting T   three o'clock QT say fact
     desu  | a. ne  |
     BE    |    IP  |
           | b. *yo |
           |    IP  |
     'Manager, so the meeting is at three, isn't it?'
```

Even when one addresses one's boss to remind him or her of the time of the meeting--which means that the speaker assumes that the boss doesn't know or is likely to have forgotten about the meeting, a case of [Sp-M]--, *ne* is the preferred choice. After all, the information provider gains instant power in human interaction and a social subordinate is expected to avoid disrupting the hierarchy of dominance by his or her higher accessibility to and/or stronger possessorship of the relevant information.

Our examination of *yo* and *ne* so far points to a curious complementary phenomenon between information and interaction. When one has the upper hand on information, so to speak, one foregrounds it while defocusing the interaction process itself--including the concern toward (the feelings of) the partner. On the other hand when one has little information and faces a partner whom one assumes to have more information access and possession, one is more likely to focus on the possessor of the information, i.e., the addressee. In fact, armed with only insufficient information, one finds an urge to have his or her information legitimized by someone who knows more. In this sense a casual information exchange becomes an emotional tug of war forcing the informationally weak to become interaction dependent. I find this tendency the key to understanding the complementary functional relationship between *yo* and *ne*.

Yo and *ne* show additional distributional characteristics, the first of which is syntactic as shown below.

```
[13] Kare wa Oosaka e  itta to omoimasu ga    | a. ne  |
     he   T  Osaka  to went QT think     but   |    IP  |
                                                | b. *yo |
                                                |    IP  |
     'I think he went to Osaka, but...'
```

Here while *ne* can follow the discourse connective *ga* 'but,' *yo* cannot. When the connective *ga* is added syntactically, the utterance is not complete and therefore it does not offer a sentence-final environment for the particle. *Yo* as an insertion particle is stylistically severely limited. If [13] is changed into blunt male casual speech, it is possible to add *yo*, as in [14].

```
[14] Aitsu    Oosaka e  itta to omou kedo yo(o).
     that guy Oosaka  to went QT think but
     'Yo, I think he went to Osaka, but...'
```

Another notable difference between *yo* and *ne* reveals itself when we combine them. While it is possible to construct multiple particles *yo ne* as in [15a], the *ne yo* combination is not appropriate as shown in [15b].

```
[15] Ano hito   Oosaka e itta n   desu  | a. yo ne.  |
     that person Oosaka to went NOM BE  |    IP IP   |
                                         | b. *ne yo. |
                                         |    IP IP   |
     'He went to Osaka, didn't he?'
```

Why is this constraint? As suggested by Watanabe (1968) and others, *yo* and *ne* must operate on qualitatively different levels of communication and the two levels can be only unidirectionally combined. In fact Watanabe categorizes *yo* as expressing *uttae* 'appeal' of communication, and *yo* as expressing *hyooshutsu* '(emotional) exposure' both of which follow, in that order, the speaker's *hantei* 'judgment.' It is widely known (See Kitahara 1970, for example) that Japanese sentence-final elements are ordered so that the closer to the end of the phrase, the more emotional and personal the message conveyed. Conversely, the farther away from the end of the phrase, the less emotional and more objective or logically-controlled is the information expressed.[5] Following this principle, then, we can fairly accurately assume that *yo* is more information-oriented than *ne* and these two particles, as similar as they are, function differently conveying varying degrees of information.

4. Relative Information Accessibility and/or Possessorship and Related Concepts

Given the situation of the Japanese particle studies where analytical concepts abound, before proceeding, perhaps I should state the rationale for introducing the concept of Relative Information Accessibility and/or Possessorship. Here I will review two representative concepts showing most resemblance to the said concept, i.e, Kamio's (1979, 1990) "speaker's territory of information" and Cook's (1988) "authority for knowledge."

According to Kamio (1979), Japanese propositions may be realized either in "direct forms" as in (16)--Kamio's (4)--, or other forms as in (17)--Kamio's (8). (Here I follow Kamio's method for data presentation.)

    (16) Usuzan ga mata hunkasita-yo.
          'Mt. Usu erupted once again.'

    (17) Usuzan-ga mata hunkasita yoo da-na/soo da-ne.
          'It appears/is said that Mt. Usu erupted once again,
          doesn't/isn't it?'

The selection of these two forms is based on whether or not the speaker exclusively has or is supposed to have the propositional information to be conveyed. In Kamio's words:

> It thus seems that a conceptual category functions within the speaker by which information that belongs to him is distinguished from information that does not. This category may be labelled as the speaker's territory of information. Given this category, it can be stated that it is information accommodated [*sic*] in the speaker's territory of information that is conveyed by statements in the direct form. (1979:221-222)

and

>...the direct form can be used to express given propositional information
>when it is held exclusively in the speaker's territory in the situation of
>utterance. (1979:227)

In reference to *ne*, Kamio (1979) makes the following points. It is extremely
strange for a person to say *atsui desu* 'it's very warm' when running into an
acquaintance in the street. Since the same awareness of the weather is available
to the listener, a non-direct form must be used. For example, *atsui desu ne* 'it's
very warm, isn't it?' While Kamio identifies *yo* as a part of "direct form" and *ne*
as a part of "other form" the distributional difference between *yo* and *ne* is not
addressed in detail. Since *yo* can occur in indirect forms as well, the concept of
whether or not the information is exclusively in the speaker's territory of
information does not seem by itself to be able to account for the occurrence or
non-occurrence of *yo* and *ne*. For example, observe [18a] and [18b].

```
[18] Usuzan  ga mata  hunkashita yoo  da     | a. yo. |
     Mt. Usu S  again erupted      seem BE   |    IP  |
                                             | b. ne. |
                                             |    IP  |
     'It appears that Mt. Usu erupted once again.'
```

In both cases though the information is not exclusively in the speaker's territory,
it can be marked by *yo* as well as *ne*.[6] This fact can be accounted for if we
introduce relative accessibility and/or possessorship of information. If the
speaker assumes that he or she has more, a case of [Sp-M], even when the
information is not exclusively the speaker's, *yo*, rather than *ne*, is chosen. In the
reverse case of [Ad-M], *ne* is appropriate.

Kamio in his 1990 work, based on a more detailed system of the "theory of
the territory of information," summarizes the use of *ne* as follows (1990:77-78,
my translation). The numbers below in parentheses correspond to the numbers
assigned by Kamio (1990).

(95) *Ne* is a marker which the speaker conveys *kyooooteki taido* 'co-
     responding attitude' with the listener. The "co-responding attitude"

refers to that attitude the speaker actively encourages the listener to
have identical cognitive state toward the relevant information.

(107) When the speaker assumes that the speaker and the listener possess
the identical information as ALI (Already Learned Information), the speaker's
utterance must accompany *ne*.

(108) When the speaker especially wants to express a co-responding
attitude by one's own expression, the speaker's utterance can be
accompanied by *ne*.

Kamio's statements (107) and (108) identify obligatory and optional use of
sentence-final *ne* in contrast with direct and indirect forms without *ne*. Since
Kamio's concern is to identify how the use of *ne* is determined by the theory of
the territory of information, his work offers only partial answer to our current
concern, i.e., the question of distributional and functional differences between
yo and *ne*. Consider, for example, the following case where the use of *yo* or *ne*
cannot be determined by Kamio's statements (107) and (108). Let us assume
that two neighbors of Tanaka, A and B, are chatting about Tanaka's daughter.
Both A and B have identical ALI and their relation to the information source
and the level of involvement are identical, and therefore, the information is
within Kamio's territory B, i.e., within both A's and B's territory of information.

```
[19.1]A:  Tanaka-san no ojoosan  wa iyoiyo sotsugyoo  da soo
          Tanaka     LK daughter T  soon   graduation BE I hear
          desu ne.
          BE   IP
          'I hear that Tanaka's daughter is soon graduating.'

[19.2]B:  Ee, soo da soo    desu | a. ne  |
          yes so  BE I hear BE   |    IP  |
                                 | b. yo  |
                                 |    IP  |
          'Yes, I hear that is so.'
```

Kamio's explanation can account for the use of *ne* in [19.2a]; but how about *yo*
in [19.2b]? In other words, the question still remains; when *yo* and *ne* are
optional, what is the difference between them? The concept of Relative

Information Accessibility and/or Possessorship introduced in this chapter can explain the motivation for the choice between these particles. While both speakers A and B share identical information, speaker B, by attaching *yo*, indicates that B thinks he or she has relatively more access to and a firmer possession of the information than A has. B finds himself or herself closer than A to the relevant information which is located in Kamio's territory B, the territory of information shared by both speaker and listener. When B feels that A has either the same or more access to and the same or firmer possession of the identical information, that relative information status is expressed by a choice of either *ne* or *yo*. Thus it is not so much whether the bit of information belongs to one of the four possible territories of information, but rather the relative proximity the speaker feels he or she has within the identical territory that the use of *yo* and *ne* in [19] can be explained. This psychological difference in Relative Information Accessibility and/or Possessorship is important because it plays a part in manipulating the information versus interaction focus explained in the next section as the functional sources for *yo* and *ne*.

Note that Kamio (1990:73) also uses the concept of *hukai kakawari* 'deep(er) involvement' in his statement (99) when characterizing the use of *ne* as shown below.

(99)   When the information provided by the speaker is more deeply involved with the speaker than it is with the listener, *ne* cannot be used.

This concept addresses the relative involvement the two participants have toward the relevant information and it resembles the proposed concept of Relative Information Accessibility and/or Possessorship. However, while Kamio's concept successfully explains the conditional constraint for the choice of *ne*, it does not provide the condition for choosing either *yo* or *ne* when both are optional as in [19.2].

Cook (1988) introduces the concept of authority for knowledge in reference to her study on the particle *no*. Cook (1988:213) distinguishes three types for sentence-final forms based on the speaker's authority for knowledge. If the speaker authorizes the knowledge with the group, *no* is added; if individually authorized, bare verbal form is used; and if the speaker chooses not to authorize the knowledge, markings such as *-tte* 'they say...,' *-rashii* 'it appears...,' and *-soo*

'I hear' which indicate the source are required. Whereas Cook builds a concept
of authority for knowledge which solves some limitations of Kamio's notion of
the speaker's territory of information (1988:211-214), Cook does not discuss *yo*
and *ne* in this framework. In her analysis of *yo* and *ne*, characteristics are
merely listed (in terms of direct meaning and indirect meanings as examined
earlier) and she falls short of discussing how *yo* and *ne* operate differently in
relation to the concept of authority for knowledge.

The proposed concept of Relative Information Accessibility and/or
Possessorship can provide more accurately the criteria used by the speaker when
making a choice between *yo* and *ne*. The concept of "relativeness" between the
speaker and the addressee reflects the interactional nature of particle choice.
As has been argued, choice is made not necessarily on the basis of the speaker's
or non-speaker's territory where information is found or whether the knowledge
is authorized individually or in a group. Rather, the level of accessibility to
and/or possessorship of information in relation to the level of the interaction
partner's is at issue.

5 Functional Sources of *Yo* and *Ne*: Manipulating Information versus Interaction Focus

Having identified the distributional constraints of *yo* and *ne*, let us examine our
data to discover their functional sources. We approach this by examining
discourse segments where a *yo* and *ne* interchange is grammatically and
pragmatically possible as in (20).

(20) At this point in the novel, the protagonist, Himiko, who is the wife of
Inspector Nikaidoo, is privately investigating the case which her friend's
sister was murdered. The murder suspect is linked to Kanazawa City by
the gradually accumulating evidence.

```
(20.1) "Kanoosei     wa takaku natte-kita wa | a. yo  |
        possibility T  high    became    IP |    IP  |
                                            | b. ne  |
                                            |    IP  |
        'The possibility is getting high.'
```

```
(20.2) Iyoiyo Kanazawa-shi  ga mijikani natta
       finally Kanazawa City S  familiar became
       kanji   | a. ne   |."
       feeling |    IP   |
               | b. yo   |
               |    IP   |
       'Finally I feel Kanazawa City has become familiar to
       us.'
```

--Saitoo 1985:94

In data set (20), the author chose the combination of *yo* and *ne* as shown in (20.1a) and (20.2a). However, if we exchange *yo* and *ne* with *ne* and *yo* respectively, as shown in (20.1b) and (20.2b), a different effect is achieved, although the semantic content remains the same. In (20.1a) Himiko comments that the possible link to Kanazawa is getting even higher by presenting (20.1a) with *yo*. Himiko has more accessibility to and/or possessorship of the relevant information than the friend and thus *yo* is chosen. The speaker's communicative intent is precisely to convey this information. When Himiko attaches *ne* in (20.2a), however, the focus of interaction changes and the solicitation of the partner's view becomes the primary concern of Himiko. This is conveyed by *ne* in (20.2a), where the addressee is marked to be the person with the same or more information, and therefore the solicitation of information is necessary. In (20.2a) Himiko solicits her friend's confirmation regarding her view that in fact she is beginning to feel increasingly more familiar with Kanazawa City.

The interpretation above must be altered when faced with (20b). In (20.1b) Himiko solicits her friend's confirmation and in (20.2b) emphatically stresses the fact that she is feeling increasingly more familiar with Kanazawa City. In short, here we witness a difference in the interpretive effect achieved by (20a) versus (20b). Note that this change is reached by merely alternating between *ne* and *yo*.

One can see more clearly the different effect discussed here in the context of where either *ne* or *yo* is more or less interactionally appropriate, as illustrated in (21).

(21) At this point in the novel, Ikebe (B) who turns out to be the murderer of Himiko's friend's sister, attempts to convince Himiko (A) that in fact the

murderer is Ikebe's fictitious friend, Takasu. Ikebe says that there are only
two choices left for Takasu. Himiko continues.

(21.1)A: "Aa, sorede moohitotsu to yuu no wa..."
           ah then   another   QT say one T
           'Ah, then, what is another choice?'

(21.2)B: "Soo desu. Kare ga jibun no shippai ni kigatsuite,
            so BE   he   S self LK mistake IO notice
           jisatsu-suru   koto desu yo.
           commit suicide fact BE   IP
           'That's right. He may notice his mistake and commit
           suicide.'

(21.3)   Boku wa sono sen   ga tsuyoi to omoimasu
           I   T that line of thought S strong QT think
           ne.
           IP
           'I think there is a strong possibility for that.'

                                        --Saitoo 1985:197

Let us pay attention to the mechanism of conversational exchange under
which (21) occurs. When Himiko asks the question (21.1), the expected pair-part
is to provide an answer. In other words, immediately following the question
(21.1), the conditionally relevant speaking turn that fills the slot is to provide
information relevant to the question.[7] Thus the center of focus lies in the
information itself. In this situation, given the choice of particles yo and ne, the
natural choice is yo which helps focus on the information itself. If ne is chosen,
the response is somewhat awkward and distant. This stems from the fact that
where the focus of information [X] is expected, [X yo] is more appropriate
simply because yo's function matches more naturally than that of ne. If [X ne]
is chosen, Ikebe's answer does not match the interactional expectation as
satisfactorily as does yo. While obviously it is possible to do so, one cannot
escape the feeling of mismatched and therefore disengaged interaction.

The same point can be made in the following casual conversation segment
taken from our conversational data (Male Pair 7) which shows phenomenon
parallel to dialogues in fiction.

(22.1)A: [Honto/ shira-nai yo, ore./]
           really know-NEG IP I
           'Really, I don't know.'

(22.2)B: [Okuyama ga itta n   ja-nai no, are./]
           Okuyama S said NOM BE-NEG NOM that
           'Didn't you, Okuyama, say that?'

(22.3)A: [Eh, uso, itte-nai yo./]
           what lie   say-NEG IP
           'What, no, not at all, I didn't say that.'

(22.4)B: [Kaette-kitara mata   sugu kaette/ mata Amerika ni
            return-COND   again soon return again America to
           modoru tte no kiita ze, ore./]
           return QT NOM heard IP I
           'I heard that when he comes back he'll return to
           America again.'

(22.5)A: [Ore shira-nai yo, soo na no./]
            I   know-NEG IP so BE NOM
           'I don't know that!'

In this discourse segment, speaker A uses *yo* three times, ending each turn with it.[8] While it is grammatically possible to substitute each case of *yo* with *ne*, such alternation gives us the impression of a disjoined interaction. For example, if A answered "*Eh, uso, itte-nai ne*" in (22.3), he expresses an attitude lacking considerateness. Although according to the generally accepted view that using *ne* should encourage rapport--for example, Cook's (1988) view that *ne* signals the participant's general attitude of mutual agreement and Kamio's (1990) notion of "cooperative attitude"--, the choice of *ne* here evokes a distant, uncaring, or even defiant attitude. The same can be said for the substitution of *yo* with *ne* in (22.1) and (22.5). Why is this effect?

The answer lies in the interactional nature of language itself. In an environment where providing information is expected--as in (22.1), (22.3) and (22.5)--using only *ne* fails to respond to the need of the listener. What the listener wants, i.e., information [X], must be foregrounded under this circumstance. Thus, we witness the appropriateness of *yo*.

This point can be further supported by the fact that in a situation depicted in [23], *ne* is in fact inappropriate.

```
[23.1]A:   Anata ga gichoo        o shita sono kaigi  itsu
           you   S  chair person O did   that meeting when
           datta n    desu ka.
           BE    NOM  BE   Q
           'When was that meeting that you chaired?'
```

```
[23.2]B:   Kinoo      datta n   desu  | a. *ne  |
           yesterday BE     NOM  BE    |     IP   |
                                       | b.  yo  |
                                       |     IP   |
           'It was yesterday.'
```

In this regard, I should refer to Kamio's (1990) explanation of the following data. Kamio (1990:76) explains that in a situation where a person is invited to go together as shown below (Kamio's data [106], glossing and translation are mine), *ne* may accompany a strong refusal.

```
(24.1)X:   Doo, isshoni  ika-nai?
           how  together go-NEG
           'How about going together?'
```

```
(24.2)Y:   Iya, ore wa ika-nai ne.
           no   I   T  go-NEG  IP
           'No, I'm not going.'
```

According to Kamio, *ne* in (24.2) indicates strong refusal because (24.2) implies that speaker Y forces the partner [X] to hold a co-responding attitude, i.e., to agree with Y's refusal of going. Since [X] is expected to have a desire of going--as expressed by his invitation--, [Y]'s solicitation is interpreted as going against X's feelings, and therefore the interpretation of strong refusal.

However, consider the following situation.

```
[25.1] A:  Ima nanji?
           now what time is it
           'What time is it now?'
```

```
[25.2]B:   Goji            da | a. ne  |
           five o'clock BE     |    IP  |
                               | b. yo  |
                               |    IP  |
           'It's five o'clock.'
```

In (25), since A is assumed not to know what time it is to begin with (as evidenced by asking the question), B cannot possibly imply a forcing of the information on A. Why then does the answer with *ne* in (25.2a) give disengaged feelings to the interaction while (25.2b) does not? I think that the disengagement between information versus interaction focus is the answer. The different focus *yo* and *ne* places in communication can further be found in the following dialogue of fiction.

(26) In this story a young man finds himself being forgotten by everybody. All his friends and acquaintances ignore him; they simply cannot identify him. A television commercial director notices this young man's ordeal and puts him in one of his television commercials. The man becomes an instant celebrity and now wherever he shows up, people recognize him. One day as he enters a restaurant, the maître d' says:

```
(26.1) "Irasshaimase. Oya, ano komaasharu no kata   desu
        welcome        oh   that commercial  LK person BE
        ne.
        IP
        'Welcome to the restaurant.  Oh, you are the one in that
        commercial, aren't you?'

(26.2) Yoku zonji-agete-orimasu yo.
        well I know              IP
        'I know you well, sir.'

(26.3) Saa, doozo kochira  e."
        well please this way to
        'This way, please.'
```

                                                    --Hoshi 1976:151

Note that this information represented by (26.1)--you are the one in that commercial--is not information that is exclusive to the maître d'. Obviously the young man has direct access to this same information. In this case *yo* results in awkwardness because there is no need to focus on the already shared information. If the maître d' is telling a third person this information, utterance (26.1) with *yo* instead of *ne* may be appropriate, since under this circumstance the third party may not necessarily have more information. The maître d' uses *yo* in (26.2) because his knowledge that he himself knows the young man is exclusive information, and therefore the speaker requesting attention from the addressee to the information itself is appropriate.

Based on these and other similar observations made so far I characterize the semantic sources for *yo* and *ne* as follows.

1. The sentence-final *yo* in the [X *yo*] structure is a marker by which the speaker demands the listener's communicative behavior of "paying attention to [X]" by foregrounding [X]. This is supported by the fact that the speaker has exclusive or more accessibility to and/or possessorship of information and being such, requesting such attention is communicationally justifiable. Information flows from the speaker (more) to the addressee (less). The speaker, possessor of more information, exhibits power, thus the use of *yo* can be a social marker for power and dominance. When sentence-final *yo* appears in discourse, both participants are encouraged to engage primarily in the process of information exchange, backgrounding the concern regarding the participants' emotional involvement.

2. The sentence-final *ne* in the [X *ne*] structure is a marker by which the speaker solicits the addressee's confirmatory attitude and/or requests the addressee's transfer of information, even if it may only be in the form of recognition. Information is requested to flow from the addressee (more) to the speaker (less). Both participants engage primarily in the interpersonal act of co-solicitation and granting of approval. Interaction is foregrounded here and the information exchange is backgrounded. In the context where information is requested, ignoring the request and marking the utterance with *ne* results in disengaged discourse.

We have seen that other DM indicators such as *da* and *desu/masu* verb morphology can distinguish between foregrounded versus backgrounded information. But *yo* and *ne* offer a unique function of foregrounding and backgrounding the two aspects of communication, i.e., object-information-oriented and person-interaction-oriented. Many of the specific functions attributed to *yo* and *ne* in previous studies originate from the basic characteristics described above. For example, when Cook (1988) states that *yo* expresses an attitude of assertiveness, such interpretation is possible simply because *yo* marked information is more the center of attention than information without *yo*. A variety of speech acts Cook claims to represent *yo*'s indirect meanings--warning, advice, instruction, announcement, explanation, report, request/command, insistence and contradiction--can be attributed to *yo* simply because these acts require specific focused information and *yo* provides a mechanism to do just that. Cook's (1988) characterization of *ne*--it indexes the speaker's and addressee's general attitude of mutual agreement--must be modified in light of our discovery that if the context requires a focus on information, *ne* can result in disengaged discourse, sometimes resulting in an expression of defiance. As Cook (1988) discusses, *ne* certainly can be associated with speech functions such as displaying and seeking agreement, confirmation, cooperation and mitigating FTA's, all originating from the functional source of *ne* as I stated above.

Admittedly the functional sources of *yo* and *ne* I propose here are similar to what has been proposed in previous studies. What is new is that I provide a perspective to the study of *ne* and *yo* by focusing on the different, and in many ways complementary functions these particles offer in a single turn. This can serve as a starting point in understanding the speaker's motivation not only for using and not using *yo* and *ne* but also for mixing them in a single speaking turn. I also emphasize the interactional nature of the particle choice in two ways; first, by incorporating the relative degree of information accessibility and possessorship through the degree of Relative Information Accessibility and/or Possessorship, and second, by pointing out that the appropriateness of the foregrounding strategy is not controlled by the speaker alone, but rather, by both speaker and addressee as discussed regarding data sets (21), (22) and (26).

6. Mixture of *Yo* and *Ne* and Conversation Management

Although so far we have discussed the functional aspects of *yo* and *ne* based on Relative Information Accessibility and/or Possessorship, we have not answered the question: Why do speakers find it necessary to use *yo* and *ne* in conversation at all? Or, why do speakers mix them in a seemingly careless manner? In an effort to answer this question, I examine two aspects of conversation management, i.e., listener responses and conversation topic introduction. Let us

first focus on the listener responses encouraged by *yo* versus *ne* in our casual
conversation data. Let us observe (27).

(27) In this segment of conversation speaker A reports to his friend B that even
     though his older friends are interested in becoming teachers, they
     discourage him from becoming one. (Male Pair 2)

    (27.1)A: [Daitai toshiue no sa/
                mostly older   LK IP
                'Mostly older people'

                          (B: Un.)
                          yeah
                          'Uh-huh.'

    (27.2)   onna   no hito   ga ooi wake./
               female LK person S many reason
               'are many, you see.'

                          (B: Un.)
                          yeah
                          'Uh-huh.'

    (27.3)   Moo ooeru   yamete naru   toka ne./
               soon office worker quit   become or   IP
               'For example, they quit office work and become
               (teachers).

                        (B: head nods repeated twice)

    (27.4)   Sooyuu hito   ga sa/
               that   person S IP
               'That kind of person,'

                          (B: Un.)
                          yeah
                          'Uh-huh.'

    (27.5)   mottainai yo to ka yuu n   da yo./]
               a waste   IP QT Q say NOM BE IP
               'says to me, "What a waste to be a teacher!"'

B gives back-channel expressions such as *uh-huh*'s and head nods when speaker A pauses after making a phrasal utterance with falling intonation and/or after marking it with particles *sa* and *ne*. At the end of his turn in (27.5) A marks the utterance with *yo*, immediately after which speaker B takes a turn. By closely observing how a listener responds to utterances marked by different particles, we can understand some of the interactional functions of these two particles. Admittedly the listener response is under a variety of constraints and encouragements which go far beyond the mere existence of certain sentence-final interactional particles. However, since particles appear at the very end of the utterance and are expected to exert a strong influence not only as to how the utterance itself is contextualized but also as to how the consequent listener's response is shaped, this approach is useful. Here unlike Tsuchihashi (1983) our attention is focused strictly on the conversational strategic device, i.e., back-channel responses and the exchange of speaking turns.

I examined all tokens of sentence-final *yo* and *ne* which are followed by a pause in our conversational data. I excluded two cases where *ne* appeared sentence-finally but not followed by a pause. For example, sometimes the speaker marked the sentence with *ne* but left no pause between *ne* and the next utterance. Here an encouraging environment for the potential listener response did not exist in the first place, and therefore I excluded these cases from the frequency count. The frequency tabulation resulted as shown in Table 6.3.

As shown in Table 6.2, out of a total 130 cases of *ne*, 75 cases (or 57.70%) received listener back-channels, while out of a total 87 cases of *yo* expressions, 29 cases (or 33.33%) received listener back-channels. Following *ne* expressions, at 40 locations new turns were taken by the partner, while following *yo* expressions, the turn exchange took place at 39 locations. As for the frequency where back channels did not follow where they could potentially have occurred, i.e., locations where the turn exchange did not occur, for *ne* expressions only 15 cases were observed out of 90 total possible locations (or 16.67%), while *yo* expressions were not responded to by back-channels at 19 locations out of the total of 48 possible locations (or 39.58%). *Ne* is followed significantly more frequently by the partner's back-channel responses--an aspect directly linked to the interpersonal aspect of communication. We observe here that *ne* and *yo* function as conversation management devices by encouraging listener back-channel response to different degrees. This result provides empirical evidence for characterizing *ne* and *yo* as more and less interaction-oriented respectively.

Table 6.2. *Listener Responses following Particles Ne and Yo in 3-minute Segments of Conversation Among 20 Pairs*

Type of Listener Responses:	Number of Particles		Percentage of Particles	
	Ne	*Yo*	*Ne*	*Yo*
Back channels	75	29	57.70	33.33
New turns	40	39	30.77	44.83
No response where back channels may be sent	15	19	11.54	21.84
Total	130	87		

Another aspect pertinent to conversation management is topic introduction. According to Cook (1988:157), "*ne* indirectly indexes the speech function of introducing a new topic (or sub-topic) in conversation." As Cook (1988:159) points out, "logically speaking a new topic in conversation can be introduced either with *yo* or *ne*." But since "*ne* seeks the addressee's cooperation by eliciting his/her involvement" (Cook 1988:158), *ne* marks the new topic significantly more frequently than *yo*. After examining a one-hour adult conversation she concludes that, out of a total of 55 new topic introductions, *ne* functions as a new topic introducing device 26 times (or 46.3%) and *yo* only once (1.8%) and the question 17 times (30.9%).

Note, however, that Cook seems to tabulate cases of *yo* and *ne* appearing both at sentence-final and sentence-internal positions. While Cook's (1988:158) data (35) points out a sentence-final *ne*, *nee* in her data (36) (1988:159) is used as an insertion particle, where the speaker introduces new (sub-)topic by stating *Mekishiko no temae no nee, (Ee?) San Jego* 'Before (one gets to) Mexico, (What?) San Diego.' Since *yo* is much more restricted in its use, to include the frequency count of *ne* where *yo* cannot potentially appear and to conclude that *ne* characteristically marks new topic introduction (versus *yo*) is misleading. New topics are not necessarily introduced by *ne* (versus *yo*); it may simply be that *ne* appears more frequently merely because it can be inserted intrasententially while *yo* cannot.

In fact, I examined *yo* and *ne* appearing at sentence-final position only and I reached significantly different results. As shown in Table 6.3, my study shows that new (sub-)topics are most frequently introduced by questions (without *yo* or *ne*). *Ne* occurs only 12.95% of the time in comparison to Cook's report of 47.3%. Unlike Cook's study which minimizes the function of *yo* as a new (sub)topic introducing device, in my study *yo* occurred 13 times (5.8%).

Table 6.3. *Sentence-final Strategies at the Time of New (Sub-)Topic Introduction in 3-minute Segments of Conversation among 20 Pairs*

Linguistic Strategies	Number of Sentence-final Strategies	Percentage of Sentence-final Strategies
Ne	29	12.95
Yo	13	5.8
desho/ja-nai	12	5.36
Question	66	29.46
Others	104	46.43
Total	224	

The result of my study seems to indicate that associating the function of *ne* to new topic introduction while minimizing such function of *yo* does not accurately reflect what actually transpires in conversation. Beyond the failure of not distinguishing sentence-final versus intrasentential particles, Cook (1988) offers no tabulation as to how not-new (or old) topics are maintained. Considering the fact that *ne* appears more frequently than *yo*, not-new topics are likely to be also maintained by *ne* more frequently then *yo*. In my data, sentence-final *ne* appears a total of 132 times, 103 times of which mark not-new topics. Similarly *yo* appears 13 times at the time of new topic introduction. Thus not-new topics are marked by *yo* 74 times out of a total occurrence of 87 times. Obviously, *ne* appears much more frequently in all segments of conversation, and this simple fact may characterize topic introduction as well as topic maintenance.

The discrepancy between Cook's study and mine discussed here can be attributed to several factors including the difference in the type of data--my 20 diadic conversations versus her single conversation with eight participants. But it seems reasonable to conclude here that the true functional difference between *yo* and *ne* does not lie so much in the presentation of new or not-new topics. The speaker motivation for the use and the mixture of *yo* and *ne* must be found elsewhere.

As already stated, my answer lies in that the interactional function of *yo* and *ne* consists of the speaker's manipulation and integration of information and interaction, which falls into the realm of Discourse Modality. More specifically, by focusing and defocusing on the different aspects of communication, the speaker designs the speaking turn not only to fit appropriately within the flow of information exchange but also, and if not more importantly, to establish and to secure interpersonal relationships as each social encounter allows. By integrating these two processes of Modal Contextualization, the speaker forms the "posture" the utterance or the speaker turn takes in the on-going conversation. As suggested many times in this chapter, conversation participants achieve this by inserting or not inserting *yo* or *ne* (and possibly avoiding particles totally, or using the *yo ne* combination). The possible effect of the particle manipulation is summarized in Figure 6.2.

Figure 6.2. *Functions of Particles* Yo *and* Ne *in Relation to Information and Interaction*

Particles	Aspects of Communication	
	Information	Interaction
Yo	Focused	Defocused
Ne	Defocused	Focused
Yo ne	Somewhat Focused	Focused
Not *Yo/Ne*	---	---

When information is relatively focused, the participants hope to successfully complete the information exchange as desired. *Yo* is a signal that participants should be aware of this intention. If the information exchange does not occur as expected, a variety of emotional reactions can be evoked. Such reactions include an impression of inconsiderateness, self-centeredness and uncooperativeness. Consequently instead of achieving emotional resonance, a disappointing emotional response may result. *Ne* is a device to avoid or to remedy this potential failure in interpersonal emotional involvement. It defocuses information and instead calls attention to interpersonal feelings to assure some level of emotional engagement. Additionally, the speaker may choose not to use *yo* or *ne* at all, or both *yo* and *ne* together. The mechanism observed here significantly operates both personally and interpersonally. For although the particle choice expresses the speaking self's own personal voice which contextualizes the information conveyed, it also reflects what he or she thinks is expected of him or her from the addressee.

In actual discourse segments, *yo* and *ne* help direct the information flow and help create and secure emotional involvement. Let us examine the following segment taken from fiction with a special focus on *yo* and *ne*.

(28) At this point in the novel Morioka (B), the former prosecutor and now a fugitive, in investigating the trap someone set up to incriminate him, talks to a taxi driver (A). The taxi driver once had a woman customer who was connected to the crime.

(28.1)A: "Soo desu ne.
           so BE IP
           'Well, let's see.'

(28.2)   Tsugumi no hanashi o shimashita | a. yo | ."
          thrush LK talk   O did | IP |
                                            | b. ne |
                                            | IP |

          'We talked about a thrush.'

(28.3)B: "Tsugumi to yuu to?"
           thrush QT say when
           'What? You say a "thrush"?'

(28.4)A: "Kotori no tsugumi desu | a. yo |.
           bird LK thrush BE | IP |
                                   | b. ne |
                                   | IP |
           'I mean the bird "thrush."'

(28.5)   Dareka ga eagan   de tsugumi o utta rashii n   desu.
           someone S air gun by thrush O shot seem   NOM BE
           'It seems that some one shot it with an air gun.'

(28.6)   Hane ga kizutsuite tobe-naide-iru tsugumi o ano
           wing S hurt   fly-NEG   thrush O that
           kata   ga hirotta   n   da soodesu.
           person S picked up NOM BE I hear
           'I hear that she took home the thrush whose wing was
           hurt and couldn't fly.'

(28.7)   Ninjoo   no aru   kata   desu | a. ne |."
           feelings S   there is person BE | IP |
                                           | b. yo |
                                           | IP |
           'She is a compassionate person, indeed.'

(28.8)B: "Sore dake desu ka?"
           that only BE   Q
           'Anything else?'

(28.9)A: "Ee, matchi o kashite-kure to iimashite ne,
           yes matches O lend   QT say   IP
           'She asked for matches;'

(28.10)   Tabako   o sutte-iru uchini hutto   omoidashita
           cigarette O smoke   while suddenly recollect
           yooni 'Untenshu-san, tsugumi ga tabako   no kemuri
           as   Mr. driver   thrush S cigarettes LK smoke
           taberu tte no wa okashii wa ne..'
           eat   QT NOM T strange IP IP
           soo | a. itta n   desu yo |."
           so | say NOM BE   IP |
               | b. iimashita ne |
               | said   IP |

'and while smoking, as if that suddenly reminded her,
she said, "Driver, don't you think it strange for a
thrush to 'eat' cigarette smoke?"'

(28.11)B: "Tsugumi ga tabako   no kemuri o taberu no desu
           thrush S cigarette LK smoke O eat   NOM BE
           ka?"
           Q
           'You mean a thrush eats cigarette smoke?'

(28.12)   Tawainonai kaiwa   da to Morioka wa omotta.
          silly   conversation BE QT Morioka T thought
          'Morioka thought it was a silly conversation.'

(28.13)A: "Sore ga ne, tabako   no kemuri ga nagarete-iku
           that but IP cigarette LK smoke S flow
           to   kizutsuita hane o batabata-yatte, shikirini
           when hurt   wing O bat   incessantly
           kemuri o tsuibamu n da soodesu | a. yo |."
           smoke O peck at   NOM BE I hear | IP |
                                           | b. ne |
                                           | IP |
          'But, when the cigarette smoke enveloped the thrush,
          the thrush batted its wounded wings and then the
          thrush kept pecking at the smoke, she said.'

(28.14)B: "Myoona tsugumi | a. da ne |."
           strange thrush | BE IP |
                           | b. desu yo |
                           | BE   IP |
          'It's a strange thrush, isn't it?'

(28.15)   Sono hokani wa nanika   hanasa-nakatta desu ka."
          that beside T something talked-NEG   BE   Q
          'Didn't she talk about anything else?'

(28.16)B: "Iie, hanashita no wa sore dake desu."
           no talked   NOM T that only BE
          'No, that's all we talked about.'

                              --Nishimura 1980:107

In our discussion we exclude non-sentence-final *yo* and *ne*. These include the non-underlined particles in (28.1), (28.10) and (28.13).[9] We also exclude the particle *ne* appearing in direct quotation in (28.10). We find six cases , i.e., (28.2), (28.4), (28.7), (28.10), (28.13) and (28.14) where the particles *yo* or *ne* appear sentence-finally, the first five of which appear in the taxi driver's utterances and the last appearing in Morioka's utterance. As predicted by our findings, all utterances marked by *yo*, i.e., (28.2a), (28.4a), (28.10a) and (28.13a) show that information flows from the speaker (taxi driver) to the addressee (Morioka). When *yo* is replaced with *ne* as shown in (28.2b), (28.4b), (28.10b) and (28.13b), one feels a sense of awkwardness. This is because the direction of the information flow as characterized in this discourse segment does not match that of the direction of the information flow signaled by the replaced *ne*.

A similar point can be made for the use of *ne* in (28.7) and (28.14). When *ne* is replaced with *yo*, awkwardness rises. The reason for the disengaged discourse with the particles altered lies in the contradictory direction of information flow. Although each use of *yo* and *ne* is syntactically appropriate, given a context of meaningful conversation, *yo* and *ne* must appear according to the direction that the relevant information flows. The use of particles chosen by the author also exhibits a manipulative mixture between information- and interaction-focus. In (28.7a) and (28.14a), the taxi driver and Morioka use *ne* in order to reaffirm the level of emotional resonance, to verify a feeling of friendliness and rapport.

At this point I should also briefly mention the issue of *yo* and *ne* as insertion particles, an issue which has been intentionally pushed aside throughout this chapter. *Ne* as an insertion particle is an extension of *ne* as a final particle. Since *ne* focuses on the addressee's feelings, it can appear phrase-finally as well as sentence-finally to enforce frequent emotional check-points. This is why *ne* as insertion particle marks utterances regardless of their new or old information status. And this is also why phrase-final *ne*'s are often followed by listener back channels in casual conversation. Unlike *ne*, since *yo* focuses on information, its appearance at the phrase-final position is strained. *Yo* functions in a meaningful way only when the sentence is semantically complete. Precisely because of this, the use of *yo* as an insertion particle is limited.

Before I conclude this section I should mention an obvious limitation of my analysis of *yo* and *ne*. *Ne* is known to have its variant such as *nee*, and to be used with varying intonation and pitch. Although my casual conversational data did not contain *ne* used for a straightforward question, I have ignored other variables of *ne* and treated all occurrences of *ne* as a single category (as opposed to *yo*). An analysis of different uses of *ne(e)* awaits future study.

7. Particles *Yo* and *Ne* as Devices for Discourse Modality Manipulation

Ultimately the particles *yo* and *ne* contribute to, along with other Discourse Modality indicators, aspects of Modal Contextualization. As we have seen, *yo* and *ne* operate primarily in four aspects of Modal Contextualization, i.e., Perspective, Exchange Structure, Designing Speaker Turns and Personal Emotion as summarized in Figure 6.3.

In this chapter I have argued that the interactional particles *yo* and *ne* function to focus on different aspects of Discourse Modality, i.e., the informational and the interactional aspect, respectively. So instead of simply characterizing *yo* and *ne* as "interactional" particles, identifying their related but distinct, indeed complementary, functions within an analytical framework such as Discourse Modality is beneficial.

Throughout this chapter we have observed that casual conversation and dialogues of fiction exhibit similar phenomena with regard to *yo* and *ne*. Since dialogues are manipulated by the author to a great extent, certainly it is difficult, and perhaps of little use, to explore primarily interactionally attributable aspects of *yo* and *ne*--such as listener responses--in dialogues of fiction. Nonetheless, our data examination shows that the primary distinction we noted for *yo* and *ne* is observed in both of these discourse types. This implies that a broader generalization of certain aspects of Discourse Modality is possible when mixing data from similar but different genres.

What is ultimately achieved through the manipulation of *yo* and *ne* is a personal expression of the speaking self. The personalization of discourse revealed here, however, differs from the cases of other DM indicators examined earlier. Note that the speaking self manipulates how the communication encounter itself should be viewed, whether the information or interaction is in primary focus. In fact we saw many examples where the speaking self engages in shifting the focus between these two essential but different aspects of communication by the appropriate choice of *yo* and *ne* in relation to the addressee's level of knowledge. Thus we must now view the concept of the

Figure 6.3. *Summary of Modal Contextualization Effects Realized by Interactional Particles Yo and Ne*

Semantic Source:	Context-bound Meaning Distribution:	Modal Contextualization, Aspects of Modality:
Mixture of *yo* and *ne*: relative focus on information versus interaction	1. [X *yo*] where [X] is requested and important 2. [X *ne*] solicits other's response (where [X] is not requested)	1. Information Qualification: Perspective (*yo* focusing on [X]; *ne* defocusing on [X]) 3. Participatory Control: Exchange Structure (encouraging different kinds of listener responses) Designing Speaker Turns (manipulation between information versus interaction focus) 4. Interactional Appeal: Personal Emotion (*ne* soliciting confirmation, emotional support)

expressiveness of language in an even broader context. The manipulation of the communicative event itself is a part of the speaking self's expression of his or her intention to qualify the communication encounter. Thus we can say that ultimately through the particles *yo* and *ne* one expresses one's subjectivity, emotion and voice.

CHAPTER 7

To Yuu in the Clause-Noun Combination

1. Introduction

In this last analysis chapter, I examine *to yuu*, one more case of the multi-phrase DM indicator. Unlike other DM indicators, *to yuu* presents a grammatically unique situation; it occurs at the sentence-internal location where a clause and noun are combined to form a complex nominal phrase. Thus from the Discourse Modality perspective, an analysis of *to yuu* is expected to offer new insight, especially into the process of Modal Contextualization within the context of subordinate clause and the clause-noun combination.

The Japanese noun-modifying construction is known to exhibit a grammatical feature in addition to what is normally identified as the relative clause structure. For example, contrast the following.

```
[1]  Asoko de sakana o yaite-iru hito    ga atarashii itamae-san
     there at fish    0 grill     person S  new       cook
     yo.
     IP
     'The person who is grilling the fish over there is the new
     cook.'

[2]  Dokoka    de sakana o yaku  nioi  ga suru.
     somewhere at fish    0 grill smell S  do
     'There is the smell of fish being grilled somewhere.'
```

In [1], the man who grills the fish is the grammatical subject (agent) of the relative clause, *asoko de sakana o yaite-iru* '(who) is grilling the fish there.' Hence [1] exhibits a structural resemblance to the English relative clause construction. In [2], however, we cannot identify a grammatical relationship between the *nioi* 'smell' and the modifying clause *dokoka de sakana o yaku* 'fish being grilled somewhere.' Fish grilling and its resultant smell are a cause/effect relationship that one can readily associate closely, but only in semantic and pragmatic terms. Let us call the structure represented in [2] an "explanatory" clause since the clause does not "modify" in the sense of relative clause construction, but "explains" about the relevant noun in some way or another.[1]

Teramura (1981) calls the clause-noun combination depicted in [1] *uchi no kankei* 'internal relationship' while the type depicted in [2] is referred to as *soto no kankei* 'external relationship,' and treats both as subtypes of the *rentai-shuushoku* 'nominal modification.' According to Teramura (1981:108), the "external type" is structurally characterized by (1) that the content of the noun can be expressed by a statement (in the form of a sentence) and (2) that in some cases the modifying clause (which he calls "content clause") cannot directly precede the noun in which case the phrase *to yuu* is necessary.

In order to follow Teramura's points, let us observe [3] and [4] both of which exemplify "external" nominal modification, our "explanatory" construction.

```
[3]   Kare wa tanin o amari    shin'yoo-shi-nai seikaku
      he   T  others O (not) so trust-NEG       personality
      datta.
      BE
      'He was of a personality not to trust others much.'

[4]   Kare wa tanin o amari    shin'yoo-shi-nai to yuu
      he   T  others O (not) so trust-NEG       QT say
      seikaku      datta.
      personality BE
      'He was of a personality (such that) not to trust others
      much.'
```

Note that the relationship between "personality" and *tanin o amari shin'yoo-shi-nai* 'not to trust others much' is that the latter expresses the content of the former; this meets the first condition of the "external" nominal modification. Note also that, as predicted by Teramura's (1984) second characteristic of the "external" nominal modification, this relationship can be grammatically expressed with or without *to yuu*. Here we face an intriguing question: Why and for what purpose does *to yuu* appear in [4] while it does not in [3]?

The distributional constraints of *to yuu* raise many varied and complex issues surrounding the Japanese relative clause construction, noun phrase modification and the complementizers such as *koto*, *no* and *to*. Obviously I cannot address these multiple issues in this work. My immediate concern in this

TO YUU IN THE CLAUSE-NOUN COMBINATION   223

chapter lies with the cases where use of *to yuu* is optional primarily in "external" noun modification. Again, the purpose here is to explore the motivation of the speaking self for use and non-use of *to yuu* within the Discourse Modality framework.

In order to answer this question, I first review some previous works that describe distributional constraints of *to yuu* in Japanese clause-noun combination. Based on the results of previous works and results of data analysis conducted in this study, I address the questions posed above and other related issues. This chapter concludes that *to yuu* is another example of a DM indicator for expressing personal voice of the speaking self in the Japanese clause-noun combination. What *to yuu* brings to the language is a "bridge" for connecting two different modes of communication, i.e., the act of "saying" and the act of "describing" in the process of the clause-noun combination in Japanese.

The data selected for this analysis consists of both dialogue and narrative portions of contemporary Japanese fiction as described in chapter 1. The rationale for choosing both dialogue and narrative discourse is that the use of *to yuu* is expected to be quite extensive in both types of discourse. Additionally, *to yuu* itself is expected to have a function connecting these two types of discourse and therefore the mixture of both types is thought to provide useful clues for our understanding of *to yuu* as well as the nature of Discourse Modality.

2. Background

In investigating the clause-noun combination with and without *to yuu*, let us use the structural descriptions [X *to yuu* Y] and [X Y] respectively for convenience. According to Josephs (1976), *to yuu* has an inherent meaning of "non-factive." Thus when an expression [X *to yuu* Y] occurs, [X] represents hearsay or something that the speaker cannot guarantee or has not verified. This point is refuted by Terakura (1980:216) in which she points out that this "non-factive hypothesis is not adequate because *to yuu* can occur even if the embedded predication represents something that the speaker knows or is certain to be true."

Terakura (1980) claims that in Japanese what [X] expresses in the structure [X *to yuu* no/koto] is PROPOSITION. PROPOSITION is defined as an idea expressed in the form of a sentence which remains subjective because somebody created it. Although her discussion is limited to the combination of clause and the complementizers *no* and *koto*, her arguments are relevant here. Terakura (1980) offers the following seven points regarding the use and non-use of *to yuu*. (Here I follow Terakura's method of romanization as given in her work.)

1. There are examples in which *to yuu* is obligatory and, if a sentence requires the presence of *to yuu*, the complement clause of that sentence cannot be separated from the matrix sentence to independently become a sincere utterance of the same speaker.

2. If a complement clause ends with a "modality auxiliary" such as -*daroo* 'probably,' -*mai* 'may not...,' -*no da* 'it is that...,' which indicate that the embedded predication represents someone's subjective conjecture or judgment, i.e., PROPOSITION, it requires the presence of *to yuu*.

3. The "modal" predicate *ariuru* 'possible or likely' requires *to yuu koto* whereas the predicate *dekiru* 'can or capable of' requires *koto*.

4. The presence of *to yuu* is obligatory if an embedded sentence modifies a "subjective P-noun" such as *kangae* 'idea or thought,' *iken* 'opinion,' *kakushin* 'conviction,' whereas it is optional if an "objective P-noun" such as *zizitsu* 'fact,' *kekka* 'result,' is the modified head-noun.[2]

5. Verbs such as *meiziru* 'order,' *yookyuu-suru* 'request or demand,' do not allow *to yuu*--for the reason that the embedded predication being CONCEPT rather than PROPOSITION.

6. Verbs such as *miru* 'see,' *kikoeru* 'hear,' *kanziru* 'feel,' which take "S *no*" as their object complement clause, do not allow the presence of *to yuu*.[3]

7. "S *to yuu koto*" is most natural as the object complement clause of verbs such as *imi-suru* 'mean,' *anzi-suru* 'imply or suggest,' *simesu* 'indicate or demonstrate.'

Each of these distributional constrains of *to yuu* is based on the idea that *to yuu* follows PROPOSITION, rather than EVENT or FACT.

In his extensive study on nominal modification in Japanese, Teramura (1981:110) offers the following list of conditions for the use of *to yuu*. The clause that requires *to yuu* exhibits typically the following features:

1. It may contain the topic marker *wa*;
2. It is a sentence expressing strong assertion ending with *da* and *desu*;

3. It is an expression of demand or request with phrases such as *-shiro*, *-nasai* 'do it,' and *-shite-kudasai* 'please do it';
4. It expresses invitation and suggestion as with *-shiyoo* 'let's do it';
5. It contains final particles such as *ka, na, kana*, or it ends with similar sentence-final expressions.

In addition, Teramura (1981:109-119) characterizes the noun [Y] that appears in the structure [X (*to yuu*) Y]; those that take *to yuu* obligatorily, optionally or those that do not at all.

To yuu is obligatory for the following categories of nouns:
1. Nouns related to "saying"--work, letter, answer, telegram, telephone, proposal, rumor, grumbling, complaint, order, invitation, request, etc.;
2. Nouns related to "thinking"--opinion, expectation, thought, idea, imagination, feeling, decision, will, belief, etc.;
    (*To yuu* is obligatory when the noun [Y] is preceded by a clause with features listed above, but optional when preceded by a clause ending with past or non-past forms of the adjectives and verbs.)
3. Nouns that refer to facts;
4. Nouns referring to concepts of action, event and state.

To yuu cannot cooccur with the following noun categories:
5. Nouns related to sense and perception--sound, smell, taste, appearance, figure, picture, photograph, scene, shape, feeling, touch;
6. Nouns expressing relational concepts--above, below, right, left, inside, outside, front, back, cause, reason, result, one side, one aspect, other, contrary to, etc.
    (Teramura states that some nouns in this category ("result" is cited) may take *to yuu*, however.)

While both Terakura's (1980) and Teramura's (1981) work provide many characteristics of the clause-noun combination in Japanese, some questions remain unanswered. For example, while Teramura offers detailed description of constraints for the use and non-use of *to yuu*, some essential and theoretically more significant questions remain unaddressed. Why are these constraints imposed upon nouns that cooccur and do not cooccur with *to yuu*? Can the answer to this question explain the motivations for optional uses of *to yuu*?

The traditional understanding of the *to yuu* expression in Japan suffers from shortcomings similar to the points raised above. For example, Shoogakukan's *Nihon Kokugo Daijiten* (1975) lists seven subcategories of meanings and functions for all *to yuu* expressions. Among them, the category represented by the example *shinu to yuu hoo wa nai* 'dying is not the solution' is relevant to our present concern. The function of this [X *to yuu* Y] structure is, according to *Nihon Kokugo Daijiten* (1975:395), *to no ukeru kotogara o tokuni toritateru* 'to specially mention what precedes *to*.' While this functional characterization is somewhat similar to what I propose in this chapter--obviously when a piece of information is specially mentioned, some degree of focusing and foregrounding is involved--, this characterization by itself cannot answer the questions posed above. Concentrating on the cases where *to yuu* is optional, in the following sections I attempt to answer these and other related questions.

2. Distributional Characteristics of *To Yuu*

Let us begin by observing some data taken from modern fiction. First, let me concentrate on one short story by Hoshi (1982) titled *Atama no ookina robotto* 'A large-headed robot.' The plot of this story (in English) is provided in Appendix 1. This story contains three cases of clause-noun combinations that are similarly structured and that use similar nouns repeatedly. In all cases *to yuu* is grammatically optional, and yet some appear with and others appear without *to yuu*. For the purpose of discussion I present here one case as shown in (5). The number after 5 indicates the sentence number given to each sentence in the story. In the data to follow, I use square brackets to segment the lexical items relevant to the [X (*to yuu*) Y] structure.

```
(5.3)   Kare ni wa [wasureppoi to yuu ketten] to, tanin  o
        him  for T  forgetful    QT say weakness and others
        amari     shin'yoo-shi-nai to yuu seikaku      ga
        (not) so  trust-NEG        QT say personality  S
        tomonatte-ita.
        accompanied
        'He had a flaw of being forgetful and had a personality
        of not being able to trust people much.'
```

(5.5)   Shikamo   [wasureppoi seikaku]   dearu node
        additionally forgetful personality BE   since
        monooboe no ii   yuushuuna hisho   de-nakutewanaranai.
        memory   S good excellent secretary must
        'Additionally, since he is of a forgetful personality,
        his secretary must be capable and must remember things
        well.'

(5.23) [Wasureppoi to yuu Enu-shi no seikaku]   wa, kore
        forgetful   QT say Mr. N   LK personality T   this
        de   oginaeru.
        with can be supplemented
        'Mr. N's personality of being forgetful can now be
        supplemented.'

(5.82) Enu-shi wa [wasureppoi seihitsu]   na node, kagi
        Mr. N   T   forgetful personality BE as   key
        o sugu   dokoka   ni okiwasurete-shimau.
        O right away somewhere at leave
        'Since Mr. N is of a forgetful personality, he easily
        forgets where he put his keys.'

                        --Hoshi 1982:37-41

Data set (5) lists four sentences in which Mr. N's characteristic description (being forgetful) is offered, some with *to yuu* and others without. [Y] in [*wasureppoi (to yuu)* Y] structure is not identical in all four sentences; *ketten* 'weakness,' *seikaku* 'personality,' *Enu-shi no seikaku* 'Mr. N's personality,' *seihitsu* 'personality, personal characteristics.' However, each shows semantic similarities and *to yuu* is optional in each case. Thus I believe that the difference in [Y] does not affect the following argument in a significant way. First, note that in (5.3) when Mr. N's forgetfulness is introduced for the first time in the narrative, *to yuu* is used. Let us here make a note of the fact that one of the distributional characteristics of *to yuu* is that of presenting [X] as new, not yet shared information, while the expression without *to yuu* assumes [X] to have been introduced earlier.

    In this regard I should mention Kinsui's (1988) study of *to yuu*. Although Kinsui concentrates on the Japanese personal reference strategy using the [Noun *to yuu* Noun] structure unlike our focus on the clause-noun structure, the use of *to yuu* he develops is relevant to our discussion. For example, when, say,

Tanaka (unknown to the partner) is identified by the speaker by using *to yuu* in conversational discourse, the partner must continue identifying Tanaka by using *to yuu* or by using the *so*-reference. In order to identify Tanaka as Tanaka-san or *kare* 'he,' both participants must have experienced "meeting" Tanaka in real life. Therefore for the partner, Tanaka remains to be *Tanaka-san to yuu hito* 'person called Tanaka,' or *sono hito* 'that person,' unless the partner has actually "met" Tanaka. Kinsui warns us, however, that in narrative discourse the participant introduced as *Taroo to yuu hyakushoo* 'a farmer called Taro' can be referred to as *Taroo* in the next sentence since the narrative world falls under a different constraint of the partner's mental space. The point of relevance to our present discussion is that *to yuu* is used to identify information which the partner does not know in the [Noun *to yuu* Noun] structure just as the case in the [X *to yuu* Y] structure. Our approximation that [X] in the [X *to yuu* Y] structure refers to new information seems to apply to similar but syntactically different linguistic phenomenon in Japanese as well, which at least provides some encouragement to proceed in this direction.

However, whether the information is new or shared cannot be the only distributional characteristic for the [X *to yuu* Y] structure, for *to yuu* appears again in (5.23) where the fact that Mr. N is forgetful is assumed to be already shared. Looking for other distributional characteristics one may note that in (5.5) and (5.82) which lack *to yuu*, the [X Y] structure appears in subordinate clauses. It is known that generally subordinate clauses offer background information rather than foregrounded and focused information, and the difference in the type of information may have some consequence for the speaker's choice of the optional *to yuu*. Taking into consideration the observation just made, I propose that what is in operation here is that the [X *to yuu* Y] structure is used when [X] is in focus--including but not limited to when [X] offers new information--and when the author wants to dramatize such description. Obviously the option of not inserting *to yuu* in (5.23) is available to the author, but the narrative context in (5.23) calls for foregrounding of the description of being forgetful. Note that the semantically important point of (5.23) is that the robot can now compensate Mr. N's personality weakness, namely, being forgetful. Thus 'being forgetful' becomes crucial and therefore foregrounded information here.

Marking focus and/or new information, however, does not seem to be the only function of the [X *to yuu* Y] structure that separates itself from the [X Y] structure. Observe manipulated data [6].

[6.1]A: Enu-shi no koto desu kedo, seikaku   wa doo
        Mr. N   LK fact BE   but   personality T how

        deshoo ka.
        BE   Q
        'About Mr. N's personality, what is he like?'

[6.2]B: Enu-san nee, nikumenai   hito   desu yo.
        Mr. N   IP   cannot hate person BE   IP

        Maa, chotto wasureppoi | a. Ø |
        well a bit   forgetful | |
                                | b. to yuu |
                                | QT say |
        seikaku   desu kedo mo.
        personality BE   but although
        'Mr. N, he is a lovable man. Well, he is a bit of a
        forgetful personality, though.'

Here let us assume a situation where speaker A asks a specific question about Mr. N's personality in [6.1] to which B responds. Note that [6.2a] (without *to yuu*) is perfectly adequate as an answer which provides new and focused information. When *to yuu* is added, however, one senses that someone qualifies Mr. N's forgetful personality as his or her own opinion. In other words, when *to yuu* is added, we sense more strongly the text producer who "says" [X]. In this case B's personal voice echoes more strongly than in the [X Y] structure.

A similar interpretation can be made in regard to data set (5). In (5.3) and (5.23), more than (5.5) and (5.82), one senses that [X] represents a view of the text producer who qualifies it as his or her expression. In this narrative segment it seems most reasonable to interpret that *to yuu* qualifies the narrator's expression itself.

To recapitulate, I propose the following characterization of *to yuu*:

In the Japanese clause-noun combination, when *to yuu* is optional, the [X *to yuu* Y] structure appears when [X] is foregrounded due to its newness

or unexpectedness of information or due to its relative importance in
discourse and the speaker finds it necessary to add a dramatic effect. The
[X *to yuu* Y] structure gives an impression that [X] is qualified as a text
producer's expression.

The distributional constraints described above are not isolated incidents
limited to the story under investigation but are observed universally in other
fictional works examined for this study. For example, (7) represents a case
where [X] offers information that requires foregrounding since the narrative
context is such that the readers are anxious to find out what kind of disease the
friend has.

```
(7)  [Shoojoo  ga susumu  nitsure, warai    ga takamaru to yuu
      symptoms S  advance as        laughter S  increase QT say
      byooki] na no  desu.
      disease BE NOM BE
      'It is a disease in which one's laughter increases as the
      symptom advances.'
```

                                        --Hoshi 1982:245

In order to illustrate the point under discussion more explicitly, let us
examine the following manipulated data [8] assuming the situation as depicted
below.

[8] Tanaka's friend has been behaving strangely lately. The rumor says that
     the friend has caught a "laughing sickness." And in fact people say that a
     doctor (A) diagnosed his friend as such. As strange as it may sound,
     observing the friends' behavior, Tanaka (B) is beginning to take this rumor
     seriously. Tanaka visits the doctor, and asks what's wrong with his friend...

```
[8.1]A:  Kore wa hushigina byooki  deshite ne, shoojoo  ga
         this T   strange    disease BE       IP  symptoms S
         susumu  nitsurete warai    ga takamaru
         advance as        laughter S  increase
         | a. to yuu  | byooki  desu.
         |    QT say  | disease BE
         | b. Ø       |
```

'This is a strange disease; as the symptom advances the laughter increases, and such is this disease.'

```
[8.2]B:  Yappari      soo deshita ka.  Wakarimashita.  Warai
         as expected so  BE      Q     understood      laughter
         ga takamaru  | a. to yuu  | byooki  dakara na n
         S  increase  |    QT say  | disease because BE NOM
                      | b. Ø       |
         desu ne, ikura    warauna    to ittemo warai-tsuzukeru
         BE   IP  however don't laugh QT say    continue to
             no  wa.
         laugh NOM T
```
'Just as I thought. I get it. It is because he has this disease that makes him laugh that he keeps on laughing and laughing no matter how sternly I order him not to laugh, isn't it?'

Although it is possible to create four different cases of clause-noun combinations with or without *to yuu* (i.e., a/a, a/b, b/a, b/b) all of which are grammatically correct, the effect is different. When *to yuu* occurs, [X] becomes a relatively important piece of information which warrants the reader's attention. But more than the mere importance of the information seems to be involved here. When the [X *to yuu* Y] construction is used, it is as if the author introduces [X] first and then adds the noun category [Y] for [X] to be categorized into. When *warai ga takamaru to yuu byooki* 'the disease that laughter increases' is used, the focus is on the *warai ga takamaru* 'the laughter increases' itself giving the impression in the English translation of something like 'the laughter increases, and that is the disease.' Note that utterance [8.1] itself is structured in such a way as to focus on *shoojoo ga susumu nitsurete warai ga takamaru to yuu byooki* 'the disease such that as the symptom advances the laughter increases' with the *n da* structure.

On the other hand in the case of the [X Y] combination without *to yuu*, the reverse is true. The relatively important information is [Y], which itself provides information within a subordinate clause. Here the information provided by the [X Y] structure is defocused. *Warai ga takamaru byooki* 'the disease that laughter increases' gives the impression in the English translation of something like 'the disease which, as you know, has the symptom of laughter increasing.' Perhaps the most expected combination of the *to yuu* options in the narrative situation as described in [8] is the a/b combination where the doctor's

information is given as new foregrounded information with *to yuu*, while
Tanaka's commentary is given in a backgrounded subordinate clause without *to
yuu*. Tanaka had already suspected that the friend suffered from the laughing
disease and therefore he was willing to accept the information as if he were
confirming the incoming information.

At this point I should go back to the question raised earlier. I stated that
both [3] and [4] are acceptable and yet to date the functional differences
between these statements have not been addressed. Following the discussion
above, we can now see that while [3] describes the personality in the preceding
modifying clause, [4] presents the author's intention to foreground the kind of
personality the man has and then this qualification is labeled as being a
personality. Therefore, although [3] and [4] are identical in terms of referential
semantics, they differ pragmatically, each answering different pragmatic needs
in discourse. The choice between the [X *to yuu* Y] and the [X Y] structure is
not syntactic but fundamentally a discourse pragmatic one, and we continue to
explore this aspect in more detail in the following sections.

4. *To Yuu* as a Bridge between "Saying" and "Describing"

Let us continue our observation of the data where *to yuu* is optional in the
clause-noun combination.

```
(9)  "Issakujitsu              karini yakusoku doori
      the day before yesterday if    promise  as is
      attemo        dokoka    e  iku  | a. to yuu  |
      even if meet  somewhere to go   |    QT say  |
                                      | b. Ø       |
      yotei wa nakatta rashii.
      plan  T  BE-NEG  seem
      'It seems that even if they met each other as promised the
      day before yesterday they did not have a plan to go
      anywhere.'
```

                                              --Yuuki 1977:25

It is possible to construct a sentence *dokoka e iku yotei* 'a plan to go somewhere'
without *to yuu*. But when *to yuu* appears as it does in Yuuki (1977:25), it gives

the impression of having a sense of *to yuu yoona* 'one may express as, such as'--
resulting in the English translation of something like 'it seems that even if they
met each other as promised the day before yesterday they did not have a plan
such as to go anywhere.' *To yuu yoona* is another option here to connect [X]
and [Y], and it conveys the speaker's qualification of the utterance itself--
something like 'I may say as' or 'I may express it such as.' When this
interpretation is incorporated into (9) the reader senses that *dokoka e iku* is
uttered by someone, rather than it being a descriptive statement integrated into
the noun *yotei*. In other words as alluded to earlier, in [X *to yuu* Y], [X] is
interpreted as representing a direct discourse uttered by someone representing
his or her voice, regardless of whether it is the author, the narrator or the
character in the narrative.

This sense of someone saying [X] obviously stems from the literal meaning
of the phrase *to yuu* itself, i.e., 'to say that.' Thus it is not difficult to assume
that the literal meaning of the linguistic signs *to yuu* is retained in some way in
the [X *to yuu* Y] expression. In fact this explains why the [X] in [X *to yuu* Y]
structure can take many (although not all) features permissible in direct
discourse while that is not the case for the [X Y] structure. It is well known, and
as Teramura (1981) points out, when [X] contains, for example, a final particle
ka, *to yuu* is obligatory. So is the case when [X] contains an expression of
demand or request. In fact each of the conditions 1 through 4 cited earlier from
Teramura (1981) points to the inherent characteristics of direct discourse in [X].
Due to this direct nature of discourse facilitated by the [X *to yuu* Y] structure,
the reader senses someone's implicit or explicit responsibility for making the
statement [X]. This awareness of the producer of the statement [X], however,
is absent in the [X Y] structure. In the [X Y] noun modification structure, the
information given in [X] does not normally reflect someone's direct discourse;
rather [X] is a part of the total information integrated into a description of [Y].

Note that grammatically, the [X Y] structure becomes a nominal, and as
Brown and Levinson (1987:208) state, "the more nouny an expression, the more
removed an actor is from doing or feeling or being something." The [X Y]
structure changes the status of the clause [X] into that of a nominal with the
subordinate clause [X] now integrated into the nominal; [X] often does not claim
or disclaim, affirm of deny; it is often amodal. The amodal nature of the
nominalized string makes the content more objectified and less involved. It is
true that [X] in [X Y] can take modal features such as tense and aspects, but
these are limited to some auxiliary verbs and auxiliary adjectives; the [X Y]

structure exhibits a nominal structure that is highly integrated where the [X]'s clausal independence is severely jeopardized.

It is also noteworthy to think of the conceptual effect of nominalization. When a clause is changed into a nominal, the event described is treated as a "thing" or a "fact," rather than an event that takes place by an agent initiating an action performed on or with something else. The event is no longer an active "event," but it becomes a "state." Thus, a nominalized clause exhibits some distance between the event and the speaker. It tends to represent a perspective of a distant observer, rather than that of an involved participant. In contrast to this, the [X *to yuu* Y] structure allows [X] to resemble directly quoted discourse and to carry most of the modality features. *To yuu*, then, is a device to introduce a vivid image, if not only an awareness, of the person whose "voice" is foregrounded.

I propose that structurally at least two distinct strategies exist in combining Japanese clauses and nouns in the noun-modifying construction. First is the strategy in which [X] constructs almost an independent statement which is marked by *to yuu* followed by a noun. The second is the clause noun combination in which, similarly to the English relative clause, [X] is a subordinate clause modifying the noun [Y]. While [X] in [X *to yuu* Y] structure retains the nature of an independent clause resembling direct speech, the [X Y] structure does not evoke a sense of this direct discourse. In my view, *to yuu* functions to connect two modes of linguistic expressions, one, to "say" something as expressed by [X], and the other, to "describe" something as expressed by the predicate in which [Y] is a syntactic constituent.

The two strategies of the clause-noun combination are summarized below with Figure 7.1 providing the contrast.

[X *to yuu* Y]: "quotative explanation"

[X] is syntactically an independent clause connected to [Y], with [Y] presenting a generalized category for the explanation offered by [X] to fall into. This structure presents [X] and [Y] in a manner that can be characterized as "information [X] (which is [Y])." X often offers new or unexpected (intended to foreground) information that is conveyed by the speaking self. In "quotative explanation" one senses more intensely than otherwise the existence of the producer of [X] who qualifies the mode of expression of [X]. [X] bears many features of direct discourse although it cannot take some features. [X] often represents the content of speech and thought with *to yuu* being a device to connect two modes of expression, "saying" and "describing." For this reason I refer to the [X *to yuu* Y] structure as clause-noun combination of "quotative explanation." [X Y]: "nominal modification"

[X] is a subordinate clause providing information for the pragmatically more important information [Y]. This structure presents [X] and [Y] in a manner that can be characterized as "information [Y] (such as [X])." [X] offers information already assumed to be accepted or known; [X] functions to identify [Y] in a more specified manner. There is no merging of the two different modes of expression here; this strategy offers in essence a description of [Y] without foregrounding the producer of [X].

Figure 7.1. *The Level of Information Focusing and the Foregrounding of the Producer of [X] in [X* to yuu *Y] versus [X Y] Structure*

	[X *to yuu* Y] "Quotative Explanation"	[X Y] "Nominal Modification"
Focused Information:	[X]	[Y]
Information Added to the Above:	(which is Y)	(such as X)
Producer of [X] foregrounded:	Yes	No

The proposal made here that in the clause-noun combination of "quotative explanation," the clause [X] is structurally independent--and not a part of a subordinate clause--is further supported by several types of evidence as listed below. Some of the constraints referred to here are those of Teramura (1981) introduced earlier.

1. Topic-marking *wa* requires [X *to yuu* Y] structure:
    The function of *wa* is to topicalize the entity preceding *wa*. The widely observed fact that *wa* does not normally appear in subordinate clauses

(unless being contrastive) stems from the reasoning that topicalization of information and subordination of information in a single clause is pragmatically contradictory. Therefore, if [X] in the [X *to yuu* Y] structure is considered not as a subordinate clause but as an independent clause connected to [Y] by *to yuu*, the above mentioned condition can be better understood.

2. Particle restriction:

The particle *no* that can replace *ga* in the subordinate clause [X] of the [X Y] noun modification cannot cooccur in the *to yuu* structure as given in [10].

[10] Warai | a. no | takamaru byooki ni kakatta.
     laughter | S | increase disease IO caught
              | b. ga |
              | S |
     'He caught a disease in which his laughter increases.'

[11] Warai | a. *no | takamaru to yuu byooki ni
     laughter | S | increase QT say disease IO
              | b. ga |
              | S |
     kakatta.
     caught
     'He caught a disease in which his laughter increases.'

This implies that syntactically [X] of the [X *to yuu* Y] structure retains the nature of an independent clause.

3. Modal adverbs require the [X *to yuu* Y] structure:

When a modal adverb is intended to express the attitude in direct discourse, noun-modification without *to yuu* is ungrammatical as shown in [12].

[12] Sono otoko wa [yappari   Bosuton e iku no wa yameru
     that man   T as expected Boston to go NOM T quit
     | a. to yuu | ketsui] o shita.
     | QT say | decision O did
     | b. *Ø |
     'The man decided not to go to Boston after all.'

Recall that the use of the modal adverb *yappari* 'as expected' is limited in that it appears only in direct discourse. If *to yuu* is used as in [12a] *yappari* can be attributed to the voice of *sono otoko* 'the man.' Here *yappari* is within the scope of [X] in the [X *to yuu* Y] structure. But if *to yuu* does not occur as in [12b], *yappari* cannot be interpreted as the expression of "the man." Rather, the only interpretation is that *yappari* is outside the modifying clause [X] and it is attributed to the speaker of the utterance [12] as a whole. One must interpret it this way since the only other possible direct discourse available in the utterance [12b] is that of the speaker's. The [X Y] structure cannot take a modal adverb such as *yappari* within [X]; this is because [X] represents subordinate indirect discourse while *yappari* requires direct discourse, and the combination of these two results in contradictory perspectives. *To yuu* makes it possible to mark [X] as an independent clause expressing direct discourse in the [X *to yuu* Y] structure.

An additional piece of information that [X] of the [X *to yuu* Y] structure can take direct discourse while [X] of the [X Y] structure cannot is found in the following.

[13] Ima demo Sasaki-san wa sono jiken no shinsoo o shiri-tai
now even Mr. Sasaki T that case LK truth O want to
    | a. <u>to yuu</u> | hanashiburi   da.
know | QT say | way of talking BE
    | b. ?∅ |
'Even now Sasaki talks in such a way as if to say "I want to know the truth of that case."

[14] Ima demo Sasaki-san wa sono jiken no shinsoo o shiri-
now even Mr. Sasaki T that case LK truth O want to
tagatte-iru | a. ?<u>to yuu</u> | hanashiburi   da.
know | QT say | way of talking BE
         | b. ∅ |
'Even now Sasaki talks in a way that he wants to know the truth of the case.'

As has been repeatedly mentioned, Japanese makes an epistemological distinction between one's own desire and someone else's by marking with *-tai* and *-tagaru*, respectively. When a third person's desire is expressed from the speaker's point of view using *-tagaru*, *to yuu* is not necessary as seen in [14b]. But when a third person's desire is expressed as direct discourse as in [13], the clause-noun combination without *to yuu* which helps to connect two different perspectives--one, the direct discourse expressed from Sasaki's perspective and the other, the indirect description of Sasaki by the speaker of [13]--the statement [13b] as a whole will present two contradicting perspectives. In other words *to yuu* makes it possible to mix two discourse types by marking what precedes as direct discourse which constitutes an independent clause.

4. The selectional constraints of nouns related to "saying":
    To yuu is obligatory when the nouns in the [Y] position are related to "saying". The reason for this constraint is that these nouns report the content of the "saying" which can be conveniently and perhaps most authentically expressed as direct discourse.

5. Selectional Constraints of nouns related to sense and perception and the nouns expressing relational concepts:
    The reason for this constraint can be explained in the following way. The relational noun, for example *mae* 'front' in [15], by itself lacks its necessary specificity. The concept of *mae* 'before' requires explanation which is given in the preceding clause, i.e., before (you) came to the store today.

```
[15] Kyoo   omise ni kuru  | a. *to yuu | mae
     today  store IO come  |    QT say  | before
                           | b. Ø       |
     dokoka      yotta?
     somewhere  stopped by
     'Did you stop by somewhere before you came to the store
     today?'
```

The relationship between [X] and [Y] in [15] is such that [Y] is dependent on [X] which offers specific information. The fact that [X] constitutes an integral part of the meaning of [Y] encourages structurally closer integration of [X] and [Y]; in this case both [X] and [Y] are expected to represent the same mode of verbal expression, i.e., description. Therefore a preference exists for the structure [X Y] rather than [X *to yuu* Y].

6. Constraints of nouns of sense or perception:
    Similarly to the case immediately above, the characterization of the sense/perception must be described to define what it is. For example, *nioi* 'smell' fails to independently offer specificity if the type of smell needs to be described; the explanatory clause such as *sakana o yaku* 'grilling fish' is

necessary. Thus the relationship between X and Y is that X offers necessary explanation to be immediately integrated into Y; thus a preference exists for the [X Y] structure as shown in [16].

```
[16] Dokoka    de sakana o yaku  | a. to yuu  | nioi  ga
     somewhere at fish   O grill |    QT say  | smell S
                                 | b. Ø       |

     suru.
     do
     'There is a smell of fish being grilled somewhere.'
```

Having said this I must raise a point related to item 6 above. Contrary to Teramura's (1981) characterization, a noun that indicates sense, for example, *nioi* 'smell' may occur in a "quotative explanation" given appropriate context as in [17].

```
[17.1]  Kono hen  ni kunsei     koojoo demo        aru
        this area in smoked food factory or something exist
        n    daroo ka.
        NOM BE  Q
        'I wonder if there is a smoked food factory around here.'
```

```
[17.2]  Kore wa nanika    o kunsei  ni shite-iru to yuu nioi
        this T  something O smoking IO do        QT say  smell
        da ga...
        BE IP
        'This is a smell (caused by) something being smoked.'
```

In the situation depicted in [17], the speaker qualifies the description in a way to express hesitancy. Thus if the intention of the speaker is to qualify his or her speech action itself by adding the meaning of "one can say," it is possible to add *to yuu* to nouns of perception. In fact a similar point can be made in regard to [15]. If the intention of the speaker is to foreground the speaking self, *to yuu* may be added--deriving the meaning "before you came to the store today, which is what you said, did you stop by somewhere?"[4] The points raised here then can serve as further evidence to support that when *to yuu* is used, the effect is that it retains the flavor of something being said by someone, while the [X Y] structure does not hint at such effect.

In fact the image of the speaker evoked by *to yuu* as described here is not limited to the "external relationship" noun-modifying construction alone. It applies to all cases of noun-modifying construction in Japanese. For example, let us examine data [1] which is reproduced here for convenience.

[1]   Asoko de sakana o yaite-iru hito   ga atarashii itamae-san
       there at fish   O grill   person S new   cook
       yo.
       IP
       'The person who is grilling the fish over there is the new
       cook.'

If *to yuu* is added to create *asoko de sakana o yaite-iru to yuu hito*, the reader is forced into awareness of a person who claims that someone is grilling the fish over there. I conclude here that the basic function of *to yuu* in the clause-noun combination is (1) to add an awareness of the speaker, (2) to present [X] as a direct discourse constituting an independent clause, and (3) to focus on [X] followed by the ensuing labeling of [X] as [Y]. Ultimately *to yuu* makes possible a bridging between the act of "saying" and the act of "describing" in the process of linguistic expression.

The distinction between the [X *to yuu* Y] and the [X Y] structure emerging here may be best understood when we place them in the context of reporting and reported speech. It is often said that the (authorial) reporting of what is reported by someone else involves shifts in points of view and the process reveals varying degrees of multiple voices representing various sources. Here Bakhtin's following characterization is helpful.

The words of the author that represent and frame another's speech create a perspective for it; they separate light from shadow, create the situation and conditions necessary for it to sound; finally they penetrate into the interior of the other's speech, carrying into it their own accents and their own expressions, creating for it a dialogized background. (1981:358)

The [X Y] structure offers the textual construction where its text producer's voice consumes the voice of the producer of [X] itself. Thus the effect of choosing the [X Y] structure is the kind that Bakhtin (1981) characterizes as above. On the other hand, by marking [X] with *to yuu*, the [X *to yuu* Y] structure offers an opportunity for its producer to explicitly qualify the voice of the producer of [X]. Many of the direct speech features are retained in this "quotative explanation." The two different ways of merging the voices represent what Vološinov (1973) calls "linear style" and "pictorial style." The linear style "construct(s) clear-cut, external contours for reported speech, whose own internal individuality is minimized" (1973:120), while the pictorial style "obliterate(s) the precise, external contours of reported speech" and it includes "not only the referential meaning of utterance, the statement it makes, but also all the linguistic peculiarities of its verbal implementation" (1973:120-121). Although the structures [X *to yuu* Y] and [X Y] resemble "pictorial style" and "linear style" respectively, neither is as clear-cut as depicted by Vološinov (1973). Especially the case of [X *to yuu* Y] is perhaps best understood as quasi-"pictorial style," since [X] can contain only limited aspects of verbal implementation. At any rate we observe here that linguistic devices and rhetorical strategies contribute to the manipulation of varying degrees of merging voices attributable to different language producers. Here I again borrow Bakhtin's words.

> The word used in quotation marks, that is, felt and used as something alien, and the same word (or some other word) without quotation marks. The infinite gradations in the degree of foreignness (or assimilation) of words, their various distances from the speaker. Words are distributed on various planes and at various distances from the plane of the authorial word. (1986:120-121)

The Japanese *to yuu* clause-noun combination represents a place in discourse where reporting and reported voices merge similarly to the case of quotation strategies in literary text.

5. *To Yuu* and the Narrative Voice

Due to the pragmatic characteristics assigned to the *to yuu* clause-noun combination as discussed above, the juncture of [X] and [Y] offers a space where multiple textual voices may be expressed and manipulated. The term "voice" is not unfamiliar in Western literary theory; it is frequently used as in "narrative voice," "dialogized voice" (Bakhtin 1981) and "multivoicedness" (Wertsch 1991). One useful definition of voice is how Bakhtin (1981) conceives it. According to Holquist and Emerson (1981:434), Bakhtin's concept of "voice" refers to "the speaking personality, the speaking consciousness,"--of course, in the context of the Bakhtinian "dialogized voice." In applying this fundamentally psychological concept of "voice" in my analysis, I mean by this term the language producer's-- including the author's, the narrator's and the character's--personal attitude toward the content of the expression, toward the verbal event itself and toward the interacting characters.

For understanding narrative voices, two immediate questions come to mind. First, whose voices are expressed in text? And second, how are these voices linguistically coded? In narrative discourse, the narrator's and the characters' voices constantly intertwine, and yet it is possible to identify whose voice is foregrounded. First, let us examine a case where we primarily hear the narrator's voice as depicted in (18).

(18) After a shipwreck, a man finds himself lying on the shore of a deserted island in the middle of nowhere. Looking for some clues of civilization he climbs a tall tree and looks around. However, there seems to be absolutely no sign of civilization. He comes down from the tree and rests in the shade. Then a new paragraph starts as follows.

(18.1) Nan to yuu koto da.
        what QT say thing BE
        'What a thing (of disaster) this is!'

(18.2) Erai   tokoro e, kite-shimatta.
        terrible place to ended up
        'I've ended up in an awful place.'

(18.3) Karadajuu kara, kiboo to yuu kanjoo ga nukete-yuku.
        whole body from hope QT say feeling S escape
        'A feeling of hope escapes from his whole body.'

(18.4) Otoko wa yakegimide hi o sugoshita.
        man   T desperately day O spent
        'The man spent days in desperation.'

(18.5) Toitte, shi ni chokketsu-suru to yuu jootai
        but   death IO directly connect QT say condition
        dewa-nakatta.
        BE-NEG

```
'But his condition was not so serious as to be directly
linked (threatening) to death.'
```

                         --Hoshi 1976:108

The author uses a stream of consciousness strategy in (18.1) and (18.2) representing the man's feelings directly. (18.3) serves as a transition from the man's consciousness to the narrator's description of the man as given in (18.4) and (18.5). As the phrase *otoko wa* 'the man' in (18.4) indicates, the narrator takes the perspective of an observer offering a description of the man. Given this narrative context, let us pay attention to the only optional *to yuu* found in (18), i.e., *to yuu* in (18.5). If *to yuu* is absent in (18.5), the reader is under the impression that the narrator is simply describing the situation from a distance-- the condition was not linked directly to death. However, when *to yuu* is used as Hoshi (1976) does, the reader is under the impression that the narrator's consciousness is directly involved. Specifically, the narrator qualifies the narrative act itself by saying that the condition is the kind that the narrator himself considers not directly linked to death. In other words, *to yuu* in the [X *to yuu* Y] structure in a narrative can be used to remind the reader that what precedes is the narrator's view representing the narrator's voice. Consequently the reader is made aware of the author's narrative act itself. By marking the [X] with *to yuu*, the feeling of [X]'s direct discourse nature returns, and as a result the narrative act is brought back into the reader's consciousness. The noun-modifying construction in Japanese offers a potential opportunity for the author to mark strongly or weakly his or her narrative presence.

A similar point can be made in the following example.

```
(19) Doa  ga aite, marude ginkoo no madoguchi kara
     door S open  as if back   LK counter   from
     chokusetsu kaketsuketa to yuu yoosu      no, sebiro
     directly   rushed       QT say appearance LK  suit
     sugata       no seinen    ga haitte-kita.
     appearance LK young man S  entered
     'The door opened and a young man clad in a suit entered who
     looked as if he had rushed out directly from behind the
     counter of a bank.'
```

                         --Akagawa 1984a:41

Here *to yuu* bridges the narrator's voice and the description given in (19); by adding *to yuu* the narrator conveys his personal judgment that the visual impression is similar to how one may look when rushing out directly from a bank. The narrator signals that the judgment is his; the reader is made aware that the narrator is there offering his personal judgment. Although one can interpret (19) as expressing the view of the heroine who is observing this young man and the judgment is hers, the argument still holds. [X] is a personalized statement of the heroine, but its voice is controlled by the narrator himself. The fact remains that [X] is not completely incorporated as a subordinate clause into the main clause; one cannot deny the presence of speakerhood in (19).

In short, the use of *to yuu* makes the reader more aware of the reality that a narrator is narrating the story. This heightened awareness of the narrator's presence adds to the story-telling effect. When using the [X *to yuu* Y] structure, then, [X] is syntactically more independent than the [X Y] structure and therefore, more potential exists for expressing aspects of Discourse Modality. Thus, the availability of the two types of noun-modifying construction can offer the choice of two narrative modes; (1) narrator's telling directly to the audience and (2) a defaced narrator telling the story from a distance. As a result, this strategy makes it possible for the author to manipulate between the role of a narrator and the role of a defaced story teller, thus making it possible for the author to freely cross between the narrator's world and the narrated world.

In narrative discourse, the perspective may be also expressed in direct discourse of characters. For example, observe the following.

```
(20.1)   Enban         datta.
         flying saucer BE
         'It was a flying saucer.'

(20.2)   Daga kare wa sahodo        odoroka-nakatta.
         but  he   T  (that) much  was surprised-NEG
         'But he was not too surprised.'

(20.3)   Nazeka, konna koto daroo to yuu yoona ki
         somehow such  fact BE    QT say like  feeling
         ga shita.
         S  did
```

'Somehow, he had the feeling that this perhaps was bound to happen.'

--Hoshi 1980:81

Here the [X] in [X *to yuu* Y] structure belongs to the discourse of the character "he." True, it is the author who controls all the voices in the narrative. However, the nature of direct discourse displayed by the expression *konna koto daroo* 'this perhaps was bound to happen' offers a reasonable basis to interpret it as a direct discourse representing the voice of "he."

The reader may argue that attributing narrative voices to a certain language producer is interpretive, and therefore problematically ad hoc. For example, in both (19) and (20), one can argue the opposite of what I have just described. For example, one can interpret (19) as expressing the view of the heroine who is observing this young man and so one can conclude that the judgment is hers instead of the narrator's. In (19), however, I find a linguistic clue to support the position that the *to yuu* construction signals the narrator's voice. The verb *kaketsuketa* 'rushed' indicates a direction which is unspecified; if the author takes the heroine's perspective, i.e., if the event in (19) is seen from the heroine's perspective, *kaketsukete-kita* 'rushed (toward self)' is likely to be used, instead. Note that the main predicate of (19) takes the directional morpheme -*kita* 'came' as in *haitte-kita* 'entered (toward self).' Similarly in (20), one may argue that the *to yuu* discourse belongs to the narrator's perspective. The expression used, *konna koto* '(lit.) this kind of thing' indicates the direct discourse of the character; if it represents the narrator's voice, the author is likely to use *sonna koto* '(lit.) that kind of thing' instead.

Although it is true that some ambiguities remain as to whose voice is foregrounded, one cannot deny the fact that [X] in the [X *to yuu* Y] structure is not wholly incorporated into the main clause; one cannot therefore deny the presence of the personal voice which is responsible for [X] in (19) and (20). In fact, this ambiguity itself offers evidence that the fictional and/or novelistic discourse does not represent an object-oriented world characterizable by logical or semantic relationships alone. Rather, one finds in the narrative world a mixture and collusion of voices. When quoted speech transforms itself into the narrative text, the text is constructed as a mosaic of quotations. Thus for example in (19), the author manipulates two voices representing two perspectives in one utterance while foregrounding the narrator's voice. In other words, the author has under his or her control several spaces where different voices are foregrounded and the *to yuu* "quotative explanation" offers a mechanism for binding and merging them and consequently creating another.

I propose that at least the following voices are recognizable at the juncture of [X] and [Y] in the "quotative explanation."

1. Narrator's voice,
2. Character's voice,
   a. Character's direct discourse,
   b. Second person discourse (from the perspective of the character),
   c. Third person discourse (from the perspective of the character).

Data (19) and (20) represent cases of [1] and [2a], respectively. (21) and (22) provided below represent cases of [2b] and [2c], respectively.

(21.1)   C no yatsu kimi o urande-iru ze.
         C LK guy you O blame   IP
         'C blames you, you know.'

(21.2)   Kane o nusunde nigeru toki, jibun o ichiban atoni
         money O steal   flee   when self O most   late
         shita to ne.
         did   QT IP
         'When you fled after stealing the money, you left him last.'

(21.3)   Jibun o tsukamae-sase, sono hima ni toosoo-shiyoo
         self O apprehend-CAUS that time in escape
         to yuu tsumori datta no daroo to.
         QT say intention BE   NOM BE   QT
         'And (he thought that) while letting them apprehend him you intended to escape.'

                               --Hoshi 1980:70

(22)   Roojin   de kinodoku da ga kane de keisatsu o
         old person BE pitiful BE but money with police   O
         sayuu-shiyoo to yuu no wa yuruse-nai koto da."
         influence   QT say NOM T forgive-NEG fact BE

'He is an old man and it is pitiful, but one cannot forgive that he tried to influence the police with money.'

--Hoshi 1980:12

Note that in all cases presented above, the language producer's voice is most directly marked by the modal features accompanying the clause [X]. As stated earlier, the environment provided by *to yuu* makes it possible to express modality, and at the same time the narrative modes of "saying" and "describing" are incorporated into each other.

6. Discourse Functions of *To Yuu*

The bridging function of *to yuu* can also offer a discourse organizational function. *To yuu* may bridge more than the clause immediately preceding it. For example, see (23).

(23.1)   Mooree shachoo   wa, Yoshikawa no kaisha o mite,
         Morley President T   Yoshikawa LK company O se
         baka-ni suru   dokoroka,   sukkari
         make a fool of rather than totally
         kanshin-shite-shimatta.
         was impressed
         'President Morley, visiting Yoshikawa's company, was
         very impressed contrary to the expectation that he may
         ridicule it.'

(23.2)   Soshite sooko   ni   haitte, kare ga dashita   hon
         and   warehouse into enter   he   S pulled out book
         o miru ni oyonde, [genga   demo, sore o karaafirumu
         O see at reach   original or   that O color film
         ni shita no ,demo okuru kara, zehi,   Yoshikawa
         IO make one or   send as   by all means Yoshikawa
         ni hon ni shite-hoshii.
         IO book IO want to make
         'And as soon as he (President Morley) entered the
         warehouse and saw the books that he (Yoshikawa) pulled
         out, he (President Morley) proposed by saying, "I will

> send the original paintings or their color films to you
> and I want you to publish them as a book."

(23.3)   Jibun wa sore o oobei   ni urisabaku,]
          self T that O Europe and America IO sell
          to yuu teian   o shita.
          QT say proposal O did
          'I will send them to European countries and the United
          States, he proposed.'

                                              --Miura 1985:27

As reflected in the translation, [X] spans over (23.2) and (23.3) whose boundary
with [Y] is marked by *to yuu*. In other words, *to yuu* signals a discourse segment
of [X] in the [X *to yuu* Y] construction even when [X] involves multi-sentential
segments. If *to yuu* is absent in (23.3), it is likely that only [X] within the same
sentence is directly related to [Y]. The desire expressed in (23.2) and President
Morley's sale in Europe and America are considered separate facts and not
segmented to constitute an identical [X] as described above. Since *to yuu*
functions as a device for interfacing two modes of communication, it can
segment the discourse accordingly, and consequently play a discourse
organizational role across sentential boundaries.

7. Interpersonal Functions of the Variants of *To Yuu*

The functions of *to yuu* discussed so far all point to one basic notion, i.e., the
personalization of discourse. By using *to yuu* when optional, the speaking self
achieves an expression of [X] as his or her personal judgment or attitude. The
modality features appearing in the nominal clause are not the only way in which
the textual voices are expressed, however. *To yuu* provides another strategy, i.e.,
expressing modal features in the *to yuu* expression itself. Exploring this
interactional aspect, in this section I examine variants of *to yuu*. Since *yuu* is a
verb meaning 'to say,' various modal features may accompany it. Instead of
using *to yuu*, one may use a variety of similar forms, for example, *to itta* 'such
that,' *to ka yuu* 'something as,' *to yuu yoona* 'such as,' *to mo ieru* 'something that
can be said as,' and so on. Let us first concentrate on *to itta*. As Fujita (1987)
argues, when *to itta* appears instead of *to yuu*, it expresses the speaker's

qualification on expression in a broader sense. For example, compare the
following examples given by Fujita (1987).

(24) Amerika, huransu, nishi-doitsu | a. *to yuu |
     America   France   West Germany | QT say |
                                        | b. to itta |
                                        | QT said |

     kuni
     country
     'countries such as the United States of America, France,
     West Germany'

(25) Tsutsumi | a. to yuu | otoko
     Tsutsumi | QT say | man
              | b. *to itta |
              | QT said |
     'man called Tsutsumi'

As made evident in (24) and (25), when [X] suggests other possibilities in a
defined set, *to yuu* is not appropriate as in (24a), whereas when [X] is specific
and does not allow other possibilities in a set *to itta* results in inappropriate
form as in (25b). The use of *to itta* then can make the statement [X] less
specific and consequently leaves some room for the semantic option and for a
possible semantic negotiation.

Let us observe an occurrence of *to itta* in fiction shown in (26) and
compare it with (27).

(26)   "...Ichiryuu gaisha   no juuyaku to itta
            top-ranking company LK director QT said
        kanji   no hito   deshita..."
        impression LK person BE
        '...He was the kind of person who gave the impression of
        being a director in a top-ranking company.'

                        --Hoshi 1976:85

(27.1) "Iya, ojisan wa kinodokuna   koto o shimashita nee."
         no   uncle T regrettable fact O did   IP
        'Uh, I'm sorry to know about your uncle's misfortune.'

(27.2)   Dokoka   no kaisha no juuyaku da <u>to yuu</u> taipu
         somewhere LK company LK director BE QT say type
         no sono otoko wa itta.
         LK that man   T said
         'The man who gave the impression of being a director of
         some company said so.'

                                          --Akagawa 1984a:94

The situation of (26) in the narrative is that a taxi driver describes one of the customers he picked up the night before to another customer who is in his taxi tonight. The story develops that in fact the taxi driver believed that the man he picked up the night before was a ghost. By describing the man with some sense of hesitation, saying [X *to itta* Y] in (26), the taxi driver leaves some room for the addressee to question his assessment of the situation. Of course *to yuu* is possible; this will also qualify the statement by personalizing the description. But *to itta* conveys a greater degree of uncertainty on the taxi driver's part--an interactional style more accommodating to the addressee. (27) represents a similar construction except that *to yuu* is used instead. Here the narrator chose to express his assessment of the man being a director with greater certainty; the narrator expresses a personal judgment stronger than the case observed in (26).

Similar arguments can be made for other variants of *to yuu*. For example, *to yuu/itta yoona, to iwareru/iwarete-iru, to ka yuu/itta* and *to mo ieru* all express varying degrees of uncertainty and/or commitment on the speaker's part regarding the content [X]. Therefore, *ichiryuu gaisha no juuyaku da to mo ieru kanji no hito* means 'a person who, I can say, gave the impression of being a director in a top-ranking company.' The availability of a host of variants of *to yuu* adds to the choice as to how the speaking self qualifies the act of speech. By uttering *to yuu* and its variants, the speaking self qualifies, mitigates and foregrounds his or her own voice in the act of discourse creation itself.

Some of the various modal and related pragmatic features coded by variants of *to yuu* in the structure of [X *to yuu* Y] include the following.

1. *To itta, to yuu yoona, to itta yoona*: offer non-specification, express hesitation--as a result pragmatically function as devices to accommodate to others and to show sensitivity to the recipient's feelings.

2. *To iwareru, to iwarete-iru*: signal that [X] represents a view accepted by others, shows little commitment of the speaking self himself or herself; a certain level of objectification of [X] is achieved.

3. *To ka yuu, to mo ieru*: signal doubt, uncertainty and hesitation; pragmatically other-accommodating.

8. *To Yuu* as a Device for Discourse Modality Manipulation

Unlike all other DM indicators examined in this study, *to yuu* functions to connect a clause with a noun to form a complex noun phrase. In other words, *to yuu* offers intrasentential manipulation of Discourse Modality, as it bridges two modes of communicative action, i.e., "saying" and "describing." In terms of Modal Contextualization *to yuu* offers evidence that proposition may be contextualized intrasententially by attaching DM indicators to clauses. Specifically *to yuu* contributes in forming aspects of Discourse Modality as summarized in Figure 7.2.

As a final remark I would like to briefly discuss the implication of our findings to the literary style in Japanese. In literary terms *to yuu* offers an opportunity to express multiple voices of the narrator as well as of characters in the fictional/novelistic discourse. This study has revealed that the *to yuu* "quotative explanation," which in many ways resembles direct speech, is strategically integrated as hidden dialogues into written discourse where a multitude of voices proliferate. Although it is possible to insert phrases comparable to *to yuu* and its variants in English nominal modification--for example, *a person who, I can say, gave the impression of being a director in a top-ranking company*, its usage seems much more restricted. The Japanese language offers an intrasentential location where such operation is routinely performed as we observed in our examples. Note that the *to yuu* clause-noun combination in Japanese achieves the effect similar to quotation more realistically than the [X Y] structure. The availability of this strategy in Japanese may very well be directly correlated to the preference toward direct discourse style observed in Japanese speech and literary discourse.

In fact, although based only on cursory observation, a preference for direct style over indirect style exists in the modern Japanese fictional/novelistic writings. In Maynard (1984) I discussed the functional differences of *to, to yuu*

Figure 7.2. *Summary of Modal Contextualization Effects Realized by To Yuu in the Clause-Noun Combination*

Semantic Source:	Context-bound Meaning Distribution:	Modal Contextualization, Aspects of DM:
To yuu connects between two modes of interaction, "saying" and "describing"	When *to yuu* is optional, [X *to yuu* Y] foregrounds [X] more than the [X Y] structure	1. Information Qualification: Perspective (manipulating narrative voice) / Discourse Cohesion (defining scope of *to yuu* clause)
		2. Speech Action Declaration and Qualification: (manipulating between "saying" and "describing")
		3. Participatory Control: Designing Speaker Turns (variants of *to yuu* offering other-accommodating strategy)

koto o and *koto o* in speech and thought representation in Japanese literary discourse. One of the findings in that study was precisely that such a preference exists in the choice of quotative style. The skewed preference toward direct discourse has a profound influence on literary effect because the direct mode represents the text producer's personal voice more clearly and it allows the reader easy access to modal features of the speech delivery. It is also true that the availability of the quotative explanation offers an environment conducive to mixing different voices intrasententially. This points to the fact that, in Japanese, the shift and maintenance of points of view are less rigidly controlled than in English. As a result, the Japanese language producer and consumer alike are likely to have easy access to the fluidity of viewpoints as expressed by different voices within a single utterance.

In this chapter we have seen that the presence and the absence of optional *to yuu* in the clause-noun combination signals the narrative voice manipulation. When so-called options exist in language and its use, one must search for the reason for each choice. By analyzing *to yuu* as a process of Modal Contextualization within the Discourse Modality framework, we have learned that indeed *to yuu* expresses the speaking self's personal decision as to how to choose between and to combine "saying" and "describing"--the two most basic speech actions we engage in as language manipulators.

Part 3

Reflections

CHAPTER 8

Discourse Modality in Perspective

1. Subjectivity, Emotion and Voice in Language

To state intuitively that language is subjective, emotional and ultimately expresses the speaker's voice offers little in the way of insight, nor is it particularly meaningful. Certainly behind every expression there has to be a person who creates it, and whose voice resonates from it. In this study, by examining some of the Discourse Modality indicators in Japanese, I have provided evidence that it is indeed the case that language, at least some part of its property, serves the primary purpose of expressing subjectivity and emotion. In fact DM indicators have proved to be the kind of linguistic signs whose meanings cannot be understood unless we view them primarily as non-referential, therefore "modal" signs.

Analysis of DM indicators conducted in this study comprises part of the more general analysis of speaker subjectivity as manifested by linguistic expressions. Ultimately we are interested in understanding how the speaking self and the addressee jointly manipulate different types of meanings to make overall sense of what is expressed in language. Our specific concern, however, has been directed toward understanding how the speaking self's discourse modality is coded in the language, and how the speaker's effort to express oneself is reflected in his or her choice of linguistic signs. I have addressed this concern by concentrating on specific linguistic signs, our DM indicators.

While this modality-centered view of language diverts from the dominant theories of modern linguistics, when placed in historical perspective, it presents itself not necessarily as a diversion but as a shift of the pendulum. In fact historically linguists have vacillated between the two views of language; one, the view of language as expression and two, the view of language as a logical referential tool. In this century, with the advent of structuralism, linguistics has been transformed by Bloomfield, Saussure, Chomsky and their followers into the study of the objectifying system. Objectifying language promises control over the domain of its study. Here the meanings are not muddled nor mysterious, but neatly presented; and the theory of language becomes a welcome soldier to enhance the canons of modern natural science.

But as repeatedly stated, 19th century Japan offers a very different perspective. During the Edo period, following the scholars of *kokugaku* 'Japanese studies' such as Motoori Norinaga (1730-1801), the Japanese grammarians perceived language not as *mono* 'thing,' but as *koto* 'event' which requires active participants--both the speaking self and the other. And it was to overcome the rational thinking (which Motoori conceived to be represented by Chinese ways of thinking) that he introduced a concept of emotion *mono-no-aware* 'the pathos of nature, an aesthetic emotion' to unite the events of human life. As being symbolized by Suzuki Akira's phrase, *kokoro no koe* 'voices from the heart,' *kokugaku* 'Japanese studies' found in human emotion the answer for giving meanings to often unrelated and isolated events--including human lives.

19th century Europe also provides a linguist, Wilhelm von Humboldt (1767-1835), whose view in some way resonates with this Japanese tradition. For Humboldt, language is not *ergon* 'product' but *energeia* 'speech, activity'; language is not the already given product but a creative power. Aarsleff, in his introduction to Heath's translation of Humboldt, summarizes Humboldt's view as the following.

> Only by virtue of language do we gain self-awareness, knowledge, and mastery of reality. It is like a second world in which we know both our own selves and the outward face of things, like a middle ground between subjective being and objective existence. This philosophy does not have room for the copy-theory of knowledge; language is not merely designative; it is not representation but expression. (1988:*xix*)

As Humboldt himself claims (Heath 1988:48), when one looks upon language, not as a dead "product," but far more as "producing," one cannot ignore the importance of the speaker and the addressee in the study of language. For in the event/activity-centered view of language, language's essence lies in the "voices from the heart," the will and the emotion of the speaking self which in turn control and define the language's referential function.

In this century also there were voices questioning the linguistic formalism fostered by structuralism. For example, Jesperson stated:

The essence of language is human activity--activity on the part of one individual to make himself understood by another, and activity on the part of that other to understand what was in the mind of the first. These two individuals, the producer and the recipient of language, or as we may more conveniently call them, the speaker and the hearer, and their relations to one another, should never be lost sight of if we want to understand the nature of language and of that part of language which is dealt with in grammar. But in former times this was often overlooked, and words and forms were often treated as if they were things or natural objects with an existence of their own... (1965:17, originally 1924)

Thus it was not the presence of anti-structuralist awareness that was lacking but rather the decision to relegate these voices to the intellectual backwaters of linguistics that has characterized the field over the past half century.

With the increasing acceptance of the so-called post-structuralism, we witness in the West an academic movement which questions the formalization of objectified thoughts and which focuses on the emotionality and the interactionality of language, especially in anthropological linguistics under the heading of "language of affect." As mentioned in chapter 2, works by Ochs and Schieffelin (1985) and Schieffelin and Ochs (1986) exemplify this movement.[1] The field of linguistics itself is beginning to embrace "humanistic linguistics" especially through studies in discourse analysis, conversation analysis, sociolinguistics, pragmatics and so on.

Of course it was not that no linguist in the past paid attention, if only cursory attention, to the affective meaning of language. Vendryes (1925:138) once said that "apart from technical, and especially scientific, language, which by definition is outside ordinary life, the expression of an idea is never free from some emotional tinge," and therefore, the complete content of a sentence "is not exhausted when the words composing it are known and its grammatical elements analyzed." And Vendryes (1925:139) contends that the sentence "still has an effective value which must be taken into account." While pointing out the existence of a variety of feelings and maintaining that the task of understanding these feelings is hardly the linguist's affair, Vendryes (1925:139) still maintains that feelings are indeed the linguist's concern "in so far as they are expressed by means of language." Vendryes suggests a study of an affectivity in language which focuses on two linguistic manipulations; the choice of words and the position they occupy in the sentence.

In retrospect Vendryes' view was correct. For, as we have seen in the study of Japanese DM indicators, emotion is abundantly expressed by the choice of words and the position they occupy not so much in sentences but in context. With a renewed interest in the West in "the emotional," the pendulum is again swinging toward the middle where the two views of language meet. This academic environment offers the possibility of reaching a new kind of awareness--when we maintain the view of language as expression of subjectivity, emotion and voice. If, as Vygotsky claims, in using language in social action we can come to have new thoughts which reach the higher mental functions in the form of "inner speech," then in expressing our feelings and emotions through language, we also come to have new feelings and emotions. By understanding that language is emotionally invested, we can appreciate its role in characterizing us as rational as well as emotional beings. And it is in the context of placing importance to "the emotional" that the present study of Discourse Modality can serve its purpose.

At this point I would like to once again return to the concept of "voice." I have used the term "voice" in two ways; (1) in the general sense of expressing personal attitude and feelings similarly to Suzuki's *kokoro no koe*, and (2) in the sense of narrative voice especially as conceived by Bakhtin in chapter 7. I would like to explore a bit further to appreciate the concept of "voice" emerging as a result of this work. As we have discovered in this work, the voice expressed by DM indicators is not merely a single personal voice. When a person uses an interactional particle *yo*, for example, *yo* does not merely reflect the speaker's interest in focusing on the information in communication. Rather, the very use of *yo*, and therefore the very meaning of *yo*, depends on the partner and the type of discourse (i.e., between social equals or toward social inferiors in casual spoken discourse), the partner's relative accessibility and/or possessorship of relevant information, and on the prior and ensuing discourse in a given social context. In this sense *yo* is both text- and context-dependent. The voice that *yo* expresses then is not a single voice controlled in its totality by the speaker, but rather, it is a collusion of voices. These voices include not only the anticipated and mutually invested partner's voices, but also include the ideological voices of the society itself. For, the availability and the very usage of *yo* are granted by the society which finds a need for it. In this sense, the voice one expresses by manipulating DM indicators is inherently an assemblage of multi-motivated voices.

The voices characterized here may be expressed by the literary term "ambivalence." For example, Kristeva (1980:68) states that the term "ambivalence implies the insertion of history (society) into a text and of this text into history." Additionally, Kristeva states:

> Dialogue appears most clearly in the structure of carnivalesque language, where symbolic relationships and analogy take precedence over substance-causality connections. The notion of ambivalence pertains to the permutation of the two spaces observed in novelistic structure: dialogical space and monological space. (1980:72)

Obviously I am stretching the term "ambivalence" here. But the indeterminate nature of meaning and function of DM indicators within the language system itself attests to the fact that language is, or at least some linguistic devices are more dominantly, ambivalent. The meanings of DM indicators cannot be identified system-internally, i.e., by the Saussurean dichotomy of the "signifier-signified" or the Saussurean notion of "opposition." It is by applying to the social and discourse contextual factors (Kristeva's history [society]) that the meanings of DM indicators can be appreciated. As we saw, it is by incorporating extra-linguistic context--such as conversational exchange, the level of awareness of the other and so on in the place similar to Kristeva's permuted space of dialogical space and monological space--that we comprehend some of the mechanisms of DM indicators. And it is precisely for this reason that DM indicators play such an important role in communication. As indicative of Kristeva's quotation given above, and as more explicitly stated by Bakhtin as given below, it is this symbolic, non-logical and interpersonally-controlled aspect of communication that often overrides all logical relations.

Bakhtin, citing the importance of the active understanding of the word which can be reached only by the assistance of the response from the other, and by dialectically merging the two, writes:

> This new form of internal dialogism of the word is different from that form determined by an encounter with an alien word within the object itself: here it is not the object that serves as the arena for the encounter, but rather the subjective belief system of the listener. Thus this dialogism bears a more subjective, psychological and (frequently) random character, sometimes crassly accommodating, sometimes provocatively polemical.

Very often, especially in the rhetorical forms, this orientation toward the listener and the related internal dialogism of the word may simply overshadow the object: the strong point of any concrete listener becomes a self-sufficient focus of attention, and one that interferes with the word's creative work on its referent. (1981:282)

What DM indicators express are ultimately the voices given life to by the language which is simultaneously subjective, inter-subjective, as well as textual and inter-textual. As Wertsch (1991:13) aptly characterizes, "human communicative and psychological processes are characterized by a dialogicality of voices," and they always represent "multivoicedness."

2. Sources and the Nature of Emotionality and Interactionality

Throughout this study I have maintained that language is emotionally invested and interactionally controlled. I have already suggested some of the psychological and social sources for language to possess these characteristics. Let us explore further the cognitive, psychological and social sources of the modal nature of language.

Searching for cognitive sources, we can return to our earlier discussion of Watsuji (1935, 1937) and Mori (1979). The philosophical themes developed by Watsuji and Mori promote an interpersonal association and concern for the "other." Thus language, being the primary means for communication, must offer ways to provide for such concerns.

In addition to the thoughts advocated by Watsuji and Mori, Doi's psychological characterization of Japanese offers an insight in our search for the motivation for Discourse Modality. It is the desire for *amae* 'psychological and emotional dependence' that encourages the use of a variety of non-referential linguistic signs as those investigated in this study. As Doi (1971) proposes, *amae* is a key concept for the understanding not only of the psychological makeup of the individual Japanese but of the structure of Japanese society as a whole. In Japanese society great importance is attached to closed ethical organizations and groups within which one identifies oneself. This world where *amae* is allowed and encouraged, according to Doi (1971:76, my translation), "has the function of seeking to 'melt down' others by *amae* and make them lose their *tanin* 'other' quality." The desire for psychological and emotional dependence on someone else foregrounds communication on the emotional level and therefore the role Discourse Modality plays in language increases in its importance.

Doi (1971, 1976) asserts that fragmented and ambiguous expressions coupled with hesitant utterance endings in the Japanese communicational style are reflections of the Japanese desire for *amae*. Given the desire for *amae*, DM indicators are ideally suited to achieve it, since they facilitate a sharing of the ebb and flow of emotion that characterize *amae* relationships. Often the non-propositional meanings which represent all aspects of Discourse Modality actually dominate the communication, even to the extent that they effectively obscure the propositional content. The non-autonomous view of self among Japanese psychologically motivates the speaker to utilize a higher level Discourse Modality. When, to a greater intensity, one's cognitive and psychological well-being depends on the other's feelings and attitudes, one is most likely to utilize as many aspects of Discourse Modality as possible in order to guarantee that each encounter becomes psychologically and emotionally rewarding.

In pursuing these psychological and social factors further, it is perhaps useful to examine additional terms often used in analyzing Japanese psychology and society. The distinction between *uchi* 'insider, in-group' and *soto* 'outsider, out-group' has served to explain a variety of Japanese behavioral patterns. Among in-group members in Japan, a reciprocal *amae* relationship allows members to express emotion and feelings directly, even sometimes in a manner considered rude by outsiders. In this warm, all-forgiving environment Japanese typically use direct discourse with little awareness of the addressee as the "other" opposing one's self. Some DM indicators we analyzed, for example, abrupt forms of the verb followed by interpersonal particles--can add to enhance this style because they add emotional features to one's expression. Toward persons outside of one's own group Japanese normally show formal politeness. Here the speaker must be extra cautious not to hurt or offend the addressee's feelings. And again, DM indicators can play a major role since they provide a means for meeting the politeness requirements.

The style shift between formal politeness and friendly directness is an important part of Japanese communication. This shift must be appreciated in the juxtaposition of two social axes, social differentiation on one hand and the desire for *amae* on the other. While these two social factors pull in different directions--psychological distance versus closeness--, both call for non-referentially based manipulation. Both are rooted in the same assumption that places utmost importance on the emotionality and interactionality of language. Obviously the fact that a sharp social distinction exists between *uchi* and *soto* provides evidence that self-identification is based on the other, especially on the fact of whether or not the other person belongs to a specific group. In other words, the other-dependence of self-identification, coupled with other-dependence on psychological and emotional *amae*, both based on the concept of group-belongingness, necessitate the expression of emotion by linguistic signs such as, among others, DM indicators.

Perhaps the strongest social motivation for the sensitivity expressed in Discourse Modality lies in the social expectation depicted by the term "face-work" by Goffman (1955). According to Goffman (1955), for communication to function appropriately one must be able to experience an effective "line." Goffman (1955:213) defines line as "a pattern of verbal and nonverbal acts by which he expresses his view of the situation and through this his evaluation of the participants, especially himself." When effective lines operate, participants can achieve successful "face-work" where nobody loses face and everyone's positive face (including the speaker's own) is mutually maintained. It is obvious that the desire for successful "face-work" exists among all social beings. What one is willing to sacrifice in order to achieve successful facework, however, may differ from society to society and from individual to individual. Japanese, especially, but not limited to, in formal situations, are known to be exceedingly sensitive to social "facework."

Many sociological and anthropological studies on Japan have suggested that the Japanese behave in such a way as to express great sensitivity to the surrounding context, including the participants and their views toward each other. Many studies, suggesting an association between linguistic features and the social orientation in Japan, have taken similar views (Doi 1971, 1976, 1985; Itasaka 1971a; Monane and Rogers 1977; Ogasawara 1972; Suzuki 1978, Honna and Hoffer 1989). For example, Japanese people are said to be constantly preoccupied with how others feel, which Haga (1985:65) characterizes with the expression *taijinteki na choowa* 'harmony with others.'

Lebra (1976) points out similar characteristics with the term "*omoiyari* culture." According to Lebra (1976), since *omoiyari* 'consideration for others' requires suppression of one's own wishes when opposed by the other, often the Japanese speaker fully expresses a thought only after the listener's positive response is received. Specifically in reference to the final particle *ne*, for example, Lebra states:

The fear of deviating from Alter's viewpoint, or the wish to maintain consensus with Alter, is further demonstrated by the frequency with which Ego interjects his speech with particle *ne* ("isn't it?"), which sounds as if he is soliciting Alter's agreement. Here, not merely external conformity but inner agreement is being demanded. If properly empathetic, Alter assures and reassures Ego of his receptivity, congeniality, or agreement by frequently nodding and exclaiming, "I am listening," "That is so!" or "Yes." (1976:39)

These characteristics of the Japanese represented by a large volume of work enumerating similar characterizations all point to the direction of a modality-centered view of language. Discourse Modality, then, as in all languages, but perhaps more strongly, remains a primary concern for Japanese communication participants.

At this point we should remind ourselves of an important aspect closely associated with the DM indicators and their psycho-social nature. As suggested already in this study, it is not simply that DM indicators reflect already established psycho-social relationships between the speaker and the addressee. Rather, by virtue of selecting certain DM indicators, or more accurately, by virtue of the fact that the speaker feels it appropriate to select certain DM indicators, the very relationship can be created. As stated by Tokieda (1951), some of the Japanese *ji*--particles and auxiliary verbs in particular--help form intricate and complex interpersonal relationships. Our DM indicators, for example, using *doose*, or choosing *da* style, create and transform constantly changing interpersonal relationships by adding different types and degrees of emotional tone. In this sense emotion is created and transformed by language as it negotiates its way through the interpersonal relationship of which it is a part.

3. Personalization of Discourse and the Structure of the Japanese Language

The functions of DM indicators observed throughout this work may be most clearly understood in the light of what I have been referring to as "personalization of discourse." We can think of a continuum with the most personalized on one extreme, and on the other, the least personalized.

Depending on the quality and magnitude of DM indicators used, each utterance can be placed on this continuum of personalization. The continuum of personalization is also useful in characterizing a genre or a type of discourse. The more intimate the discourse, the more intimacy-encouraging personalization is needed, and therefore the more DM indicators to express interpersonal closeness are likely to be used--as in intimate face-to-face conversation. The more formal the discourse, the more polite and/or other-accommodating personalization is expected. Therefore more DM indicators are likely to be chosen to express social tact and interpersonal courtesy.

Personalized discourse uses various interactional Discourse Modality strategies and creates a highly emotionally invested style of communication. The kind of text with objective description as the main goal, on the other hand, normally contains the least number of DM indicators--as in, for example, a scientific text. This is because in an environment where one's interest lies in knowledge rather than human interaction, depersonalization becomes more appropriate.

Although at first glance the highly personalized discourse may seem to lack logical persuasion and therefore lack authority and power, ironically the reverse is true. Since highly personalized discourse is closely owned by the speaker, its validity can not be logically challenged. One can ignore but cannot "negate" the other's personal and subjective point of view. No one can speak in place of the "other," for one's voice is empowered only by oneself. The highly personalized communication style requires that one must also accept other's personalization. The high level of subjective interaction then necessitates the interactants to exercise sensitivity toward others, which encourages the other-dependency. The characterization of the Japanese view of self and society discussed earlier is intricately connected with the orientation of the Japanese language which encourages a high level of personalization.

This observation brings us to another aspect of the personalization scale. Differences in the levels of personalization are not limited to genre. It is likely that different languages have access to different levels of personalization. While obviously personalization itself is universal among languages, the ready availability of and acceptance (or even encouragement) toward a high degree of personalization differ from one genre to another and from one language to another. The Japanese language, equipped with a variety of DM indicators, ranks high among personalization-oriented languages. One may view Japanese discourse--at least certain genres of Japanese--as highly subjective with the ultimate goal of communication being the expression of one's emotion and voice.

The degree of importance Discourse Modality plays may also change through time. A variety of historical factors may play a role in shifting language to be more or less modality- or proposition-centered. For example, as Onoe (1982) suggests, in modern Japanese the decline of grammatical *kakarimusubi* 'grammatical adverb-predicate correspondence' which was abundant in classical Japanese attests to the fact that the same language may shift through time between the polarities of the personalization scale.

It was through our investigation of DM indicators that the high personalization level of modern Japanese is empirically supported. But if this essentially is the nature of Japanese language, this high level of personalization is likely to be witnessed in other characteristics as well. I suspect the Japanese's well-known topic-comment structure holds a key to this inquiry.[2]

According to Li and Thompson (1976), while English is subject-predicate prominent, Japanese is typologically characterized as both subject-predicate and topic-comment prominent. Indeed as is widely known the concept of topic-comment plays an important role in the structure of the Japanese language. For one, Japanese has a surface topic marker *wa* (among others), which overtly marks the topic. Besides, as noted by Mikami (1972) the traditional sense of subject and predicate does not play an important grammatical role as it is witnessed in the absence of grammatical person (subject-predicate) agreement. In fact Mikami (1972) goes to the extent to deny the existence of the grammatical subject in Japanese and emphasizes the difference between Japanese and European languages on the basis of *daijutsu kankei* 'topic-comment or theme-rheme' and *shujutsu kankei* 'subject-predicate.' Naturally, both topic-comment and subject-predicate play important roles in Japanese and English. The question at hand, however, is which dominates and which emerges as the primary axis in the structure of the language. If the topic-comment proves to be the dominant axis, and when the language provides linguistic devices to express this preference, the language as a whole will bear such features. That is, since topic is basically an information-based unit, the syntactic relationship of subject-predicate may be overridden by the topical structure, and those devices that have little to do with the subject-predicate relationship are likely to be abundantly available.

In Japanese it seems that the language user is primarily interested in offering commentary on a set topic rather than describing the world in terms of subject-predicate. The relative prominence in topic-comment relationship makes it easier to personalize the discourse since the very function of offering comments is subjectively controlled. Running the risk of gross simplification, I think it is possible to characterize one of the cognitive characteristics of the Japanese language in contrast with English as shown in Figure 8.1.

Figure 8.1. *The Relationship among the Speaking S(elf), the A(ddressee) and the T(hird-person) within the P(ossible) W(orld)*

Japanese Language Situation: English Language Situation:

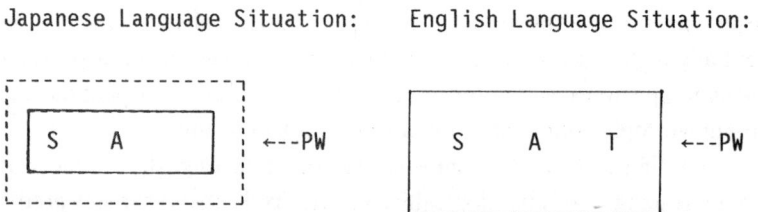

As Figure 8.1 shows, in Japanese, the speaking S(elf) and the A(ddressee) are mutually reflected in each other, thereby creating a distinct world within the P(ossible) W(orld), the world one perceives to exist. In fact the strong interdependence between S and A is substantiated by our earlier discussion on the Japanese non-autonomous self in relation to Mori's (1979) idea of "thy thou" and the "binary rapport." The main concern for S is simply that S create a world with A with little regard given to its immediate and direct significance in P-W. The lack of a clearly defined personal pronoun system in Japanese may be rooted in the way Japanese speakers typically place themselves in the perceived world as depicted here. It is also widely known, as Suzuki (1978) points out, that Japanese self-referencing terms take "other-oriented self-designation"; a middle-aged male, for example, refers to himself as a "teacher" when addressing a student, an "uncle" when addressing a small child, and so on. It is true that a similar use of referential terms is observed in English, but its use is far more limited. In these encounters, the Japanese speaker and the addressee form an immediate universe where the identification of each of whom depends on the partner. In fact actual use of pronouns such as *watashi* 'I' and *anata* 'you' are considerably limited.

On the other hand in English the speaker is most concerned with observing and describing the world within which the speaker finds S, A and T(hird-person). In fact the speaker usually finds S located in the world as an objective self, which constitutes a part of the world. The three-way personal pronoun system in English offers evidence that this distinction is one of importance. In English the way to describe this possible world is primarily through subject-predicate axis. Thus it becomes important to observe the event in such a way as to clarify who does what to whom. In fact the grammatically required subject-predicate axis forces the speaker to characterize the world based on this relationship. This restriction does not exist in Japanese. Comment is offered toward the subject, object, locative or whatever is relevant at the time of communication. The topic-comment structure and the lack of a dominant three-way personal pronoun system both seem to offer opportunities for easier personalization of the discourse. The subject matter to be expressed by the Japanese language is free from the strict subject-predicate system in which the participants must be identified within a tripartite pronoun system.

While obviously what I describe above requires further substantiation, I feel that the characterization depicted above touches upon the essence of the Japanese language. In fact a more substantial work such as Ikegami (1981) can offer additional support here. Based on contrastive analysis of various grammatical features, Ikegami (1981) contends that the Japanese language is a BECOME-language in contrast with English being a DO-language. While the English language requires an identification of who does what to whom and describes the event as "someone DO-ing something to someone," Japanese tends to describe the world as a changing state conceived as a whole, i.e., "the state is BECOME-ing another state." In Japanese the general description of a specific state may take the subject-predicate grammatical structure but such a grammaticization process is not required. In fact the speaker and the addressee can choose to observe the perceived world from a distance, as it changes itself. The topic-comment structure seems to be well-suited for this non-involvingly passive observer. For a Japanese person then the main concern lies not in the description of who does what to whom, but in the immediate human interaction which may be non-committing to the P-W. This kind of manifestation of thought encourages, and often requires, personalization through DM indicators.

In my statement above I do not mean, however, that Japanese "uniquely" expresses personalization of discourse. A personalization process exists in all languages and the interpersonal relationship mediated by such a process is coded in each and every language. What has become evident in this study is simply that the Japanese language is equipped with DM indicators which facilitate certain aspects of personalization and that the intentions, means and degree of personalization strategies differ from English.

4. Discourse Modality in Cross-cultural Communication

Throughout this study little has been said about the consequences of what our view may bring to cross-cultural communication. Although every language is equipped with DM indicators, for the reason of being what they are, some DM indicators pose problems in translation across speech communities. Of course no one would deny that communicating across languages and cultures in general can cause misunderstandings. The misunderstandings in terms of referential meanings are often clearly definable and therefore can be (one hopes) satisfactorily resolved. The kind of misunderstandings in Discourse Modality, however, can impose serious problems upon communication in that participants' emotional involvement is at stake. Unlike grammatical mistakes, which can be dismissed simply as lack of knowledge, non-referential signs in general can cause serious communication problems. For example, as I stated elsewhere (Maynard 1989:223), interactional signs in conversation such as head movement and back-channel expressions are more likely to be interpreted as a social style readily identified with the personality of the participant. This point was made by Erickson (1984) in his discussion of the difference in interactional styles between black and white Americans. According to Erickson,

> In these troublesome encounters, persons fail to understand one another's intentions, fail to get their points across and, more often than not, make unjustified negative evaluations of the sincerity, interest, intelligence and motivation of other parties in interaction. (1984:82)

The gravity of cross-cultural misunderstandings as depicted here can become increasingly more serious as we recognize that beyond the interactional style, another non-referential aspect of communication, i.e., Discourse Modality, poses a potential threat.

To illustrate some of the difficulties of communicating Discourse Modality, let me cite two examples from Japanese fiction and contrast the original

Japanese with English translation.[3] The first is taken from Abe Kobo's *Tanin no Kao 'The Face of Another.'*

At this point in the novel, the protagonist "I" is looking for someone from whom he can have a mask of his face modeled. He spots a man in a dining hall and asks if the man is willing to do him a favor. The man shows some interest. "I" responds:

> "That's a weight off my mind. I can still move my seat, but these waitresses are so sullen. However, before I do, I've just one promise I'd like you to make. Since I'll not ask you anything about you or your work, you're not to ask about me."
> "There's no work to ask about," he said, "and if I don't know anything I can save the trouble of excuses later."

--Saunders 1966:73

The underlined segment is the translation of the original Japanese as given in (1) below.

(1.1) "Doose kiite-itadaku yoona shokugyoo ja-nai.
      anyway have someone hear such as occupation BE-NEG

(1.2) Soreni shira-nakya atode dareka ni iiwake-suru
      besides know-NEG-COND later someone IO offer an excuse
      tema mo habukeru wake da shi ne."
      trouble also avoid reason BE and IP

--Abe 1968:85

The translation of (1) in English does not accurately communicate the emotional involvement felt in Japanese as evoked by the modal adverb *doose* in (1.1). As discussed in chapter 4, *doose*'s meaning is attitudinal. The feeling of being overpowered by fate (as characterized by the Surrendering unto Fate interpretation) is reflected to some degree in the English translation of 'there's no work to ask about.' But the emotional response *doose* evokes in the original Japanese is difficult to locate in this translation. The almost desperate helplessness of not being able to hold a worthy occupation and his resigning attitude expressed in (1.1) is not evoked fully by the English translation. In fact by adding *doose*, the speaker hopes to evoke some sympathy from the addressee; the speaker is indirectly sending a signal that he wants to feel emotionally connected in some way to the addressee. The feeling invested in (1.1) may be expressed as : 'Heck, don't waste your breath on me. My work isn't anything worth talking about, anyway.'

Let us take another example from Ooe Kenzaburo's novel *Kojintekina Taiken 'A Personal Matter.'* At this point in the novel, the protagonist meets a man at the hospital, the man who also has a handicapped child and who had to continue his fight to save the child. The English translation and original Japanese version follow.

"You've got to give them a battle, you know, fight! fight! fight!" he said. "It's a fight with the hospital, especially the doctors! Well, I really let them have it today, you must have heard me."

--Nathan 1969:102

(2.1) "Anata tatakawa-nakya dame <u>desu</u> yo. Tatakawa-nakya.
        you   fight-NEG-COND bad BE   IP   fight-NEG-COND
        Faito! Faito! Faito!" to kootoko wa yuu no datta.
        fight   fight   fight   QT small man T say NOM BE

(2.2) "Faito, byooingawa   to   no faito <u>desu</u> yo. Tokuni
        fight hospital side with LK fight BE   IP   especially
        isha   to   takakawa-nakereba! Watashi wa kyoo,
        doctor with must fight   I   T today
        zuibun   <u>tatakatta</u> yo. Anta kiita <u>deshoo</u> ga."
        very much fought   IP   you heard BE   but

--Ooe 1981:120

In the original Japanese the sentence-final forms within the quotation vary in an interesting way. Among utterances which end with verbals, the only *da*-ending utterance is the expression, *watashi wa kyoo, zuibun tatakatta yo.* Admittedly the *da*-ending verb is followed by an interactional particle *yo*, and therefore it is not a naked *da* form. It is obvious, however, that this utterance is not designed with strong awareness of "thou," which will require the *desu/masu* form as in fact the case at other locations. The distinct feeling evoked by this style, that of directness, friendliness and that of a somewhat self-addressed confession is identical to the naked *da* form. This feeling is not communicated fully in the English translation; English translation indicates no stylistic shift and as a result, the speaker's intention to reveal the self by *da*-ending form as if the addressee is a closer and familiar person remains uncommunicated. Of course English is equipped with devices to express similar intentions. In fact the translator uses a comma to unite the two last separate sentences in (2.2) in his English translation. This strategy reflects the original *da* style in *tatakatta yo*--which is uttered with low awareness of the other--somewhat successfully. Still, this strategy does not fully convey the effect of the stylistic change witnessed in the original Japanese. One may characterize the feeling expressed in the *da*-ending utterance in (2.2) as: 'Oh, yeah! I sure gave them a good fight today! You heard me fight, didn't you?'

As we noted above, the gap in the emotional response that a word such as *doose* evokes is not easily communicated. The same can be said for the stylistic mixture which conveys different levels of the other-awareness. Aspects of Discourse Modality are difficult to be accurately trans-appreciated across languages and cultures. And it is precisely for this reason the study of Discourse Modality with a modality-centered view of language can potentially make a significant contribution to the issues surrounding cross-cultural communication.

For, as we are all aware it is in and by language with its Discourse Modality as its essential ingredient that one projects oneself in the face of another; it is this language that makes possible human emotions and thought. Projecting oneself cross-culturally requires a special kind of awareness because when doing so, the dimensions of the projection become altered. And more problematically, the very means of self-projection, the language itself, also takes a different personality. Study of language as a broad-based interaction as captured in part by aspects of Discourse Modality can help reveal some of the often ignored emotional investment and divestment in cross-cultural communication.

In future, other languages may be examined from the Discourse Modality perspective to reveal how and to what degree personal voices and emotion are coded in different languages. Such studies will also reveal in what ways DM indicators not only reflect but also constitute reality in cross-cultural relationships.

5. Concluding Remarks

At the beginning of this book three goals were stated. First was to propose a possible new theoretical framework of Discourse Modality for analyzing the "expressiveness" of language, which I did in chapter 2. The second goal, to analyze several of the Discourse Modality indicators, was achieved in the ensuing analysis segments of the book, i.e., chapters 3 through 7. I examined selected DM indicators, i.e., modal adverbs *yahari/yappari* and *doose*, discourse connectives *dakara* and *datte*, sentence-final forms *da* versus *desu/masu* endings, interactional particles *yo* and *ne*, and finally, *to yuu* in the clause-noun combination. Our third goal was to introduce traditional Japanese scholarship, which I hope I have sufficiently achieved throughout the work. The literature review for each DM indicator has included Japanese precursors' works, some of which represent traditional *kokugogaku* studies. I have incorporated some traditional Japanese philosophical works as a foundation for my idea of Modal Contextualization. I have also searched for the cognitive and social sources for the existence and the use of DM indicators based on some of the Japanese scholarship.

Although the goals set forth at the beginning of the study have been reasonably achieved, results of the present work constitute only a partial analysis of DM indicators. Many DM indicators including paralinguistic DM strategies and syntactic DM strategies were not analyzed at all. Obviously much remains to be studied. Future research into Discourse Modality must address other DM indicators, especially paralinguistic DM strategy of intonation since intonation is known to play an important role in communicating speaker attitudes.

In terms of the theoretical perspective, I have explored an avenue of analyzing language in terms of the process of Modal Contextualization. Modal Contextualization is a concept that various DM aspects provide contexts for the interpretation of the propositional meaning. I used the concept of scene to locate a place where the semantic integration of DM aspects and proposition takes place. I have emphasized that the meaning of DM indicator does not exist a priori, waiting to be discovered in the objectified world. Only by using structures and frameworks available in discourse analysis and other related fields, could I locate its meaning and function. The meaning of DM indicator is understood only in reference to its actual text and context.

I used some of the discourse structures and frameworks as points of reference. But I do not take the position that structure exists a priori and the researcher's task ultimately lies in its discovery--which is the fundamental tenet of structuralism. Instead, my goal has been to explain the reason why DM indicators are used in the first place and how they come to mean (or imply) what they mean. The structure and the concepts were used only to realize this goal.

The nature of meaning of DM indicators reported in this study suggests that a theory of meaning must in some way be able to account for the non-referential semantics, personal intentions and interpersonal expectations. Establishing a general theory to account for all these simultaneously is indeed a formidable, if not impossible, task. This is partly because once we rescue and (re)introduce the concept of the speaking person in the study of linguistics, his or her sociocultural diversity comes into play. The philosophical differences across time and space become so wide-spread that the sweeping generalization which was once possible at the expense of the obscured speaking self now becomes almost impossible.

As we have discussed, cross-cultural variation exists in the very definition of the self and such difference warrants care in analyzing language and in building a theory of language. Since the psychological makeup of self and society is an integral part of language and its study, the linguistic research itself must be accountable to the psycho-social context of that community. At the same time, the theory itself is conceived by a researcher who is bound by some, out of the many cross-culturally diverse, psycho-social contexts. Thus, ultimately theory building must be conducted in such a way as to answer this diversity; it must avoid comforting dependence on pre-determined models and already available theories. Forcing ready-made theories on every language can only distort the true picture. Perhaps the goal of the study of language and communication--at least in the initial stage--should be to explore multiple theories, rather than hurriedly endorse and cling to a one and only "universal" theory. As suggested in this study, a theory of language is, at least in part, an outcome of one's view toward self. And since we the researchers are products of different cultures and academic philosophies of our time, our theories and disciplines are themselves particular to the culture and society. For this reason, differing views toward language including the view that has emerged in this study must be received not with tolerance but with a ready acceptance.

I am not advocating an extreme relativist view--as expressed by empty claims such as "everyone is entitled to his or her own theory," or "linguistic activity is unique at every occasion, and therefore there is no possibility to make some generalization." Obviously not all theories are equally meaningful and a certain degree of generalization is prerequisite to research.

But this does not justify an extreme universalist position either, which claims that one linguistic theory can be forced on all human languages. When faced with linguistic, cultural, social and philosophical diversity across speech communities, our answer seems to lie in the process of dialogic exploration of differing views toward language. In this process we will proceed to hold a more all-embracing and tempering view toward language itself. Hence I put forward my analysis of Discourse Modality as an attempt to offer an emotion- and interaction-based view of language derived from analysis of modern Japanese, which I hope will become one voice among many voices in language research. And, more specifically, I hope the study reported here helps gain insight into the diverse ways the Japanese language as an expression of voices comes to mean what it means through its subjective and emotional subtext.

Appendix 1

Plot of the story "A Large-headed Robot":
  (The number appearing in parenthesis is the sequential number assigned to each sentence in the story, which corresponds to the number given in data set (5) in chapter 7. The underlined English portion roughly corresponds to the [X *to yuu* Y] expression of the original Japanese.)

Mr. N was a very fortunate person with money and talent who owned his own business. But he had two personality flaws: (3) being forgetful and not trusting others. He needed a secretary who could remember important things for him (5) because he was forgetful, but he was also plagued with fear that his secretary might expose important information to others. Having money and talent, he resolved this problem by building a robot-secretary. The robot accurately remembered everything he said. (23) Mr. N's forgetful personality could be compensated by the robot. Besides, since it is a robot, it won't be bribed by an industrial spy, Mr. N. thought.

So one day Mr. N takes the robot to a bar where it tells the waitresses that Mr. N is planning to evade his taxes. Mr. N realized that although the robot would not betray him, it would answer any questions asked by any person. Mr. N developed a system in which the robot would respond only to his own voice. The robot's head grew in size with this new technological improvement. But one day Mr. N discovered that the kids from the neighborhood recorded his voice and used it to get the robot to respond to them. So, in order to solve this problem Mr. N taught the robot a password. But one day Mr. N overhears the robot muttering a response to what he thinks he said in his sleep.

Mr. N now developed a system that unless a person inserts a key and says the password the robot will not respond. Again the robot's head grew in size due to the additional improvement. But (82) being forgetful, Mr. N frequently forgot the key. So, in order to solve this problem, this time Mr. N develops a system attached to the nose of the robot which identifies the fingerprint of Mr. N's right index finger. But he was worried that someone may make an artificial finger which has a fingerprint identical to his. Thus he installed in the robot's head an additional system that responds only to the fingerprint of a real finger.

Mr. N finally felt secure and began drinking to celebrate. But he drank too much and began staggering around the room. For a moment Mr. N. held onto the robot which now had such a large head that it easily lost its balance. The robot fell on Mr. N and smashed Mr. N's right index finger.

Nowadays Mr. N is leading a miserable life. None of the good ideas Mr. N made the robot remember was in Mr. N's forgetful mind. However hard Mr. N begs the robot to speak, the robot fails to utter even a single word. (Hoshi 1982:37-43, my translation)

Notes

CHAPTER 1

[1] This quote is my translation of Tokieda's words: "--*Mottomo kyakutaiteki sonzai to kangaerare yasui gengo wa mottomo shutaiteki naru mata shinteki naru sonzai toshite kangaenakereba naranai koto ni naru*." The word *shinteki* is difficult to translate into a single English word. The word *shin* (or *kokoro*) in Japanese refers not only to mental and psychological activity, but also spirit, knowledge, emotion and consciousness.

[2] The order of first and last names of Japanese scholars in the present work follows the Japanese convention (of last name appearing first) unless it is conventionalized to be otherwise, as in the field of linguistics.

[3] In Watsuji's original work: *Son no honrai no igi wa shutaitekina jikohoji dearu. ... "Zai" no honrai no igi wa shutai ga aru basho ni iru koto dearu. ... Tokorode shutai no iru basho wa yado, taku, goo, yo nado no shakaitekina basho dearu. Iikaereba kazoku, mura, machi, seken to yuu gotoki ningenkankei dearu. Shitagatte zai wa shutaiteki ni koodoosuru mono ga nanraka no ningenkankei no naka o kyoraishi-tsutsu, sono kankei ni oite aru koto ni hokanaranai.*(22-23) *Sonzai to wa masani aidagara to shite no shutai no jikohaaku, sunawachi ningen ga kore jishin o motsu koto dearu. Wareware wa sarani kantanni sonzai to wa "ningen no kooiteki renkan" dearu to ieru dearoo.*

[4] In Mori's words: *Sate watashi wa, "nihonjin" ni oite "keiken" wa hukusuu o, sarani tantekini wa hutari no ningen (aruiwa sono kankei) o teigisuru to itta. Sore wa ittai nani o imishite-iru no dearoo ka. Hutari no ningen o teigisuru, to yuu koto wa, wareware no keiken to yobu mono ga, jibun ikko no keiken ni made bunsekisare enai, to yuu koto dearu. ... Honshitsutekina ten dake ni kagitte yuu to, "nihonjin" ni oite wa, "nanji" ni tairitsusuru no wa "ware" dewa-nai to yuu koto, tairitsusuru mono mo mata aite ni totte no "nanji" na no da, to yuu koto dearu. ... Oyako no baai o tote-miru to, oya o "nanji" to shite toru to, ko ga "ware" dearu no wa jimei no koto no yooni omowareru. Shikashi sore wa soo dewa-nai. Ko wa jibun no naka ni sonzai no konkyo o motsu "ware" dewa-naku, toomen "nanji" dearu oya no "nanji" to shite jibun o keikenshite-iru no dearu.*

[5] According to Kristeva (1980:74), Francis Ponge offers his own variation of "I think therefore I am": "I speak and you hear me, therefore we are." The view presented here by Mori and the view I subscribe to may be best characterized as "you hear me as I speak, therefore we are."

[6] For detailed discussion of the procedures for the collection of casual conversational data and its preparation for analysis, see Maynard (1989), chapter 2.

CHAPTER 2

[1] The translation of Japanese grammatical terms is problematic, to say the least. Particularly the term *chinjutsu* has been used by linguists in so many different ways that it is difficult to find one, single appropriate English equivalence. *Chinjutsu* has been translated as 'predicate' and 'modal' or 'modality' most frequently. In order to avoid further confusion, I will continue to translate *chinjutsu* as 'modality.'

[2] Although in *Ayuishoo* Fujitani explains poetry by using *satogoto* 'spoken Japanese of the time,' the main purpose of his study, and all other *kokugogaku* studies of the period for that matter, was to provide a manual for the better and deeper interpretation and appreciation of Japanese literature, especially the classical *tanka* poetry.

[3] In Fujitani's words: *Mata iwaku, uchiai wa kono shoo no joo gotoni yuu ga gotoku, sono ayui gotoni sadameru nori aru uchini, "nabikizume," "kakusu uchiai" no hutatsu arite bechi ni yomubeki yoo ari. "Nabikizume" to wa, ooyoso yosoi, ayui no nabiki wa kanarazu "zo-ie," moshiwa utagai no kazashi, ayui nado ni uchiau beki o, samonakute yomitsumetaru o yuu. Kore wa kokoro o hukumete nagame sutsuru nari. Nabiki no shita ni "koto yo" "koto kana," aruiwa "mono o" nade kuwaete kokoroubeshi. ... "Kakusu uchiai" to wa, "zo-ie" wa shita ni uchiau bekiyoo sadamareru o, sadakani yomitsumezu shite yomimote yuku o yuu.*

[4] In his English translation of *Gengyo Shishuron*, Bedell (1968) chooses English phrases different from my translation. For example, Suzuki's term *kokoro no koe* is translated as "gesture (words)" in Bedell (1968:238) where he translates: "When we examine the particles in comparison with the other three categories, we see that the latter have reference, whereas the former have none. The latter are concept words, whereas the former are gesture words. The latter become concept words by referring to things, whereas the former are gestures which attach to the concept words." Although I am aware that any translation is potentially misleading, I find the term "gesture (words)" a bit strained; I will use the term "voices from the heart" throughout this study.

[5] In Yamada's words: *Shi wa te-ni-o-ha to tano shi tono kubetsu o tada hiyu o motte ieru nomi naru ga yueni, sono hongi wa tsuini hosokusuru koto kanawazaru nari. Sonouchi hikakutekini teigi ni chikaki mono o toreba "shi ni tsukeru kokoro no koe" to yuu koto nari. Kokoro no koe to wa ikanaru mono ka. Shisoo o arawasu seion no gi ka. Shikaraba izureno go ka kokoro no koe narazaru. Shi ni tsukeru kokoro no koe to wa tsuini kaishaku subekarazaru nari.*

[6] In Tokieda's words: *Sasu tokoro to wa gainenka kyakutaika no i deari, kokoro no koe to wa, kannen naiyoo no chokusetsuteki hyoogen o imisuru mono to kaisanakereba naranai. Watashi wa ima, jiko no ronriteki ketsuron kara mite, Akira no setsu o tadashi to suru no dewa-naku, mushiro, subete kokugogakushi o choosashite Akira no gakusetsu o ginmishita sai, kare no tootatsushita shisoo ga, taisei no gengogakusetsu no imada itarie-nakatta ue ni dete-iru koto ni kyootanshi, soko ni keihatsusarete, koko ni ronritekini kare no gakusetsu no tenkai o kokoromita no dearu. Yamada Yoshio hakase ga Akira no setsu o hyooshite, sono hongi wa tsuini hosokusuru koto*

kanawazaru nari to iware, kokoro no koe to wa ikanaru mono ka. Shisoo o arasasu seion no gi ka, shikaraba izure no go ka kokoro no koe narazaru to iwareta no wa, gokooseikan ni tatte no hihyoo dearu ga, kakuno gotiki gengokan ni tatsu kagiri, Akira no shin'i wa tsuini seitooni kaishakusuru koto wa dekinai no dearu.

[7] In Tokieda's words: *Soshite chinjutsu no honshitsu o kangaete mireba, sore wa kyakutaitekina mono de naku, mattaku shutaitekina kooteihandan sono mono no hyoogen dearu kara, akirakani sore wa ji to kyootsuu shita mono o motte-iru no dearu.*

[8] In Yamada's words: *Yoogen no mottomo taisetsuna tokuchoo wa, sono chinjutsu sayoo o arawasu to yuu ten ni aru no dearu. Kono sayoo wa ningen no shisoo no tooitsu sayoo de, shui ni tatsu gainen to hin'i ni tatsu gainen to no idoo o akirakani shite kore o musubitsukeru chikara o sasu no dearu.*

[9] In Watanabe's words: *Chinjutsu to wa, toojo niyotte totonoerareta jojutsunaiyoo, mata wa mutoojo no sozaiteki yooso ni taishite, gengoshutai ga, sono sozai, aruiwa taishoo, kikite to jibunjishin to no aidani, nanraka no kankei o koosei-suru kankeikooseiteki shokunoo dearu. Chinjutsu no shokunoo o takusareru naimenteki igi to shite wa, gengoshutai no dantei, gimon, kandoo, uttae, yobikake ga mitomerareru.*

[10] My recent works related to this theme includes (Maynard 1990a, 1990b, 1991a, 1991b, 1991c, 1992a and 1992b).

[11] In original Japanese Tokieda states: *...basho no gainen ga tanni kuukanteki ichitekina mono dearu no ni taishite, bamen wa basho o mitasu tokoro no naiyoo o mo hukumeru mono dearu. Kono yooni shite bamen wa mata basho o mitasu jibutsu, jookei to aitsuuzuru mono dearu ga, bamen wa dooji ni, korera jibutsu jookei ni shikoo-suru shutai no taido, kibun, kanjoo o mo hukumu mono dearu.*

[12] It should be mentioned that Nagano (1952) also insists on the importance of the speaker's view in identifying the listener. Nagano (1952) uses the term *aite* 'partner' to refer to the listener as subjectively identified by the speaker. A similar view has been put forward by Goffman (1964).

[13] In original Japanese Nishida states: *Hutsuu ni wa ware to yuu gotoki mono mo mono to onajiku, shujunaru seishitsu o motsu shugoteki tooitsu to kangaeru ga, ware to wa shugoteki tooitsu de nakerebanaranu. Hitotsu no ten dewa-nakushite hitotsu no en de nakerebanaranu. Mono de wa-naku basho de nakerebanaranu.*

[14] Obviously all linguistic phenomena are inherently connected to the issues of perspective. For a study that explores how subjectivity--especially the epistemological perspective--operates in Japanese grammar, specifically in tense forms and the switch-reference morpheme, see Iwasaki (forthcoming).

CHAPTER 3

[1] Following van Dijk (1979), I will use the term "connectives" instead of "conjunctions" in my analysis. The grammatical category of conjunctions is more limited than the devices categorized under "connectives" which include other grammatical items, for example, adverbs such as *moreover*.

[2] Although the term "discourse particles" is used in Schourup's (1985) earlier work, Schourup (1988) suggests that "discourse marker" is more appropriate than the term "discourse particle."

[3] In Tokieda's words: *Setsuzokushi wa, ippanni, go, ku, bun o tsuzukeru go dearu to teigisarete-iru ga, kono teigi kara, setsuzokushi ga atakamo mono to mono to o renketsusuru renketsuki no yoona yakume o suru mono to kangaerare yasui.*

[4] For convenience I use 'so' and/or 'therefore' in English translation of *dakara* in this study. I am aware that the English *so* has similar yet different functions from the Japanese *dakara*. The reader should be aware that all translations for data given in this work are provided for the purpose of convenience and quick reference only.

[5] Refer to Takahara (1990) for a contrast between English *because* and Japanese *kara*.

[6] This is my translation. In Yokobayashi and Shimomura: *Mae no kotogara no toozen no kekka toshite ato no kotogara ga okoru to yuu hanashite no handan o shimesu.*

[7] In Japanese there is a conjunctive particle *kara* 'because' which is attached to informal forms of verbs and adjectives to constitute a subordinate clause expressing cause. When it is preceeded by the verb *da* 'BE,' it gives the combination *da kara* as shown in (3.20). Although the connective *dakara* is etymologically related to the conjunctive particle *kara*, here it is considered to be a grammatically separate element. The cases of *da kara* are transcribed as such and are excluded from my analysis.

[8] By "narrative coda" I mean, following Labov (1972), the ending phrase which often bridges the gap between the moment of time at the end of the narrative proper and the current goings-on of the conversational interaction.

[9] In Nagano's words: *tenkai-gata--mae no bun no naiyoo o ukete, ato no bun de iroironi tenkai-saseru kankei.*

[10] In Nagano's words: *hosoku-gata--mae no bun no naiyoo ni taishite, ato no bun de setsumei o oginau kankei.*

[11] I do not mean that in general backward directing is an abnormal order for expressing the cause-and-result relationship between utterances. As stated by Halliday and Hasan (1976:257),

the reversed form of the causal relation also occurs in English with expressions such as *the reason was that* or *for*. The point made here, however, is that one and the same conjunction *dakara* in Japanese can appear in two seemingly contradicting positions.

[12] The distinction I make here between two functions is similar to but different from Posner's (1980) distinction between "literary meaning" and "conversational suggestion." While it is true that the cause-and-result meaning of *dakara* may be characterized as having "literary meaning," the explanatory function differs from what Posner (1980) means by "conversational suggestion"--which is based strictly on the meaning associated with the usage of linguistic sign. The explanatory function of *dakara*, along with its extended functions, are interactionally based and may best be considered as adding another dimension to interactional strategies.

[13] The two types of usage of *dakara* resemble in part the two ways that the English conjunction *so* can be used. While *so* occurs in the context of connecting "cause-result" relationship in English, it also functions to mark a transition in conversation, as in "so how was your vacation?" and "so what's new?" Although the latter function is not observed in Japanese *dakara*, *dakara* functions at least in a similar way in that it can signal a new unit of discourse as we observe in data set (5).

[14] I use the term "(conversational) move" to refer to a semantically and pragmatically meaningful unit of the conversation participant's communicative action as intended by the speaker as well as perceived by the partner. A move may consist of one or more speaking turns. See Maynard (1989, chapter 6) for the definition of the speaking turn in Japanese casual conversation.

[15] According to Mio (1948:83), *genshoobun* expresses phenomena perceived and reflected emotionally which are arrived at without the process of judgment. There is no gap between the phenomenon and its descriptive expression. Since there is no subjective view to intrude between the phenomenon and the expression, there is no responsibility on the part of the user in regard to the semantic contents. In original Japanese: *Genshoobun wa genshoo o arinomama, sonomama o utsushita mono dearu. Handan no kakoo o hodokosanaide, kangan o tsuujite kokoro ni utsutta mama o sono mama hyoogenshita bun dearu. Genjitsu to hyoogen no aida ni nan no sukima mo nai. Genshoo to hyoogen to no aida ni hanashite no shukan ga mattaku hairikomanai no dearu kara, soko ni wa shukan no sekinin mondai wa nai.*

[16] Recall that in data set (3), *dakara* also appears toward the end of the explanatory discourse unit. That *dakara* could also function as a turn-end or turn-yielding signal.

[17] Note that in this function of *dakara*, the portion [X is already mentioned in discourse] is deleted and an actual utterance starts with [so (*dakara*) I add explanatory statement Y relevant to X], retaining the original meaning of cause-and-result on the interactional level. I thank Matsuo Soga for pointing this out to me when I presented a shorter version of the paper at the Association of Teachers of Japanese conference in Washington D.C. in March, 1989.

[18] See Smith and Frawley (1983) for differences in use of English conjunctions in four different genres-fiction, journalism, religion and science.

[19] See Doi (1971) for further discussion of the concept of *amae*.

[20] In Yokobayashi and Shimomura: *hutatsu no kotogara o ronriteki kankei de tsunagu hyoogen* and *saki ni ketsuron o nobe, ato kara sono riyuu o noberu iikata.*

[21] In Yokobayashi and Shimomura: (1) *mae no bun no riyuu o yuu,* and (2) *kaiwa de aite no kotoba ni hantai-suru kimochi o arawashitari iiwake o shistari suru.*

[22] I am aware that it is not impossible to think of a context where [23.2] may make sense. For example, B made his position known earlier in the interaction that he wanted to stay at the store much longer. A's inquiry may be taken as a threat to his position and B provides [23.2] as a supporting argument that it's not yet late at all. My point here is merely that an environment such as [23]--where one recognizes a straightforward question/answer adjacency pair--is not conducive to the occurrence of *datte.*

[23] Note that *datte* glossed "even" in (30.1) is not a discourse connective *datte.*

CHAPTER 4

[1] Original Japanese definition given by Yamada is: *Chinjutsu no hukushi wa honbun ni yuu yooni yoogen no jisshitsujoo no igi sunawachi, sono shimesu zokusei ni wa kankei ga naku, sono chinjutsu no hoohoo dake o sootei-suru mono dearu.*

[2] This relationship between the guidance and the corresponding predicate type is reminiscent of *kakarimusubi* 'grammatical adverb-predicate correspondence' recognized in classical Japanese. Although *kakarimusubi* in a strict sense does not exist in modern Japanese, I find this notion very useful in characterizing modal adverbs in modern Japanese.

[3] The literal translation of *yakusokuteki hukushi* is 'promising adverb,' meaning the adverb "promises" how the utterance will be delivered. For example, *watashi ga yuu made mo naku* '(lit. without my mentioning) needless to say,' "promises" that the following statement is delivered in such a way as to reflect the feeling of "needless to say."

[4] For example, the narrow view--taken by Halliday and Hasan (1976:14)--states that "form of presupposition, pointing BACK to some previous item is known as anaphora" (original emphasis).

[5] The point that in a nominalized phrase the actor is usually more removed from the event has been pointed out by Brown and Levinson (1987:208). Also refer to Maynard 1992b (in press)

for the exploration of the nominalized clause of the *no da* expression which I call "commentary predicate."

CHAPTER 5

[1] In data presentation for the main verbal ending in each utterance, either formal or abrupt style is assigned, and it is indicated at the end of each utterance in parenthesis.

[2] This chapter does not discuss the distinction between two predicate forms of Japanese copula, *da* 'BE' and *dearu* 'BE.' See Maynard (1985) for the functional differences between *da* and *dearu* in written Japanese. In this study I categorize *dearu* as *da* form and *dearimasu* as *desu/masu* form.

[3] In Kindaichi's words: *Da-tai no tokoro wa hitorigototekina tokoto, naishi wa, bunshoo ga chiisaku kirete-iru tokoto, desu-tai no tokoro wa, hanashikake-choo no tokoro, naishi wa bunshoo ga ookiku kirete-iru tokoro de, awasete zentaitoshite henka no myoo o misete-iru.*

[4] See Maynard (1989) chapter 3 on this regard.

[5] Refer to Neustpuný (1983) for the sociolinguistic issue of politeness avoidance among Japanese speakers.

[6] For a detailed analysis of the *no da* construction within the proposed Discourse Modality framework, see Maynard (1992b).

[7] I informally asked six native speakers to guess a likely narrative setting in which conversations (1) and [7] might take place. All informants responded in writing and expressed similar differences between the two types of discourse. In fact one informant came very close to the situation I present here although she was told merely that the conversation was taken from a mystery novel without a hint of the narrative situation. In summary, she stated that the situation appropriate for (1) is such that the speaker announces that one person unexpectedly shows up (*Hitori dete-kita*), and then the speaker points out that the person who just showed up is the child of their concern (*Ano ko desu yo*). The situation appropriate for [7] is such that the child is expected to appear and the speaker reports the fact (*Hitori dete-kimashita*) and unexpectedly finds out that that child is someone the speaker was looking for (*Ano ko da*).

[8] Here I should point out a similar observation made by Noda (1989). Noda discusses two types of sentences--sentences with genuine modality (*shinsei modariti o motsu bun*) and sentences without (*shinsei modariti o mota-nai bun*)--and comments that sentences without genuine modality which express low levels of independence (*dokuritsusei no hikui bun*) are not likely to take formality markings.

[9] Although (10.16) ends with *da*, since it contains the *no da* predicate, I categorize this not as a naked abrupt style.

[10] At this point the reader might think of another closely related aspect of verb morphology interacting with the *da* and *desu/masu* forms, i.e., their tense. See Soga (1981:289) for his comments on tense switching in Japanese narratives based on Hopper's notion of foregrounding and backgrounding. According to Soga, (1) foregrounded events tend to be stated in the *-ta* form, and backgrounded events, in the *-ru* form, and (1) for the purpose of "vividness" effect, even foregrounded events may sequentially be stated by the *-ru* form. In fact Soga's comments offer interesting combinatory possibilities of tense and *da* and *desu/masu* forms. Such discussion, however, is beyond the immediate concern of this study.

[11] It should also be mentioned that the choice of the self-referencing term also reflects a different perspective. Note that in (12.1) and (12.6) *watashi* 'I-formal' is chosen whereas in (12.5) *boku* 'I-informal/familiar' is selected.

[12] It is known that folktales and children's stories often take the *desu/masu* style which gives a sense of the author directly telling a story to the reading audience.

[13] For further discussion of the contextualization of self, see Maynard (1989) in which I discuss the concept of "self-contextualization."

[14] The reader may wonder at this point how we can understand the abrupt style speech used at the time of confrontation and conflict. Note that in such a situation one refuses to be considerate to the addressee and ignores "thou"--a case of intentionally created low awareness situation. Thus ironically the stylistic choice of the <u>da</u> style in this context works to achieve the opposite effect of a feeling of closeness. Although this is an intriguing point which demands further exploration, its discussion must await future study.

CHAPTER 6

[1] *Ne* accompanied by a rising tone can also occur when asking a question. However, in our data, no obvious use of *ne* in a straightforward interrogative utterance was found. All cases of *ne* occur at the point in discourse where the speaker solicits general, often favorable, listener response, but not at the point where the speaker seeks a specific answer to a question.

[2] In Tokieda's (1951:8) words, *ne* is characterized as "*kokugo ni okeru isshu no kandoojoshi dearu ga, shi ni tsuite, sore ni taisuru kandoo o hyoogen-suru to yuu yori mo, kikite o doochoosha to shite no kankei ni okoo to suru shutaiteki tachiba no hyoogen dearu.*" *Yo* (along with *zo*) is characterized as "*kikite ni taishite hanashite no ishi ya handan o tsuyoku oshitsukeru hyoogen.*"

[3] For the concept of F(ace) T(hreatening) A(cts), see Brown and Levinson (1987). Brown and Levinson state that the speaker can threaten the addressee's positive face (i.e., a desire to be appreciated) by performing acts such as expressing that the speaker has a negative evaluation of the addressee or does not care about the addressee's positive face.

[4] I am aware that the shortened version of *n desu*, i.e., *no*, can be followed by *ne*--as in *Raishuu wa Oosaka e ikitai no ne*. However, since *no* is a nominalizer and when appearing without *da/desu* it retains its phrasal nature, I will consider such use as insertion particle. As will be suggested later, the *ne* as insertion particle also focuses on the interactional aspect of comunication and in fact seems to be more flexible in its use. *Ne* as insertion particle can cooccur regardless of the new or old information status.

[5] In Kitahara (1970:33) he states: "*Jodooshi soogo shoosetsu no gojun wa, ue kara tadoreba kanjooteki seikaku no kokunatte-yuku junjo deari, shita kara tadoreba ronriteki seikaku no kokunatte-yuku junjo dearu to ieru dearoo.*" Although his discussion is limited to the ordering of Japanese auxiliary verbs and adjectives, I follow the principle proposed here to the extent that the same principle operates in the internal ordering of particles. Watanabe's (1968) ordering of particles in fact follows the same principle.

[6] It should be pointed out that Oishi (1985) makes a somewhat similar distinction of informational territory. While Kamio (1990) makes a binary distinction between speaker's territory versus non-speaker's territory, Oishi finds that the third territory, i.e., speaker and hearer's territory must be established. My [Sp-M] and [Ad-M] categories fall into Oishi's third category. However, Oishi does not take into account the relative degree of information access and possession within the territory of information.

[7] For the concept of "conditional relevance," see Schegloff (1968). According to Schegloff: "By conditional relevance of one item or another we mean: given the first, the second is expectable; upon its occurrence it can be seen to be a second item to the first: upon its non-occurrence it can be seen to be officially absent--all this provided sheerly by the occurrence of the first item." (1968:1083)

[8] Strictly speaking, *yo* appearing in (22.1) and (22.5) is not sentence-final. However, since in both cases noun phrases which follow *yo* are post-posed, I take these examples of *yo* as cases of sentence-final *yo*.

[9] Although *soo desu ne* in (28.1) is a grammatically complete sentence, *desu ne* in this expression is used as a particle-like expression (instead of *soo ne*, for example) and therefore I do not consider this *ne* in (28.1) as a sentence-final particle.

CHAPTER 7

[1] In fact the semantic/pragmatic relationship between the modifying clause and the head noun can require extensive "world-view" as suggested by Matsumoto (1987). Think for an instance of an expression such as *paatii ni korarenakatta shukudai* 'the homework (because of) which (you, etc.) could not come to the party.'

[2] The term P-noun is taken from Vendler (1972) and refers to the kind of nouns which can replace a complement clause that contains proposition. P-nouns are either "subjective" (e.g., belief, opinion, assumption, view, etc.) or "objective" (e.g., fact, cause, result, outcome, etc.).

[3] S here refers to sentence.

[4] A similar point may be made regarding [14a]. When to yuu is used, one is made aware of the speaker who evaluates [X] (i.e., the way of talking is such that Sasaki wants to know the truth of the case).

CHAPTER 8

[1] See Besnier (1990) for an overview on language and affect within anthropology and linguistics.

[2] Although in my earlier studies on Japanese *wa* I have consistently used the term theme-rheme rather than topic-comment, here I use the latter for convenience. The terms theme and rheme reflect the Praguean tradition and are less widely used; topic and comment are less restricted and are used more frequently and they are more appropriate here.

[3] I am only contrasting Japanese with English here simply because I and the majority of readers are most familiar with these languages. This does not mean, however, that one is limited to contrasting Japanese with English. Once DM indicators are studied across many languages, we will be able to reach a more balanced view of the ways in which DM indicators cause communication difficulties across many other languages and cultures.

References

Atkinson, J. Maxwell and John Herigate. (eds.)
  1984. *Structures of social action*. Cambridge: Cambridge University Press.

Austin, J. L.
  1962. *How to do things with words*. Oxford: Clarendon Press.

Bach, Kent and Robert M. Harnish.
  1979. *Linguistic communication and Speech Acts*. Cambridge, Massachusetts: The M.I.T. Press.

Bakhtin, M. M.
  1981. *The dialogic imagination*. Translated by C. Emerson and M. Holquist. Edited by M. Holquist. Austin, Texas: University of Texas Press.
  1986. *Speech genres and other late essays*. Translated by V. W. McGee. Edited by C. Emerson and M. Holquist. Austin, Texas: University of Texas Press.

Bedell, George Dudley.
  1968. Kokugaku grammatical theory. Unpublished dissertation. M.I.T.

Bedell, George D., Eiichi Kobayashi and Masatake Muraki. (eds.)
  1979. *Explorations in linguistics: Papers in honor of Kazuko Inoue*. Tokyo: Kenkyuusha.

Bellert, Irena.
  1977. "On semantic and distributional properties of sentential adverbs". *Linguistic Inquiry* 8:337-351.

Benveniste, Emile.
  1971. *Problems in general linguistics*. Translated by M. E. Meek. Miami linguistics series, 8. Coral Gables, Florida: University of Miami Press.

Besnier, Niko.
  1990. "Language and affect". *Annual Review of Anthropology* 19:419-451.

Bilmes, Jack.
  1988. "The concept of preference in conversation analysis". *Language in Society* 17:161-181.

Blakemore, Diane.
  1987. *Semantic constraints on relevance.* Oxford: Blackwell.
  1989. "Denial and contrast: A relevance theoretic analysis of *but*". *Linguistics and Philosophy*
          12:15-37.

Bobrow, Daniel and Allan Collins. (eds.)
  1975. *Representation and understanding.* New York: Academic Press.

Brown, Gillian and George Yule.
  1983. *Discourse analysis.* Cambridge: Cambridge University Press.

Brown, Penelope and Stephen Levinson.
  1987. *Politeness: Some universals in language use.* Cambridge: Cambridge University Press.

Chafe, Wallace.
  1976. "Givenness, contrastiveness, definiteness, subjects, topics and point of view". In C. N.
          Li (ed.), 27-55.

Chatman, Seymour.
  1978. *Story and discourse: Narrative structure in fiction and film.* Ithaca and London:
          Cornell University Press.

Coates, Jennifer.
  1988. Modal meanings: The semantic-pragmatic interface. Paper presented at meeting of the
          Linguistic Association of Great Britain at Exeter.

Cole, Peter. (ed.)
  1981. *Radical pragmatics.* New York: Academic Press.

Cook, Haruko Minegishi.
  1988. Sentential particles in Japanese conversation: A study of indexicality. Unpublished
          dissertation. University of Southern California.

Coulthard, Malcolm.
  1977. *An introduction to discourse analysis.* London: Longman.

Dilworth, David A. (trans.)
  1987. *Last writings: Nothingness and the religious world view.* By Kitaroo Nishida. Honolulu:
          University of Hawaii Press.

Doherty, Maria.
  1987. *Epistemic Meaning.* Berlin: Springer-Verlag.

Doi, Takeo.
   1971.   *Amae no koozoo*. Tokyo: Koobundoo.
   1976.   "The Japanese patterns of communication and the concept of *amae*". In L. A. Samovar and R. E. Porter (eds), 188-193.
   1985.   *Omote to ura*. Tokyo: Koobundoo.

Dressler, Wolfgang. (ed.)
   1978.   *Current trends in textlinguistics*. New York: de Gruyter.

Duncan, Starkey and Donald W. Fiske.
   1977.   *Face-to-face interaction: Research, methods, and theory*. Hillsdale, New Jersey: Lawrence Erlbaum.
   1985.   *Interaction structure and strategy*. Cambridge: Cambridge University Press.

Erickson, Frederick.
   1984.   "Rhetoric, anecdotes, and rhapsody: Coherence strategies in a conversation among Black American adolescents". In D. Tannen (ed.), 81-154.

Espinal, Teresa M.
   1987.   "Modal adverbs and modality scales". *Lingua* 72:293-314.

Fillmore, Charles.
   1982.   "Frame semantics". In The Linguistics Society of Korea (ed.), 111-137.

Fujita, Yasuyuki.
   1987.   "Kenkyuu nooto: To yuu to to itta". *Kokugogaku Ronsetsuz Shiryoo* 24:486-489.

Fujitani, Nariakira.
   1938.   (originally 1767). *Kazashishoo*. Edited by K. Hukui. Kokugaku taikei: Gohoo sooki, Vol. 1. Tokyo: Kooseikaku.
   1960.   (originally 1778). *Ayuishoo*. In N. Nakada and M. Tekeoka.

Garvin, Paul L.
   1964.   *A Prague School reader on esthetics, literary structure, and style*. Washington, DC: Georgetown University Press.

Givón, Tamil. (ed.)
   1979.   *Syntax and semantics*. Vol. 12. New York: Academic Press.

Goffman, Erving.
   1955.   "On face-work: An analysis of ritual elements in social interaction". *Psychiatry* 18:213-231.
   1964.   "The neglected situation". *American Anthropologist* 66, 6-2:133-136.

Greenbaum, Sidney.
1969. *Studies in English adverbial usage.* Coral Gables, Florida: University of Miami Press.

Gumperz, John J.
1982. *Discourse strategies.* Cambridge: Cambridge University Press.
1984. "Communicative competence revisited". In *Georgetown University Round Table on Languages and Linguistics. Meaning, form, and use in context: Linguistic applications,* 278-289.

Gumperz, John J. and Dell Hymes. (eds.)
1972. *Directions in sociolinguistics: The ethnography of communication.* New York: Holt.

Haga, Yasushi.
1954. "Chinjutsu to wa nani mono?" *Kokugo Kokubun* 23, 4:47-61.
1962. *Kokugo hyoogen kyooshitsu.* Tokyo: Tookyoodoo.
1982. *Shintei nihonbunpoo kyooshitsu.* Tokyo: Kyooiku Shuppan.
1985. *Hanaseba wakaru ka.* Tokyo: Koodansha.

Halliday, M.A.K.
1967. "Notes on transitivity and theme in English, Part 2". *Journal of Linguistics* 3:199-244.
1970. "Functional diversity in language as seen from a consideration of modality and mood in English". *Foundations of Language* 6:322-361.

Halliday, M.A.K. and Ruqaiya Hasan.
1976. *Cohesion in English.* London: Longman.

Harden, Theo.
1983. *An analysis of the semantic field of the German particles: überhaupt and Eigentlich.* Tübingen: Gunter Narr Verlag Tübingen.

Hayashi Fiichi kyooju kanreki kinen ronbunshuu kankoo iinkai. (ed.)
1979. *Eigo to nihongo to.* Tokyo: Kuroshio Shuppan.

Hayashi, Shiroo.
1983. "Nihongo no bun no katachi to shisei". In Kokuritsu Kokugo Kenkyuujo (ed.), 43-62.

Heath, Peter. (trans.)
1988. *On language: The diversity of human language-structure and its influence on the mental development of mankind.* By Wilhelm von Humboldt, with an introduction by Hans Aarsleff. Cambridge: Cambridge University Press.

Hinds, John, Senko K. Maynard and Shoichi Iwasaki. (eds.)
1987. *Perspectives on topicalization: The case of Japanese wa.* Amsterdam: John Benjamins.

Holquist, Michael and Caryl Emerson.
1981.   Glossary for *The dialogic imagination*. In M. M. Bakhtin, 423-434.

Honna, Nobuyuki and Bates Hoffer. (eds.)
1989.   *An English dictionary of Japanese ways of thinking*. Tokyo: Yuuhikaku.

Hopper, Paul J.
1979.   "Aspect and foregrounding in discourse". In T. Givón (ed.), 213-241.

Hori, Motoko.
1985.   "Taiguu ishiki o han'ei suru gengo keishiki". In *Kokugogaku Ronsetsu Shiryoo*, 24, 3:196-204.

Hymes, Dell.
1972.   "Models of the interaction of language and social life". In J. Gumperz and D. Hymes (eds.), 35-71.

Ichikawa, Takashi.
1976.   "Hukuyoogo". *Bunpoo* 1, Iwanami kooza nihongo, 6, 219-258. Tokyo: Iwanami.

Ikeda, Yasaburoo, and Donald Keene. (eds.)
1982.   *Nichiei koji kotowaza jiten*. Tokyo: Asahi Evening News.

Ikegami, Yoshihiko.
1981.   *Suru to naru no gengogaku*. Tokyo: Taishuukan.

Itasaka, Gen.
1971a. *Nihonjin no ronri koozoo*. Koodansha gendai shinsho. Tokyo: Koodansha.
1971b. "Yahari, sasuga." *Kokubungaku Kaishaku to Kanshoo* 36, 1:216-221.

Iwasaki, Shoichi.
Forthcoming. *Subjectivity in grammar and discourse--theoretical considerations and a case study of Japanese spoken discourse*. Amsterdam: John Benjamins.

Jarvella, Robert J. and Wolfgang Klein (eds.)
1982.   *Speech, place and action: Studies in deixis and related topics*. New York: John Wiley and Sons.

Jefferson, Gail.
1972.   "Side sequences". In D. Sudnow (ed.), 298-338.

Jesperson, Otto.
1965.   (originally 1924). *The philosophy of grammar*. New York: W. W. Norton & Company.

Johnson, Mark.
1987. *The body in the mind.* Chicago: The University of Chicago Press.

Josephs, Lewis S.
1976. "Complementation". In M. Shibatani (ed.), 307-369.

Kamio, Akio.
1979. "On the notion speaker's territory of information: A functional analysis of certain sentence-final forms in Japanese. In G. D. Bedell, E. Kobayashi and M. Muraki (eds.), 213-231.
1990. *Joohoo no nawabari riron: Gengo no kinooteki bunseki.* Tokyo: Taishuukan.

Kenkyuusha.
1974. *New Japanese-English Dictionary.* Tokyo: Kenkyuusha.

Kindaichi, Haruhiko.
1982. *Nihongo seminaa,* Vol. 1. Tokyo: Chikuma Shoboo.

Kinsui, Satoshi.
1988. "Nihongo ni okeru shinteki kuukan to meishiku no shiji ni tsuite". *Osaka Joshi Daigaku Kokubungakuka Kiyoo,* Vol. 39:1-24.

Kiparsky, Paul and Steven Angerson. (eds.)
1973. *Festschrift for Morris Halle.* New York: Holt.

Kitagawa, Chisato.
1984. "Hatsugen no kaisookoozoo to kotoba no shutaisei". *Nihongogaku* 4:31-42.

Kitahara, Yasuo.
1970. "Jodooshi no soogo shoosetsu ni tsuite no koobunronteki koosatsu. *Kokugogaku* 83, 10:32-59.

Kokuritsu Kokugo Kenkyuujo. (ed.)
1982. *Kenkyuu hookokusho.* 3. Tokyo: Shuueisha.
1983. *Danwa no kenkyuu to kyooiku.* Vol. 1. Tokyo: Ookurashoo Insatsukyoku.

Kristeva, Julia.
1980. *Desire in Language: A semiotic approach to literature and art.* Oxford: Basil Blackwell.

Kudo, Hiroshi.
1982. "Johoo hukushi no imi to kinoo--Sono kijutsuhoohoo o motomete". In Kokuritsu Kokugo Kenkyuujo (ed.), 45-92.

Kuno, Susumu.
   1972.   "Functional Sentence Perspective--A case study from Japanese and English". *Linguistic Inquiry* 3:269-320.

Kuroda, S.-Y.
   1973.   "Where epistemology, style and grammar meet: A case study from the Japanese". In P. Kiparsky and S. Anderson (eds.), 337-391.

Labov, William.
   1972.   *Language in the inner city.* Philadelphia: University of Pennsylvania Press.

Labov, William and David Fanshel.
   1977.   *Therapeutic discourse.* New York: Academic Press.

Lakoff, Robin.
   1972.   "The pragmatics of modality". *Papers from the Eighth Regional Meeting of the Chicago Linguistics Society*, 229-246.

Lebra, Takie S.
   1976.   *Japanese patterns of behavior.* Honolulu: University of Hawaii Press.

Leech, Geoffrey N.
   1983.   *Principles of pragmatics.* London and New York: Longman.

Li, Charles N. (ed.)
   1976.   *Subject and topic.* New York: Academic Press.

Li, Charles N. and Sandra A. Thompson.
   1976.   "Subject and topic: A new typology of language". In C. N. Li (ed.), 450-490.

Longacre, Robert and Stephen Levinsohn.
   1978.   "Field analysis of discourse". In W. Dressler (ed.), 103-122.

Lyons, John.
   1977.   *Semantics.* Vol. 1 and 2. Cambridge: Cambridge University Press.
   1981.   *Language, meaning and context.* Suffolk: Fontana.
   1982.   "Deixis and subjectivity: Loquor, ergo sum?" In R. J. Jarvella and W. Klein (eds.), 101-124.

Makino, Seiichi.
   1983.   "Speaker/listener-orientation and formality marking in Japanese". *Gengo Kenkyuu* 84:126-145.

1990.   Some notes on intra/inter-paragraphic coherence in written narrative discourse in Japanese. Paper presented at the Association for Asian Studies Annual Meeting in Chicago.

Makino, Seiichi. (ed.)
1981.   *Papers from the Middlebury symposium on Japanese discourse analysis.*

Malinowski, Bronislaw.
1923.   "The problem of meaning in primitive language". In C. K. Ogden and I. A. Richards (eds.), 296-355.

Martin, Samuel.
1975.   *A reference grammar of Japanese.* New Haven and London: Yale University Press.

Masuoka, Takashi.
1991.   *Modariti no bunpoo.* Tokyo: Kuroshio Shuppan.

Matsumoto, Yoshiko.
1987.   Noun-modifying constructions in Japanese: A pragmatic approach. A paper presented at the Linguistics Society of America Annual Meeting.

Maynard, Senko K.
1980.   Discourse functions of the Japanese theme marker *wa*. Unpublished dissertation. Northwestern University.
1984.   "Functions of *to* and *koto-o* in speech and thought representation in Japanese written discourse". *Lingua* 64:1-24.
1985.   "Choice of predicate and narrative manipulation". *Poetics* 14:369-385.
1987.   "Thematization as a staging device in the Japanese narrative". In J. Hinds, S. K. Maynard and S. Iwasaki (eds.), 57-82.
1989.   *Japanese conversation: Self-contextualization through structure and interactional management.* Norwood, New Jersey: Ablex.
1990a. An epistemological inquiry into textual and social anaphora: A case of Japanese modal adverb *yahari/yappari*. A paper presented at the Association for Asian Studies Annual Meeting in Chicago.
1990b. Pragmatics of discourse modality: A case of the Japanese emotional adverb *doose*. Paper presented at the International Pragmatics Association Conference in Barcelona, Spain.
1991a. "Buntai no imi: Da-tai to desu/masu-tai no kon'yoo ni tsuite". *Gengo* 20, 2:75-80.
1991b. "Pragmatics of discourse modality: A case of *da* and *desu/masu* forms in Japanese". *Journal of Pragmatics* 15:551-582.
1991c. "Discourse and interactional functions of the Japanese modal adverb *yahari/yappari*. *Language Sciences*, 13, 1:39-57.

1992a. (in press) "Speech act declaration in conversation: Functions of the Japanese connective *datte*." *Studies in Language*, 16,1.

1992b. (in press) "Cognitive and pragmatic messages of a syntactic choice: A case of Japanese commentary predicate *n(o) da*". *TEXT: An Interdisciplinary Journal for the Study of Discourse*, 12,3.

Michell, Gillian.
1974. "Obviously I concede..." performatives and sentence adverbs". *Papers from the Tenth Regional Meeting of the Chicago Linguistics Society*, 436-445.

Mikami, Akira.
1972. *Gendaigohoo josetsu--shintakusu no kokoromi*. Tokyo: Kuroshio Shuppan.

Mio, Isago.
1942. *Hanashikotoba no bunpoo*. Tokyo: Teikoku Kyooiku Shuppanbu.
1948. *Kokugohoo bunshooron*. Tokyo: Sanseidoo.

Miyauchi Hideo kyooju kanreki kinen ronbun henshuu iinkai. (ed.)
1972. *Miyauchi Hideo kyooju kanreki kinen ronbun*. Tokyo: Sanseidoo.

Mizutani, Osamu and Nobuko Mizutani.
1981. *Nihongo notes*. 4. Tokyo: Japan Times, Ltd.

Monane, Tazuko A. and Lawrence W. Rogers.
1977. "Cognitive features of Japanese language and culture and their implications for language teaching". *Proceedings of the 2nd HATJ-UH Conference on Japanese Language and Linguistics*, 129-137.

Mori, Arimasa.
1979. *Mori Arimasa zenshuu*, Vol. 12. Tokyo: Chikuma Shoboo.

Motoori, Norinaga.
1902 (originally 1771). "Te-ni-o-ha himokagami". In *Zooho Motoori Norinaga zenshuu*, Vol. 9, 1-2. Tokyo: Yoshikawa.

Nagano, Masaru.
1952. "Aite to yuu gainen ni tsuite". *Kokugogaku*, 9:23-28.
1972. *Bunshooron shoosetsu*. Tokyo: Asakura Shoten.

Nakada, Norio and Masao Takeoka. (eds.)
1960. *Ayuishoo shinchuu*. Tokyo: Kazama Shoboo.

Nakane, Chie.
1970. *Japanese society*. Berkeley and Los Angeles: University of California Press.

Nakau, Minoru.
1979. "Modariti to meidai". In Hayashi Eiichi kyooju kanreki kinen ronbunshuu kankoo iinkai (ed.), 223-250.

Nathan, John. (trans.)
1969. *A personal matter*. By Kenzaburoo Ooe. New York: Grove Press, Inc.

Neustupný, J. V.
1983. "Keigo kaihi no sutoratejii ni tsuite". *Nihongogaku*, 2, 1:62-67.

Nishida, Kitaroo.
1949. (originally 1926). "Basho". In *Nishida Kitaroo zenshuu*, Vol. 4, 208-289. Tokyo: Iwanami Shoten.

Nishihara, Suzuko.
1988. "Washa no zentei, *yahari* (*yappari*) no baai. *Nihongogaku*, 7, 89-99.

Nitta, Yoshio.
1989. "Gendai nihongo no modariti no taikei to koozoo". In Y. Nitta and T. Masuoka (eds.), 1-55.

Nitta, Yoshio and Takashi Masuoka. (eds.)
1989. *Nihongo no modariti*. Tokyo: Kuroshio Shuppan.

Noda, Hisashi.
1989. "Shinsei modariti o motsu bun". In Y. Nitta and T. Masuoka (eds.), 131-157.

Ochs, Elinor and Bambi Schieffelin.
1985. Language has a heart. Paper presented at the Linguistic Society of America Summer Institute at Georgetown University.

Ogasawara, Rinju.
1972. "Nichi-bei no bunka to kotoba joron". In Miyauchi Hideo kyooju kanreki kinen ronbun henshuu iinkai (ed.), 13-28.

Ogden, Charles K. and I. A. Richards. (eds.)
1923. *The meaning of meaning*. London: Routledge and Kegan Paul.

Oishi, Toshio.
1985. A description of Japanese final particles in context. Unpublished dissertation. The University of Michigan.

Onoe, Keisuke.
1973. "Bunkaku to ketsubun no waku". *Gengo Kenkyuu* 63:1-26.
1982. "Bun no kihon koosei, shiteki tenkai". In *Kooza nihongogaku*. Vol. 2, 1-19. Tokyo: Meiji Shoin.

Ookubo, Tadatoshi.
1974. *Nihon bunpoo to bunshoo hyoogen*. Tokyo: Tookyoodoo.

Pomerantz, Anita.
1984. "Agreeing and disagreeing with assessments: Some features of preferred/dispreferred turn shapes". In J. M. Atkinson and J. Heritage (eds.), 57-101.

Posner, Roland.
1980. "Semantics and pragmatics of sentence connectives in natural language". In J. Searle, F. Kiefer and M. Bierwisch (eds.), 169-203.

Prince, Ellen.
1981. "Toward a taxonomy of given/new information". In P. Cole (ed.), 223-255.

Random House. (ed.)
1966. *The Random House dictionary of the English language*. New York: Random House, Inc.

Rumelhart, David E.
1975. "Notes on a schema for stories". In D. Bobrow and A. Collins (eds.), 211-236.

Sacks, Harvey, Emanuel Schegloff and Gail Jefferson.
1974. "A simplest systematics for the organization of turn-taking for conversation". *Language* 50:696-735.

Saji, Keizoo.
1956. "Shuujoshi no kinoo". *Kokugo Kokubun* 26, 7:461-469.

Samovar, Larry A. and Richard E. Porter. (eds.)
1976. *Intercultural communication: A reader*. Hillsdale, New Jersey: Laurence Erlbaum.

Saunders, E. Dale. (trans.)
1966. *The face of another*. By Kobo Abe. New York: G. P. Putnum's Sons (Perigee Books).

Sawada, Harumi.
   1978.   "Nichieigo bunhukushirui no taishoo gengogakuteki kenkyuu". *Gengo Kenkyuu* 74:1-36.

Schank, Roger C. and Robert P. Abelson.
   1977.   *Scripts, plans, goals and understanding.* Hillsdale, New Jersey: Lawrence Erlbaum.

Schegloff, Emanuel.
   1968.   "Sequencing in conversational openings". *American Anthropologist* 70:1075-1095.

Schegloff, Emanuel and Harvey Sacks.
   1973.   "Opening up closings". *Semiotica* 8:289-327.

Schieffelin, Deborah and Eleanor Ochs.
   1986.   "Language socialization". *Annual Review of Anthropology* 15:163-191.

Schiffrin, Deborah.
   1987.   *Discourse markers.* Cambridge: Cambridge University Press.

Schourup, Lawrence.
   1985.   *Common discourse particles in English conversation.* New York and London: Garland
           Publishing, Inc.
   1988.   Review of *Discourse markers* by Deborah Schiffrin. *Language* 64:633-637.

Schreiber, Peter A.
   1971.   "Some constraints on the formation of English sentence adverbs". *Linguistic Inquiry*
           2:83-101.

Searle, John.
   1969.   *Speech acts.* London and New York: Cambridge University Press.

Searle, John, Ferenc Kiefer and Manfred Bierwisch. (eds.)
   1980.   *Speech Act theory and pragmatics.* Dordrecht: D. Reidel.

Shibatani, Masayoshi. (ed.)
   1976.   *Syntax and semantics.* Vol. 5. New York: Academic Press.

Shoogakukan. (ed.)
   1975.   *Nihon Kokugo Daijitan.* Tokyo: Shoogakugan.

Sinclair, John and Malcolm Coulthard.
   1975.   *Towards an analysis of discourse.* London: Oxford University Press.

Smith, Raoul N. and William J. Frawley.
  1983. "Conjunctive cohesion in four English genres". *TEXT* 3:347-374.

Soga, Matsuo.
  1981. "Tense and aspect in conversations and narratives". In S. Makino (ed.), 276-294.

Sperber, Dan and Deirdre Wilson.
  1986. *Relevance: Communication and cognition.* Cambridge, Massachusetts: Harvard University Press.

Stubbs, Michael.
  1983. *Discourse analysis.* Chicago: University of Chicago Press.
  1986. "A matter of prolonged field work: Notes towards a modal grammar of English". *Applied Linguistics* 7:1-25.

Sudnow, David. (ed.)
  1972. *Studies in social interaction.* New York: The Free Press.

Suzuki, Akira.
  1979. (originally 1824). *Gengyo Shishuron.* Edited by K. Toshio and M. Tsuboi. Benseisha Bunko, 68. Tokyo: Bunseisha.

Suzuki, Takao.
  1978. *Japanese and the Japanese.* Translated by A. Miura. Tokyo: Kodansha International, Ltd.

Takahara, Paul.
  1990. Semantic and pragmatic function of causal connectives in English and Japanese. Paper presented at the International Pragmatics Association Conference in Barcelona, Spain.

Tannen, Deborah. (ed.)
  1984. *Coherence in spoken and written discourse.* Norwood, New Jersey: Ablex.

Terakura, Hiroko.
  1980. Some aspects of complementation in Japanese: A study of *to yuu.* Unpublished dissertation. University of Wisconsin-Madison.

Teramura, Hideo.
  1981. *Nihongo no bunpoo--ge.* Nihongo Kyooiku Shidoo Sankoosho, 5. Tokyo: Ookurashoo Insatsukyoku.
  1984. *Nihongo no shintakusu to imi.* Vol. 2. Tokyo: Kuroshio Shuppan.

The Linguistic Society of Korea. (ed.)
   1982. *Linguistics in the morning calm.* Seoul: Hanshin Publishing Co.

Thorndyke, Perry W.
   1977. "Cognitive structures in comprehension and memory of narrative discourse". *Cognitive Psychology* 9:77-110.

Tokieda, Motoki.
   1941. *Kokugogaku genron.* Tokyo: Iwanami.
   1950. *Nihon bunpoo koogohen.* Tokyo: Iwanami.
   1951. "Taijin kankei o koosei suru joshi, jodooshi". *Kokugo Kokubun* 20, 9:1-10.
   1954. "Shi to ji no renzoku, hirenzoku no mondai". *Kokugogaku* 19, 12:1-16.

Tsuchihashi, Mika.
   1983. "The speech act continuum: An investigation of Japanese sentence final particles". *Journal of Pragmatics* 7:361-387.

Tsukahara, Tetsuo.
   1959. "Setsuzokushi". In *Bunpoo kakuron hen.* Zoku nihon bumpoo kooza. Vol. 1., 156-174. Tokyo: Meiji Shoin.

Uspensky, Boris.
   1973. *A poetics of composition.* Translated by V. Zavarin and S. Wittig. Berkeley: University of California Press.

Uyeno, Tazuko.
   1971. A study of Japanese modality--A performative analysis of sentence particles. Unpublished dissertation. The University of Michigan.

van Dijk, Teun A.
   1977. *Text and context: Explorations in the semantics and pragmatics of discourse.* London and New York: Longman.
   1979. "Pragmatic connectives". *Journal of Pragmatics* 3:447-456.

Vendler, Zeno.
   1972. *Res cogitans: An essay in rational psychology.* Ithaca and London: Cornell University Press.

Vendryes, Joseph.
   1925. *Language: A linguistic introduction to history.* Translated by P. Radin. London: K. Paul, Trench, Trubner & Co.

Vološinov, V. N.
  1973.   *Marxism and the philosophy of language.* Translated by L. Matejka and I. R. Titunik.
          New York and London: Seminar Press.

Vygotsky, L. S.
  1962.   *Thought and language.* Cambridge, Massachusetts: The M.I.T. Press.

Watanabe, Minoru.
  1968.   "Shuujoshi no bunpooronteki imi". *Kokugogaku* 72:127-135.
  1971.   *Kokugo koobunron.* Tokyo: Hanawa Shoboo.

Watsuji, Tetsuroo.
  1935.   *Huudo: Ningengakuteki koosatsu.* Tokyo: Iwanami.
  1937.   *Rinrigaku jookan.* Tokyo: Iwanami.

Weil, Henry.
  1887.   (originally 1844). *The order of words.* Translated by C. W. Super. Boston: Ginn and
          Company Publishers.

Wertsch, James V.
  1991.   *Voices of the mind: A sociocultural approach to mediated action.* Cambridge,
          Massachusetts: Harvard University Press.

Wertsch, James V. (trans. and ed.)
  1979.   *The concept of activity in Soviet psychology.* Armonk, NY: Sharpe.

Yamada, Yoshio.
  1908.   *Nihon bunpooron.* Tokyo: Hoobunkan.
  1922.   *Nihon koogohoo koogi.* Tokyo: Hoobunkan.
  1936.   *Nihon bunpoogaku gairon.* Tokyo: Hoobunkan.

Yokobayashi, Hisayo and Akiko Shimomura.
  1988.   *Setsuzoku no hyoogen.* Gaikokujin no tame no nihongo reibun mondai shiriizu. Tokyo:
          Aratake Shuppan.

Yule, George.
  1981.   "New, current and displaced entity reference". *Lingua* 55:41-52.

Data References

Abe, Kooboo.
    1968. *Tanin no kao*. Shichoo Bunko. Tokyo: Shinchoosha.

Agawa, Hiroyuki.
    1983. "Saishuu oriento kyuukoo". In H. Agawa (ed.), 26-46.

Agawa, Hiroyuki. (ed.)
    1983. *Tabi*. Nihon no meizuihitsu, Vol. 15. Tokyo: Sakuhinsha.

Akagawa, Jiroo.
    1983. *Kakeochi wa shitai to tomoni*. Shuueisha Bunko. Tokyo: Shuueisha.
    1984a. *Hare tokidoki satsujin*. Kadokawa Bunko. Tokyo: Kadokawa Shoten.
    1984b. *Kiri no yoru ni goyoojin*. Kadokawa Bunko. Tokyo: Kadokawa Shoten.
    1986. *Kodokuna shuumatsu*. Koosseidoo Bunko. Tokyo: Kooseidoo.

Endoo, Shuusaku. (ed.)
    1983. *Kokoro*. Nihon no meizuihitsu. Vol. 13. Tokyo: Sakuhinsha.

Haniya, Yutaka. (ed.)
    1984. *Yume*. Nihon no meizuihitsu. Vol. 14. Tokyo: Sakuhinsha.

Hiraiwa, Yumie.
    1981. *Onna no katei*. Bunshun Bunko. Tokyo: Bungei Shunjuu.

Hoshi, Shin'ichi.
    1976. *Takusan no tabuu*. Shinchoo Bunko. Tokyo: Shinchoosha.
    1980. *Hitonigiri no mirai*. Shinchoo Bunko. Tokyo: Shinchoosha.
    1982. *Mirai issoppu*. Shinchoo Bunko. Tokyo: Shinchoosha.

Hukada, Yuusuke.
    1981. *Nihon akusai ni kanpai*. Bunshun Bunko. Tokyo: Bungei Shunjuu.

Komatsu, Sakyoo.
    1980. *Ashita no ashita no yume no hate*. Kadokawa Bunko. Tokyo: Kadokawa Shoten.

Maeda, Yuugure.
    1984. "Mugihumi". In K. Yamamoto (ed.), 165-172.

Matsumoto, Seichoo.
  1980. *Kyoohansha*. Shinchoo Bunko. Tokyo: Shinchoosha.
  1982. *Kami to yajuu no hi*. Koodansha Bunko. Tokyo: Koodansha.

Miura, Shumon.
  1985. *Saikai*. Shuueisha Bunko. Tokyo: Shuueisha.

Morimura, Seiichi.
  1977. *Nihon arupuru satsujin jiken*. Kadokawa Bunko. Tokyo: Kadokawa Shoten.

Murakami, Haruki.
  1985. *Hitsuji o meguru booken--joo*. Koodansha Bunko. Tokyo: Koodansha.

Natsuki, Shizuko.
  1981. *Hikaru gake*. Kadokawa Bunko. Tokyo: Kadokawa Shoten.

Nishimura, Jukoo.
  1980. *Kimi yo hunnu no kawa o watare*. Tokuma Bunko. Tokyo: Tokuma Shoten.

Nishimura, Kyootaroo.
  1981. *Nihon daabii satsujin jiken*. Tokuma Bunko. Tokyo: Tokuma Shoten.
  1986. *Yukisaki no nai kippu*. Hutaba Bunko. Tokyo: Hutabasha.

Ogawa, Kunio.
  1984. "Moeru uma". In Y. Haniya (ed.), 81-84.

Okamoto, Kanoko.
  1983. "Jihi". In S. Endoo (ed.), 142-145.

Ooe, Kenzaburoo.
  1981. *Kojintekina taiken*. Shinchoo Bunko. Tokyo: Shinchoosha.

Ooyabu, Haruhiko.
  1983. *Nisedoru o oe*. Tokuma Bunko. Tokyo: Tokuma Shoten.

Saitoo, Sakae.
  1985. *Kamakura takiginoo satsujin jiken*. Koobunsha Bunko. Tokyo: Koobunsha.

Sasazawa, Saho.
  1983. *Yuke, kodokuna kaze no gotoku*. Tokuma Bunko. Tokyo: Tokuma Shoten.

Tachihara, Msaaki.
  1976. *Adashino*. Shinchoo Bunko. Tokyo: Shinchoosha.

Tsuzuki, Michio.
    1983. *Meitantei modoki*. Bunshun Bunko. Tokyo: Bungei Shunjuu.

Yamamoto, Kenkichi. (ed.)
    1984. *Haru*. Nihon no meizuihitsu. Vol 17. Tokyo: Sakuhinsha.

Yamamura, Misa.
    1986. *Dairi zuma satsujin jiken*. Koobunsha Bunko. Tokyo: Koobunsha.

Yokota, Jun'ya.
    1985. *Taijin kamereon-shoo*. Koobunsha Bunko. Tokyo: Koobunsha.

Yoshimura, Akira.
    1988. *Aki no machi*. Bunshun Bunko. Tokyo: Bungei Shunjuu.

Yuuki, Shooji.
    1977. *Shishatachi no yoru*. Kadokawa Bunko. Tokyo: Kadokawa Shoten.

Author Index

Subject Index

A

Action, speech, 54, 106, 109, 116
    labels, 106
    structure of, 109
Affect, 56, 259
Amae, 115, 116, 178, 180, 181, 262-264
Anaphora, 134
    extended definition of, 134
    of discourse, 134
Anyway, 12, 147
    in contrast with *doose*, 147

B

Background, 135, 164, 168, 208, 232, *see also* Foregrounding
Basho no ronri, 45
Belongingness, 132, 136, 180, 181
Binary combination, 16
Binary rapport, 16, 268
Bunmatsu ikkan no gensoku, 152

C

Causality, concept of, 70-71
Cause-(and-)result, 69, 71, 80, 84, 89, 95
Chinjutsu, 26, , 30, 31-32
    Yamada's view, 31
    Tokieda's view, 31-32
    Haga's view, 32
    Watanabe's view, 32
Clause-noun combination, 221
Cohesion, concept of
    Halliday and Hasan's view, 18-19
    criticism of, 19
    in discourse, 19-20
Cohesion marker, 134
Connection types
    as proposed by Nagano, 86, 108

Connectives, 6, 67-69
    semantic, 67
    pragmatic, 67
Context of situation, 42
Cross-cultural communication, 25, 273
    examples of, 271-273

D

Da, see Da and *desu/masu, Da* style
Da and *desu/masu*, 12, 25, 49, 150-182, 274, *see also Da* style
    and the MC process, 180-182
    as a DM manipulation device, 180-182
    discourse organizational functions of 163-164
    in different genres
        in casual conversation, 155-159
        in dialogues of fiction, 159-170
        in literary essay, 170-180
    ontological basis for, 177-178
    precursors' characterization of, 152-155
    schematization of topical structure associated with, 175
Da style, 150-182, 265, 272-273, *see also Da* and *desu/masu*
    functions of,
        expressing immediacy, 156-158
        expressing narrative-internal perspective, 156-158, 181
        marking echo questions, 158-159
        marking jointly created utterances, 158-159
    interactional functions of,
        expressing *amae*, 178, 181
        expressing group belongingness, 180, 181
Dakara, 6, 25, 49, 67, 68, 69-98, 274

Modality-centered view, 20-21, 257

N

Naked abrupt forms
   of the verb, 152, 157
Nanji no nanji, 16
Narrative coda, 80-81
Narrative voice, 241-247, 252
Ne, 11, 202-209, 214-215, 220, *see also Yo and ne*
   associated with personal emotion, 208, 220
   characterization in contrast with *yo*, 208, 214-215
   signaling interaction focus, 202-209
Nikoo kankei, 16
Noun-modifying construction, 221

O

Omoiyari, 264
   culture, 264

P

Parole, 5
Participatory control, 6, 55-56
   subcategories of,
      exchange structure, 55-56, 109, 116, 139, 220
      designing speaker turns, 56, 97, 220, 252
Personal emotion, 56-57, 97, 116, 139, 148, 180, 181, 220, *see also* Interactional appeal
Personalization
   of discourse, 265-270
Perspective, 49, 51-52, 100, 126, 141, 158, 220, 252, *see also* Information qualification
   as an aspect of DM, 49, 51-52, 220, 252
   as a speaker's positioning, 100, 126, 141, 158
Place, concept of, 42-47
   in linguistics, 42-44, 46-47
   in philosophy, 44-46

Nishida's, 45-46
Tokieda's, 43-44
Point of view, 157
   conceptual, 157, 158
   perceptual, 157, 158
Politeness principle, 57
POSITION, 54, 106, 107, 113, 114, 115, 116, 118, 119

Q

Quotative explanation, 234-235

R

Recognizing realized expectations, 128, *see also Yahari/yappari*
Relative Information Accessibility and/or Possessorship, 190, 193-194, 198-202, 260
   and related concepts, 198-202
      Cook's authority for knowledge, 201-202
      Kamio's Speaker's Territory of Information, 198-201
   and the choice of *yo* and *ne*, 193-194
      schematization of, 194
   explanation of, 193-194
Relevance, 60
Reluctance marker, 55, 56, 113, 116, *see also* Dispreference marker
   datte as, 56, 113, 116
   yahari/yappari as, 56, 136, 137

S

Sanshu-no-shi, 29
Saussurean view of Language, 3, 5, 257-258
   criticism of, 261
Scene, 24, 39-42, 44, 46-47
   definition of, 40-41
   Discourse Modality as, 39-42
Sentential anaphora, 88, 100, 125, 141
Self, 4, 7, 10-11, 15-17, 266, 275
   autonomous view of, 4, 15

In the PRAGMATICS AND BEYOND NEW SERIES the following titles have been published and will be published during 1993:

1. WALTER, Bettyruth: *The Jury Summation as Speech Genre: An Ethnographic Study of What it Means to Those who Use it.* Amsterdam/Philadelphia, 1988.

2. BARTON, Ellen: *Nonsentential Constituents: A Theory of Grammatical Structure and Pragmatic Interpretation.* Amsterdam/Philadelphia, 1990.

3. OLEKSY, Wieslaw (ed.): *Contrastive Pragmatics.* Amsterdam/Philadelphia, 1989.

4. RAFFLER-ENGEL, Walburga von (ed.): *Doctor-Patient Interaction.* Amsterdam/Philadelphia, 1989.

5. THELIN, Nils B. (ed.): *Verbal Aspect in Discourse.* Amsterdam/Philadelphia, 1990.

6. VERSCHUEREN, Jef (ed.): *Selected Papers from the 1987 International Pragmatics Conference. Vol. I: Pragmatics at Issue. Vol. II: Levels of Linguistic Adaptation. Vol. III: The Pragmatics of Intercultural and International Communication (ed. with Jan Blommaert).* Amsterdam/Philadelphia, 1991.

7. LINDENFELD, Jacqueline: *Speech and Sociability at French Urban Market Places.* Amsterdam/Philadelphia, 1990.

8. YOUNG, Lynne: *Language as Behaviour, Language as Code: A Study of Academic English.* Amsterdam/Philadelphia, 1990.

9. LUKE, Kang-Kwong: *Utterance Particles in Cantonese Conversation.* Amsterdam/Philadelphia, 1990.

10. MURRAY, Denise E.: *Conversation for Action. The computer terminal as medium of communication.* Amsterdam/Philadelphia, 1991.

11. LUONG, Hy V.: *Discursive Practices and Linguistic Meanings. The Vietnamese system of person reference.* Amsterdam/Philadelphia, 1990.

12. ABRAHAM, Werner (ed.): *Discourse Particles. Descriptive and theoretical investigations on the logical, syntactic and pragmatic properties of discourse particles in German.* Amsterdam/Philadelphia, 1991.

13. NUYTS, Jan, A. Machtelt BOLKESTEIN and Co VET (eds): *Layers and Levels of Representation in Language Theory: a functional view.* Amsterdam/Philadelphia, 1990.

14. SCHWARTZ, Ursula: *Young Children's Dyadic Pretend Play.* Amsterdam/Philadelphia, 1991.

15. KOMTER, Martha: *Conflict and Cooperation in Job Interviews.* Amsterdam/Philadelphia, 1991.

16. MANN, William C. and Sandra A. THOMPSON (eds): *Discourse Description: Diverse Linguistic Analyses of a Fund-Raising Text.* Amsterdam/Philadelphia, 1992.

17. PIÉRAUT-LE BONNIEC, Gilberte and Marlene DOLITSKY (eds): *Language Bases ... Discourse Bases.* Amsterdam/Philadelphia, 1991.

18. JOHNSTONE, Barbara: *Repetition in Arabic Discourse. Paradigms, syntagms and the ecology of language.* Amsterdam/Philadelphia, 1991.

19. BAKER, Carolyn D. and Allan LUKE (eds): *Towards a Critical Sociology of Reading Pedagogy. Papers of the XII World Congress on Reading.* Amsterdam/Philadelphia, 1991.

20. NUYTS, Jan: *Aspects of a Cognitive-Pragmatic Theory of Language. On cognition, functionalism, and grammar.* Amsterdam/Philadelphia, 1992.
21. SEARLE, John R. et al.: *(On) Searle on Conversation.* Compiled and introduced by Herman Parret and Jef Verschueren. Amsterdam/Philadelphia, 1992.
22. AUER, Peter and Aldo Di LUZIO (eds): *The Contextualization of Language.* Amsterdam/Philadelphia, 1992.
23. FORTESCUE, Michael, Peter HARDER and Lars KRISTOFFERSEN (eds): *Layered Structure and Reference in a Functional Perspective.* Papers from the Functional Grammar Conference, Copenhagen, 1990. Amsterdam/Philadelphia, 1992.
24. MAYNARD, Senko K.: *Discourse Modality: Subjectivity, Emotion and Voice in the Japanese Language.* Amsterdam/Philadelphia, 1993.
25. COUPER-KUHLEN, Elizabeth: *English Speech Rhythm. Form and function in everyday verbal interaction.* Amsterdam/Philadelphia, 1993.
26. STYGALL, Gail: *Trial Language. A study in differential discourse processing.* Amsterdam/Philadelphia, n.y.p.
27. SUTER, Hans Jürg: *The Wedding Report: A Prototypical Approach to the Study of Traditional Text Types.* Amsterdam/Philadelphia, n.y.p.